Books are to be returned on or before
the last date

EXTREMES of age

The 1999 Report of the National Confidential Enquiry into Perioperative Deaths

Data collection period 1 April 1997 to 31 March 1998

Compiled by:

K G Callum MS FRCS

A J G Gray MB BChir FRCA

R W Hoile MS FRCS

G S Ingram MBBS FRCA

I C Martin LLM FRCS FDSRCS

K M Sherry MBBS FRCA

F Whimster MHM

LIVERPOOL
JOHN MOORES UNIVERSITY
AVRIL ROBARTS LRC
TEL. 0151 231 4022

WITHDRAWN

LIVERPOOL JMU LIBRARY
3 1111 00912 2217

Published 17 November 1999 by the National Confidential Enquiry into Perioperative Deaths

35-43 Lincoln's Inn Fields, London WC2A 3PN
Tel: (020) 7831 6430
Fax: (020) 7430 2958
Email: info@ncepod.org.uk
Website: www.ncepod.org.uk

Requests for further information should be addressed to the Chief Executive

ISBN 0 9522069 6 X

A company limited by guarantee Company number 3019382
Registered charity number 1075588

This report is printed on paper produced from wood pulp originating from managed sustainable plantations and is chlorine-free, acid-free, recyclable and biodegradable

Additional information

This report is available for downloading from the NCEPOD website at www.ncepod.org.uk

Copies can also be purchased from the NCEPOD office.

The analysis of data from anaesthetic and surgical questionnaires is not included in full in this report. A supplement containing additional data, and copies of the questionnaires, is available free of charge from the NCEPOD office.

Throughout this Report AQ and SQ are used to denote the anaesthetic or surgical question from which the data was obtained.

Acknowledgements

This is the ninth report published by the National Confidential Enquiry into Perioperative Deaths and, as in previous years, could not have been achieved without the support and cooperation of a wide range of individuals and organisations. Our particular thanks go to the following:

- The Local Reporters, whose names are listed in Appendix E, and those who assist them in providing initial data on perioperative deaths.
- All those surgeons and anaesthetists, whose names are listed in Appendices F and G, who contributed to the Enquiry by completing questionnaires.
- The Advisors whose names are listed overleaf.
- Those bodies, whose names are listed in Appendix C, who provide the funding to cover the cost of the Enquiry.

The Steering Group, Clinical Coordinators and Chief Executive would also like to record their appreciation of the hard work and tolerance of the NCEPOD administrative staff: Peter Allison, Fatima Chowdhury, Paul Coote, Sheree Cornwall, Jennifer Drummond and Dolores Jarman.

Dedication

This Report is dedicated to the memory of Brendan Devlin, one of the original pioneers responsible for setting up the Enquiry, who sadly died in December 1998.

Clinical Contributors

NCEPOD Coordinators

K G Callum — Clinical Coordinator, NCEPOD and Consultant General & Vascular Surgeon, Derbyshire Royal Infirmary

A J G Gray — Clinical Coordinator, NCEPOD and Consultant Anaesthetist, Norfolk and Norwich Hospital

R W Hoile — Principal Clinical Coordinator, NCEPOD and Consultant General Surgeon, Medway Maritime Hospital

G S Ingram — Principal Clinical Coordinator, NCEPOD and Consultant Anaesthetist, University College London Hospitals

I C Martin — Clinical Coordinator, NCEPOD and Consultant Oral and Maxillofacial Surgeon, Sunderland Royal Hospital

K M Sherry — Clinical Coordinator, NCEPOD and Consultant Anaesthetist, Northern General Hospital NHS Trust, Sheffield

Specialty Advisors

Children

Anaesthesia

P Crean — Royal Belfast Hospital for Sick Children

D J Higgins — Southend Hospital

S E F Jones — Birmingham Children's Hospital

J B Luntley — Barnsley District General Hospital

A Mackersie — Great Ormond Street Hospital for Children

V Sidhu — St Mary's Hospital, London

K Wilkinson — Norfolk and Norwich Hospital

Surgery

M K D Benson — Consultant Orthopaedic Surgeon, Nuffield Orthopaedic Centre

J M Graham — Consultant ENT Surgeon, Royal National Throat, Nose and Ear Hospital

P L May — Consultant Neurosurgeon, Royal Liverpool Children's Hospital

C A Reid — Consultant Plastic Surgeon, Newcastle upon Tyne Hospitals

M D Stringer — Consultant Paediatric Surgeon, The Leeds Teaching Hospitals

D Thompson — Consultant Neurosurgeon, Great Ormond Street Hospital for Children

V M Wright — Consultant Paediatric Surgeon, Bart's and The London Hospitals

Paediatrics

M Little — Consultant Paediatrician, Medway Maritime Hospital

Pathology

M Ashworth — Bristol Royal Hospital for Sick Children

K McKenzie — Royal Hospital for Sick Children, Edinburgh

The Elderly

Anaesthesia

C Dodds — South Tees Acute Hospitals

A E Edwards — Wrexham Maelor Hospital

M W Platt — St Mary's Hospital, London

K N Robinson — Northampton General Hospital

Cardiothoracic surgery

K M Taylor — Hammersmith Hospital

Care of the elderly

D Da Costa — Northern General Hospital NHS Trust, Sheffield

F G Vaz — South Warwickshire General Hospitals

General surgery

A R Berry	Northampton General Hospital
P Farrands	Royal Sussex County Hospital
M Kelly	Leicester General Hospital
C A Makin	Wirral Hospital

Gynaecology

J H Shepherd	Bart's and The London Hospitals

Neurosurgery

J Bartlett	King's College Hospital (retired)

Ophthalmology

M Beck	University Hospital of Wales

Oral and Maxillofacial surgery

E D Vaughan	Aintree University Hospitals

Orthopaedic surgery

K Daly	Kingston Hospital
A Floyd	Milton Keynes General
P Gill	Sunderland Royal Hospital
D Griffiths	North Staffordshire Hospital
M J Parker	Peterborough District Hospital
R Vickers	St George's Hospital, London

Otorhinolaryngology

M Wickstead	Norfolk & Norwich Hospital

Plastic surgery

N R McLean	Newcastle upon Tyne Hospitals

Urology

M A Stott	Royal Devon & Exeter Hospital

Vascular surgery

S Ashley	Plymouth Hospitals
S Parvin	Royal Bournemouth & Christchurch Hospitals
P Taylor	Guy's & St Thomas' Hospital

Pathology

C M Corbishley	St George's Hospital, London
M H Griffiths	University College London Hospitals
K Scott	The Royal Wolverhampton Hospitals

Contents

LIVERPOOL
JOHN MOORES UNIVERSITY
AVRIL ROBARTS LRC
TEL. 0151 231 4022

Tables, Figures and Questions

1 General Data

General data analysis

Sample groups for detailed review

Distribution and return rates for the total sample group

2 Children

General Issues

Who anaesthetises and who operates on children?

Patient profile

Time of death

Hospitals, facilities and staffing

Admission and transfer

Audit

Specific Issues

Neurosurgery

Urology

Vascular surgery

Other specialties

Pathology

Foreword

This report concentrates on the extremes of age. In detail there are obvious differences between the groups, yet many of the lessons to be drawn from this study span the age difference. This is also our first report since the introduction of clinical governance, following publication of 'The new NHS Modern Dependable' and 'A First Class Service' by the government, in which participation in National Confidential Enquiries was seen as a mandatory requirement. NCEPOD is delighted that this government has paid such attention to the issue of quality of care, which we have been promoting since our inception a decade ago. It must be remembered, however, that the data collected, and participation in this report, occurred before the introduction of clinical governance and hence the return rates cannot be viewed against this requirement and show that there is still room for significant improvement. The reasons for failure to return data are multiple, yet why there should be marked regional variation is difficult to understand.

In children's surgery it is quite evident that our previous message regarding the inappropriateness of occasional paediatric practice has been acted upon, with far fewer surgeons and anaesthetists involved in the management of children. However, this message should apply particularly to emergencies, an area where a significant number of respondents failed to see the inappropriateness of occasional practice. The division of responsibilities between surgeons in specialist paediatric units and those in district general hospitals has to be resolved. On occasions this carries with it the issue of patient transfer; the facility for this to be carried out by appropriately trained staff from the receiving centre may be indicated - yet this is a resource which is not always available. The report also highlights the lamentable fact that audit of deaths in children was less than adequate and we would hope that the introduction of clinical governance will address this failing.

The greatest problem seen in the elderly group concerned the management of fluid balance. Although coexisting medical conditions were common, surprisingly few patients were treated by a multidisciplinary team. However, the report does highlight the need for a full diagnosis to be made in these patients before surgical intervention. Issues surrounding emergency admissions throughout the week, and the availability both of emergency theatre time and of sufficiently senior clinicians, are factors behind the delays in treatment of some elderly patients that still need to be addressed. A far greater issue is that of proper preoperative evaluation and management of the patient's physiological state. Life expectancy is increasing and society understandably demands and expects successful outcomes after surgical intervention for this elderly population. This requires the involvement of more senior staff, on a multidisciplinary basis, than is currently the practice. A rigorous preoperative high dependency approach to stabilising the physiological state of the patient is required if postoperative complications are to be avoided and early mobilisation achieved. The lack of high dependency beds has been recognised but the problem of providing suitably trained nursing staff is an even greater resource issue. Unless this is addressed, it is difficult to envisage significant improvements in the care of this group of patients.

NCEPOD was concerned at the low postmortem rates in both these age groups and particularly that reports of findings failed to meet the standards set by the Royal College of Pathologists. It is highly desirable that clinicians should be present at postmortems, yet this seems not to occur, presumably due to other commitments. This results in an even greater need for postmortem reports to be communicated to the clinicians involved, but this does not occur sufficiently frequently.

Dissemination of our findings has always been a major concern, since all too frequently the clinical teams who should be the principal recipients fail to see them. We hope that this year's wider distribution of an executive summary will alert all interested parties to the availability of this full Report.

John Ll Williams
Chairman

Recommendations

Clinical

- There is a need for a system to assess the severity of surgical illness in **children** in order to gather meaningful information about outcomes. The ASA grading system is widely used by anaesthetists but, as a comparatively simple system, does have limitations for use in children (see pages 31-33).

- Anaesthetic and surgical trainees need to know the circumstances in which they should inform their consultants before undertaking an operation on a **child.** To encourage uniformity during rotational training programmes, national guidelines are required (see pages 39-41).

- The death of any **child,** occurring within 30 days of an anaesthetic or surgical procedure, should be subject to peer review, irrespective of the place of death (see page 47).

- The events surrounding the perioperative death of any **child** should be reviewed in the context of multidisciplinary clinical audit (see page 47).

- Fluid management in the **elderly** is often poor; it should be accorded the same status as drug prescription. Multidisciplinary reviews to develop good local working practices are required (see pages 68-71).

- A team of senior surgeons, anaesthetists and physicians needs to be closely involved in the care of **elderly** patients who have poor physical status and high operative risk (see pages 58-59, 62, 80).

- The experience of the surgeon and anaesthetist need to be matched to the physical status of the **elderly** patient, as well as to the technical demands of the procedure (see pages 62, 74, 81, 86).

- **Elderly** patients need their pain management to be provided by those with appropriate specialised experience in order that they receive safe and effective pain relief (see pages 75-76, 78-79).

- Surgeons need to be more aware that, in the **elderly**, clinically unsuspected gastrointestinal complications are commonly found at postmortem to be the cause, or contribute to the cause, of death following surgery (see page 102).

Organisational

- The concentration of **children's** surgical services (whether at a local or regional level) would increase expertise and further reduce occasional practice (see page 26).

- A review of manpower planning is required to enable anaesthetists and surgeons in various specialties to train in the management of small **children** (see page 26).

- In the management of acute **children's** surgical cases a regional organisational perspective is required. This particularly applies to the organisation of patient transfer between units. Paediatric units have a responsibility to lead this process (see pages 43-46).

- All Trusts should address the requirements of the framework document on **paediatric** intensive care. Most children's hospitals have a good provision but many district general hospitals are deficient (see pages 35-36, 46).

- There is a need for central guidance to ensure the uniformity of data collection on surgery in **children** (see page 16).

- If a decision is made to operate on an **elderly** patient then that must include a decision to provide appropriate postoperative care, which may include high dependency or intensive care support (see pages 61-62, 70).

- There should be sufficient, fully-staffed, daytime theatre and recovery facilities to ensure that no **elderly** patient requiring an urgent operation waits for more than 24 hours once fit for surgery. This includes weekends (see pages 61-63, 82).

- Clinicians are still unable to return data to NCEPOD as a result of missing patient records. Action is required to improve hospital record systems; this is within the remit of **clinical governance** (see pages 11-12).

- NHS Trusts must take responsibility for ensuring that all relevant deaths are reported and questionnaires returned to NCEPOD as part of their **clinical governance** duties (see page 3).

1 GENERAL DATA

Compiled by: F Whimster

RECOMMENDATIONS

- Clinicians are still unable to return data to NCEPOD as a result of missing patient records. Action is required to improve hospital record systems; this is within the remit of clinical governance.

- NHS Trusts must take responsibility for ensuring that all relevant deaths are reported and questionnaires returned to NCEPOD as part of their clinical governance duties.

1. General Data

Introduction

The NCEPOD protocol used during the 1997/98 data collection period is shown in Appendix D. This is currently under review to take into account important changes arising as a result of the white paper 'The new NHS Modern Dependable'[1], 'A First Class Service'[2] and 'Clinical Governance: Quality in the new NHS'[3]. These changes brought NCEPOD under the aegis of the National Institute for Clinical Excellence (NICE) and, most significantly, stated that *"all relevant hospital doctors and other health professionals will be required to participate in the work of the National Confidential Enquiries. Results from their findings will be fed into appropriate NICE guidance and standard setting and will be an important part of ensuring effective clinical governance locally which is to be independently scrutinised by the Commission for Health Improvement (CHI)"*[2].

It was also stated that *"NHS Trusts have responsibility for ensuring that all hospital doctors take part in national clinical audits and confidential enquiries"*[3]. This requirement, coupled with improved centralised national data should, in the future, enable clinicians to measure and compare outcomes. It is, therefore, essential that the current rates of reporting deaths and returning questionnaires to NCEPOD be increased. The profession will need to improve compliance, or explain the obstacles to participation, if criticism is to be avoided.

The introduction of clinical governance and compulsory participation from April 1999 will in no way compromise the confidentiality and anonymity with which data received by the Enquiry will be treated.

It should be remembered, however, that the data presented in this Report was gathered *before* the advent of clinical governance and mandatory participation.

Data collection

Data was requested from all NHS hospitals in England, Wales, Northern Ireland, Guernsey, Jersey, Isle of Man and the Defence Secondary Care Agency. In addition, many hospitals in the independent sector contributed data. Data was not collected from Scotland where the Scottish Audit of Surgical Mortality (SASM) performs a similar function.

Deaths occurring in hospital, between 1 April 1997 and 31 March 1998, and within 30 days of a surgical procedure, were reported to NCEPOD by the designated Local Reporter for each hospital (Appendix E). A few reports of deaths occurring at home were also received.

Figure 1.1: Total deaths reported

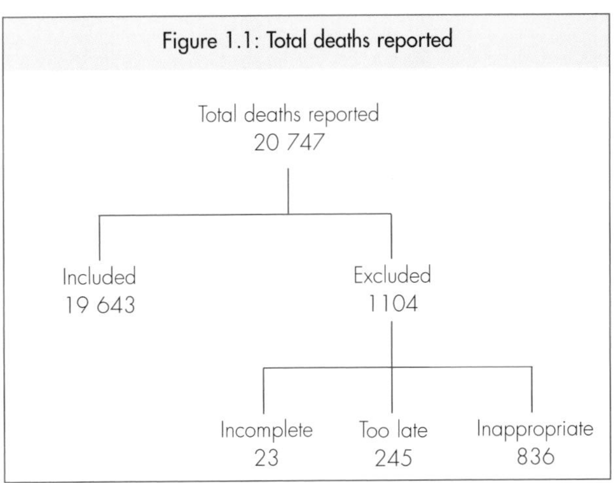

General data analysis

Figure 1.1 shows that a total of 20 747 reports were received. Of these, 1104 were excluded from further analysis: 836 were deemed inappropriate according to the NCEPOD protocol (Table 1.1 and Appendix D), 245 were received after the deadline of 30 September 1998 and 23 remained incomplete despite all efforts to identify missing information.

Table 1.1: Inappropriate reports received and excluded

Reason for exclusion	Number
More than 30 days *(day of operation to day of death)*	220
Procedure not performed by a surgeon	221
Duplicate report	271
No surgical procedure performed or procedure excluded by NCEPOD criteria	106
Procedure performed in non-participating independent hospital	14
Patient still alive	2
Maternal death	2
Total	836

These figures do not include inappropriate reports included in computer printout format. Some hospital information systems cannot easily filter out inappropriate reports, such as deaths following procedures by physicians, or deaths following procedures excluded by NCEPOD.

A regional breakdown of the remaining 19 643 deaths is shown in Table 1.2. Comparisons with previous years' figures should be treated with caution due to the effect of alterations in the regional structure of the NHS together with a lack of denominator data to indicate possible changes in the total number of operations performed.

LIVERPOOL
JOHN MOORES UNIVERSITY
AVRIL ROBARTS LRC
TEL. 0151 231 4022

Table 1.2: Deaths reported to NCEPOD by region									
	1997/98	1996/97	1995/96	1994/95	1993/94	1992/93	1991/92	1990	1989
Anglia & Oxford	1720	1578	1672	1361	1577	1862	1556	1367	1371
North Thames	2252	2292	2081	1944	2703	2515	2127	2554	2609
North West	2698	2634	2736	2618	2636	2378	2509	2736	2864
Northern & Yorkshire	3018	2870	3110	2549	2637	2671	2267	2464	2685
South & West	2288	2201	2508	2469	2561	2493	1847	1997	2306
South Thames	2202	2330	2166	2246	2531	2445	2465	2457	2840
Trent	2301	2218	2397	2386	2342	2036	2014	1722	1849
West Midlands	1559	1527	1595	1531	1578	1565	1578	1826	1902
Wales	915	1102	840	933	1078	1072	1079	1102	1162
Northern Ireland	462	480	469	497	529	474	375	316	380
Guernsey	15	27	33	12	33	26	18	39	32
Jersey	28	18	26	17	27	32	25	22	26
Isle of Man	16	26	0	0	25	41	25	25	7
Defence Secondary Care Agency	5	8	7	17	36	40	75	60	94
Independent sector	164	185	201	148	149	166	172	130	120
Total	**19 643**	**19 496**	**19 841**	**18 728**	**20 442**	**19 816**	**18 132**	**18 817**	**20 247**

Figure 1.2: Calendar days from operation to death

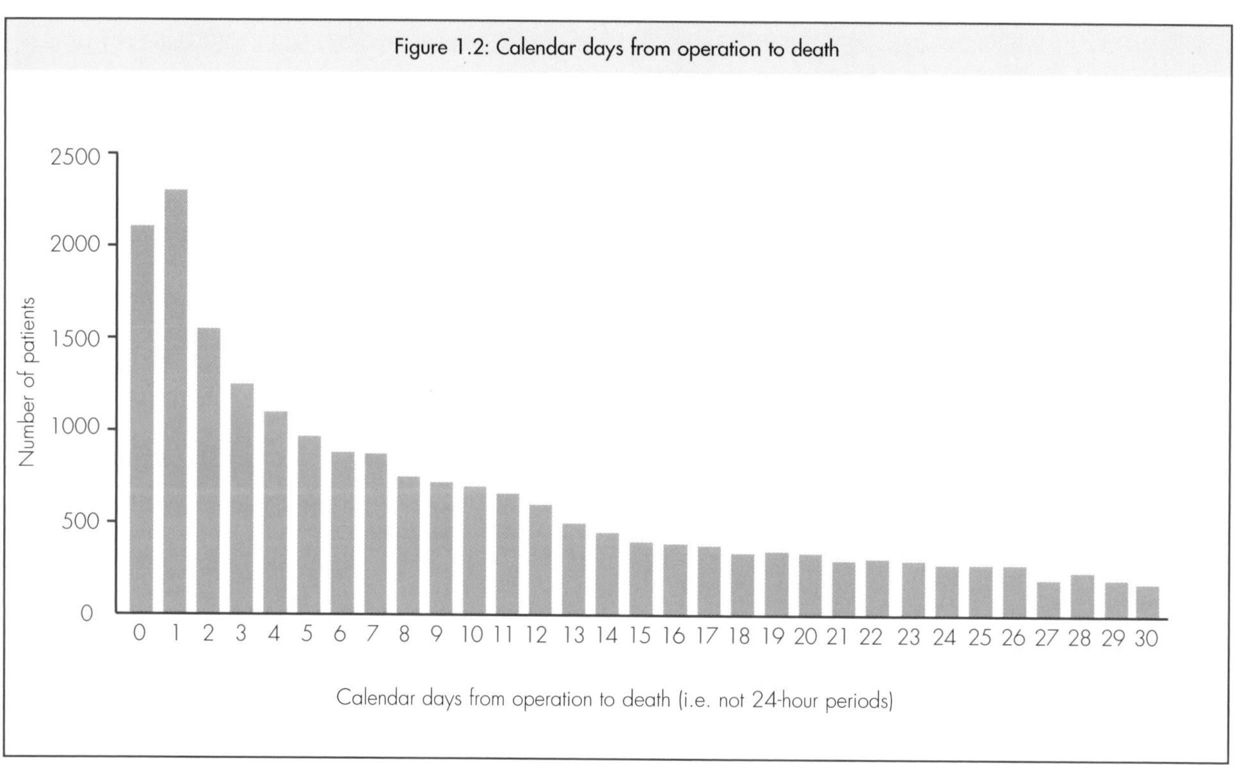

Figure 1.2 shows the distribution of the number of calendar days between operation (day 0) and death, with a peak at day 1, and almost half of deaths occurring within the first five days. This distribution has remained remarkably unchanged over the years.

Figure 1.3 shows the distribution of age and sex.

The number of days taken for Local Reporters to inform NCEPOD of deaths is shown in Table 1.3. Variations in the length of time are largely due to the different data collection methods used by Local Reporters. Whilst understanding constraints on the time available, a reduction in days taken to report deaths would undoubtedly be helpful. The sooner questionnaires can be dispatched to clinicians, the more likely it is that the medical records will be available, the case clearly remembered and the relevant clinicians still working at the same hospital. In addition, it allows more time for questionnaires to be completed and

Figure 1.3: Age/sex distribution of reported deaths

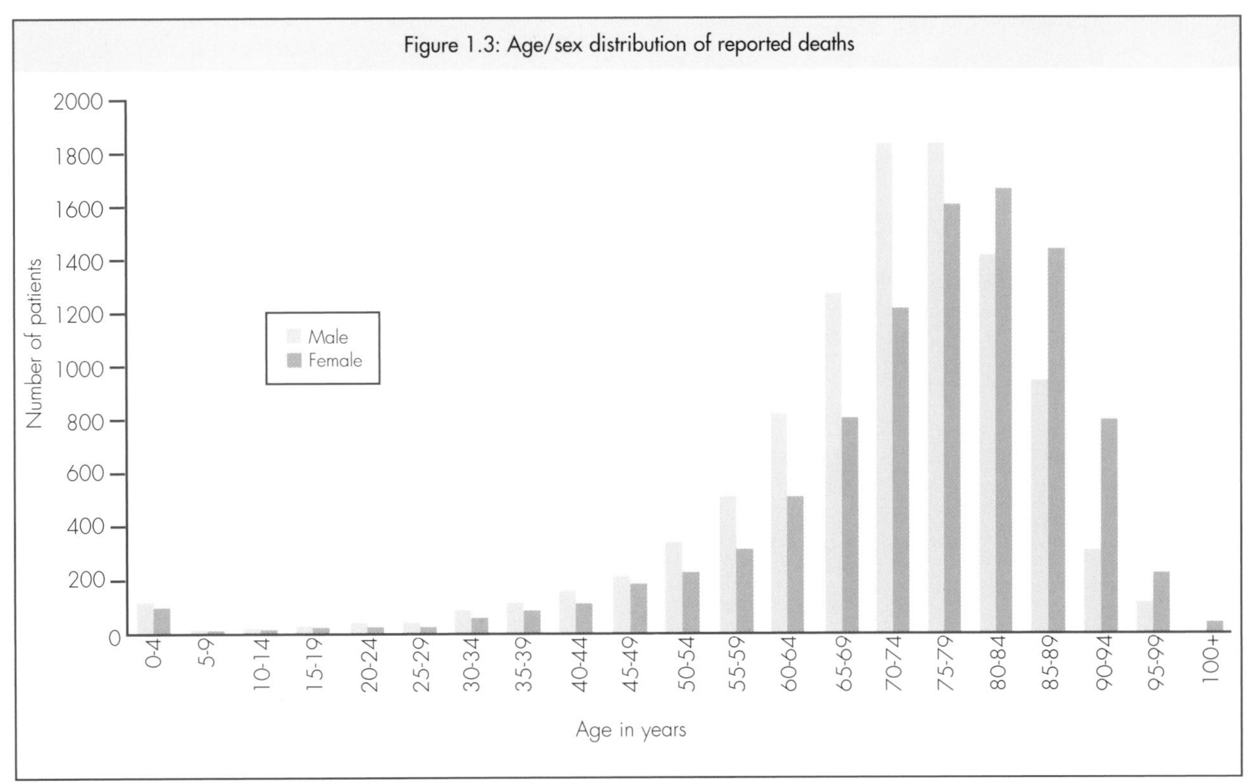

returned by the annual deadline of 31 December. For this reason, the deadline for reporting deaths has, from 1999, been brought forward to 31 August from 30 September.

Table 1.3: Calendar days between death and receipt of report by NCEPOD

Calendar days (i.e not 24-hour periods)	Number of deaths reported
1–29	4587
30–59	4245
60–89	3182
90–119	2301
120–149	1721
150–179	1170
180+	2437
Total	19 643

Sample groups for detailed review

Two sample groups were selected for detailed review: deaths of children aged less than 16 years (i.e. until the day preceding the 16th birthday) and deaths of those aged 90 years and over (i.e. from the day of the 90th birthday).

On this basis, from the total of 19 643 deaths, 1567 (8%) were initially included. This represented 139 in the less than 16 years age group and 1428 in the 90 years and over group (Figure 1.4).

Children

There were 139 deaths in the less than 16 years sample for which a surgical questionnaire was required and 120 deaths for which an anaesthetic questionnaire was needed (Figure 1.5).

Figure 1.4: Selection of sample groups

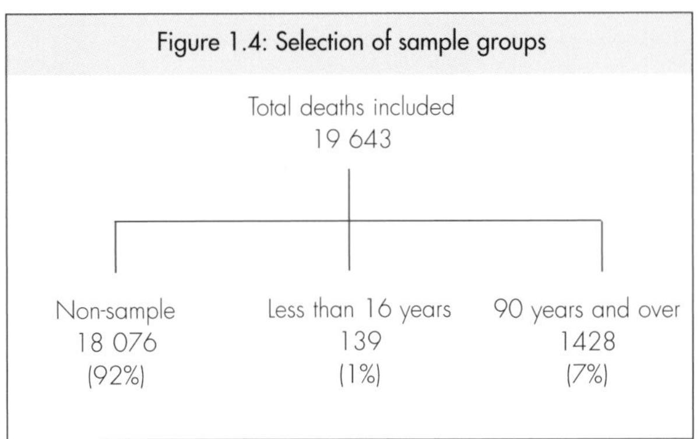

In the 19 cases where no anaesthetic questionnaire was sent this was either because the procedure was performed without an anaesthetist present (5) or because the name of the appropriate consultant was unobtainable or notified too late (14).

Figure 1.5: Distribution, return and analysis of questionnaires (less than 16 years)

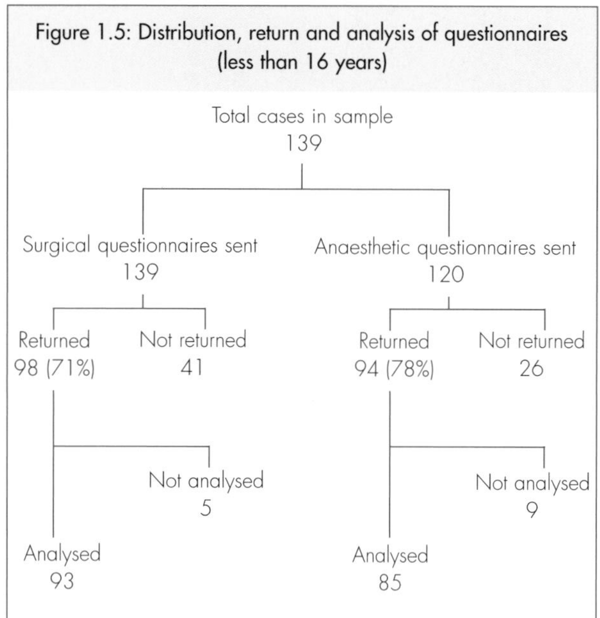

Ninety-eight surgical questionnaires (98/139, 71%) and 94 anaesthetic questionnaires (94/120, 78%) were returned (Figure 1.5). Five surgical questionnaires were excluded from analysis for the reasons given in Table 1.4. Similar exclusions occurred for nine anaesthetic questionnaires (Table 1.5).

Table 1.4: Reasons for exclusion of surgical questionnaires from analysis (less than 16 years)

Reasons for exclusion	Number
Questionnaire completed for wrong operation	2
Questionnaire received too late	1
Questionnaire related to cardiac case (excluded by the NCEPOD protocol)	2

Following the exclusion of this small number of cases there were 93 surgical and 85 anaesthetic questionnaires for consideration. This represents 67% and 71% of the sample respectively. The return rate for questionnaires must be improved.

Table 1.5: Reasons for exclusion of anaesthetic questionnaires from analysis (less than 16 years)

Reasons for exclusion	Number
Questionnaire incomplete	3
Questionnaire completed for wrong operation	4
Questionnaire received too late	1
Questionnaire related to an inappropriate procedure according to NCEPOD protocol	1

Figure 1.6: Reasons for non-return of surgical questionnaires (less than 16 years)

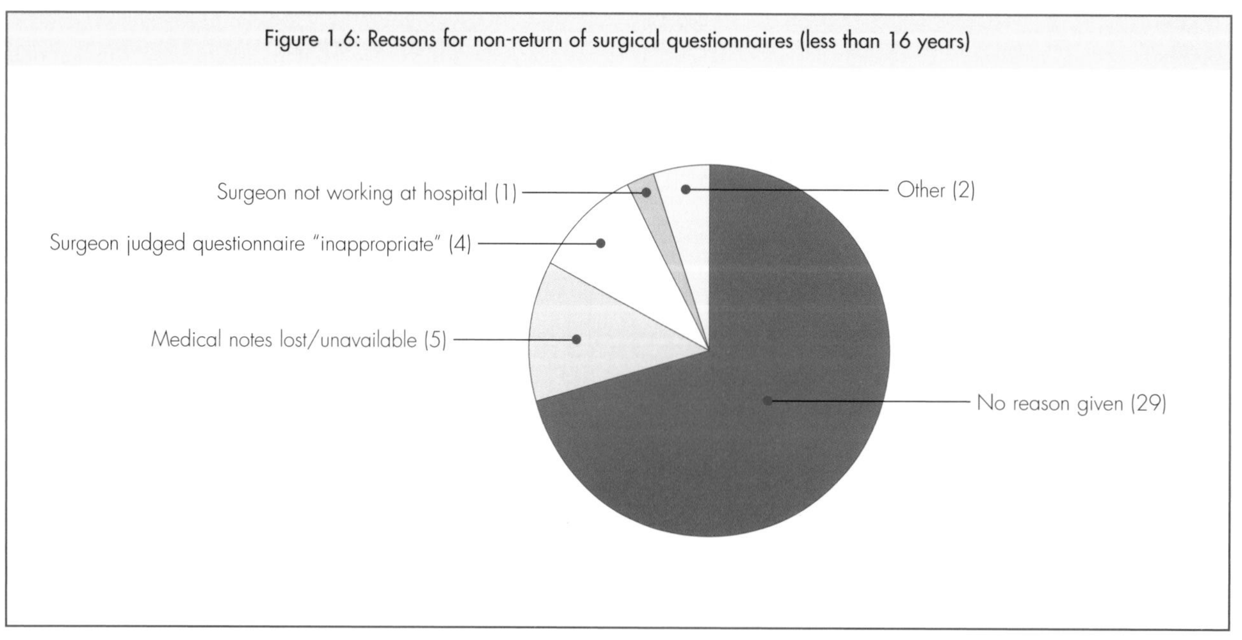

Figure 1.7: Reasons for non-return of anaesthetic questionnaires (less than 16 years)

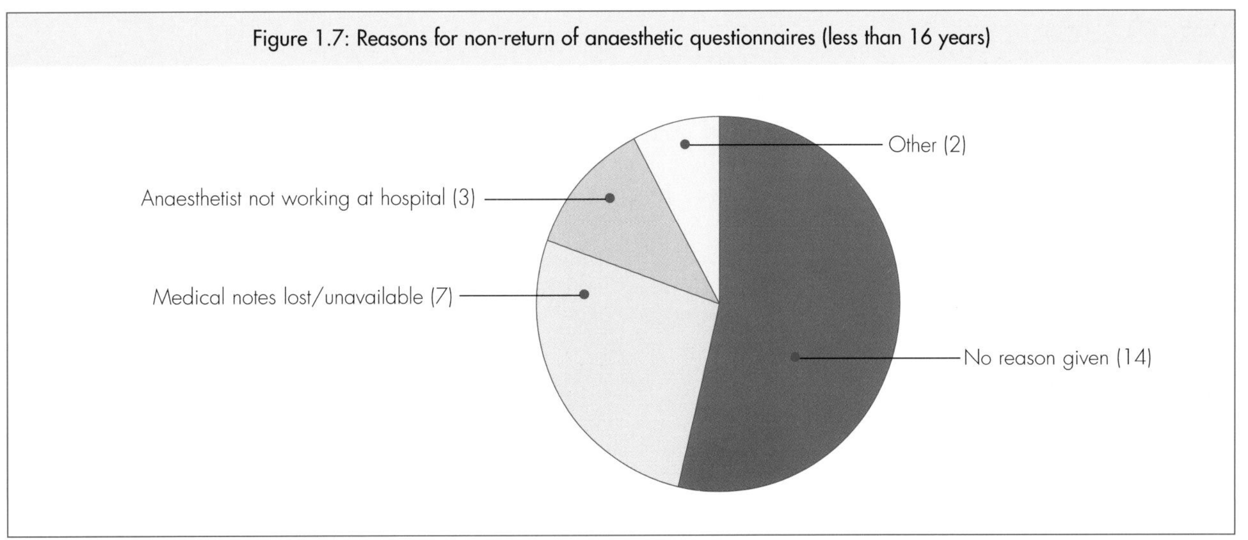

Figures 1.6 and 1.7 show that the reasons for non-return of questionnaires in the paediatric sample varied. The largest group (71% of non-returns for surgery and 54% for anaesthesia) failed to return a questionnaire and did not respond to at least two reminders.

The second most common cause for failure to return a questionnaire was the loss or unavailability of the medical notes (12% of the surgical questionnaires and 27% of the anaesthetic questionnaires not returned).

A regional breakdown of questionnaire distribution, return and analysis is shown in Table 1.6.

The return rates of anaesthetic questionnaires from South & West (36%) and South Thames (44%) are totally unacceptable and also contrast poorly with the equivalent rates for the elderly sample (Table 1.9) when anaesthetists in South & West returned 85% and those in South Thames 77% of questionnaires received. The return rates of surgical questionnaires from South Thames (56%), Wales (33%) and Northern Ireland (25%) are also poor, although the overall number of questionnaires distributed in Wales and Northern Ireland was small.

Consultant input was high. Ninety-four percent of surgical questionnaires (87/93) and 96% of anaesthetic questionnaires (82/85) were completed, or seen and agreed, by the relevant consultant.

Table 1.6: Distribution, return and analysis of questionnaires by region (less than 16 years)

SQ = Surgical Questionnaire AQ = Anaesthetic Questionnaire	Questionnaires distributed		Questionnaires returned		Return rate		Questionnaires analysed	
	SQ	AQ	SQ	AQ	SQ	AQ	SQ	AQ
Anglia & Oxford	5	4	5	4	100%	100%	5	3
North Thames	36	32	26	31	72%	97%	25	30
North West	17	16	13	13	76%	81%	13	12
Northern & Yorkshire	21	16	13	14	62%	88%	13	13
South & West	12	11	8	4	67%	36%	8	4
South Thames	9	9	5	4	56%	44%	5	4
Trent	23	20	17	13	74%	65%	15	12
West Midlands	9	8	9	8	100%	100%	7	5
Wales	3	0	1	0	33%	-	1	0
Northern Ireland	4	4	1	3	25%	75%	1	2
Guernsey	0	0	0	0	-	-	0	0
Jersey	0	0	0	0	-	-	0	0
Isle of Man	0	0	0	0	-	-	0	0
Defence Secondary Care Agency	0	0	0	0	-	-	0	0
Independent sector	0	0	0	0	-	-	0	0
Total	**139**	**120**	**98**	**94**	**71%**	**78%**	**93**	**85**

The Elderly

There were 1428 deaths in the elderly sample for which a surgical questionnaire was required and 1240 deaths for which an anaesthetic questionnaire was needed (Figure 1.8). In the 188 cases where no anaesthetic questionnaire was sent this was either because the procedure was performed without an anaesthetist present (67) or because the name of the appropriate consultant was unobtainable or notified too late (121).

Figure 1.8: Distribution, return and analysis of questionnaires (90 years and over)

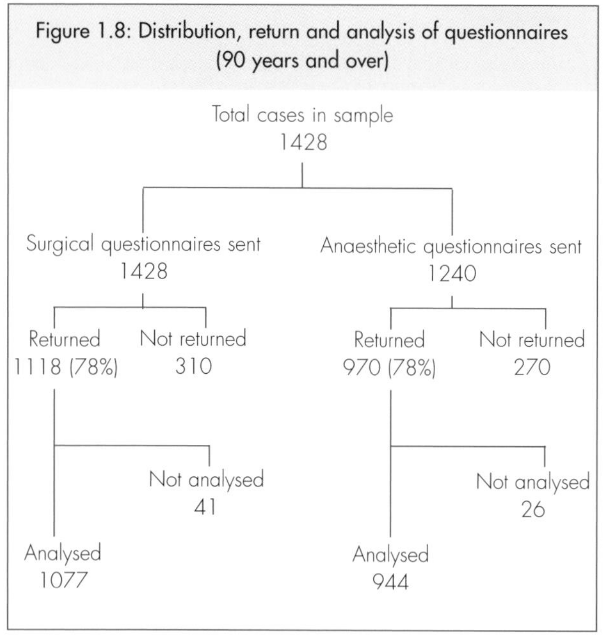

One thousand one hundred and eighteen surgical questionnaires (1118/1428, 78%) and 970 anaesthetic questionnaires (970/1240, 78%) were returned (Figure 1.8). Forty-one surgical questionnaires were excluded from analysis for the reasons given in Table 1.7. Similar exclusions occurred for 26 anaesthetic questionnaires (Table 1.8).

Table 1.7: Reasons for exclusion of surgical questionnaires from analysis (90 years and over)

Reasons for exclusion	Number
Questionnaire incomplete	16
Questionnaire completed for wrong operation	15
Questionnaire received too late	10

Table 1.8: Reasons for exclusion of anaesthetic questionnaires from analysis (90 years and over)

Reasons for exclusion	Number
Questionnaire incomplete	9
Questionnaire completed for wrong operation	6
Questionnaire received too late	9
Questionnaire related to case where no anaesthetic given	2

Following the exclusion of these cases there were 1077 surgical and 944 anaesthetic questionnaires for consideration. This represents 75% and 76% of the sample respectively.

Figure 1.9: Reasons for non-return of surgical questionnaires (90 years and over)

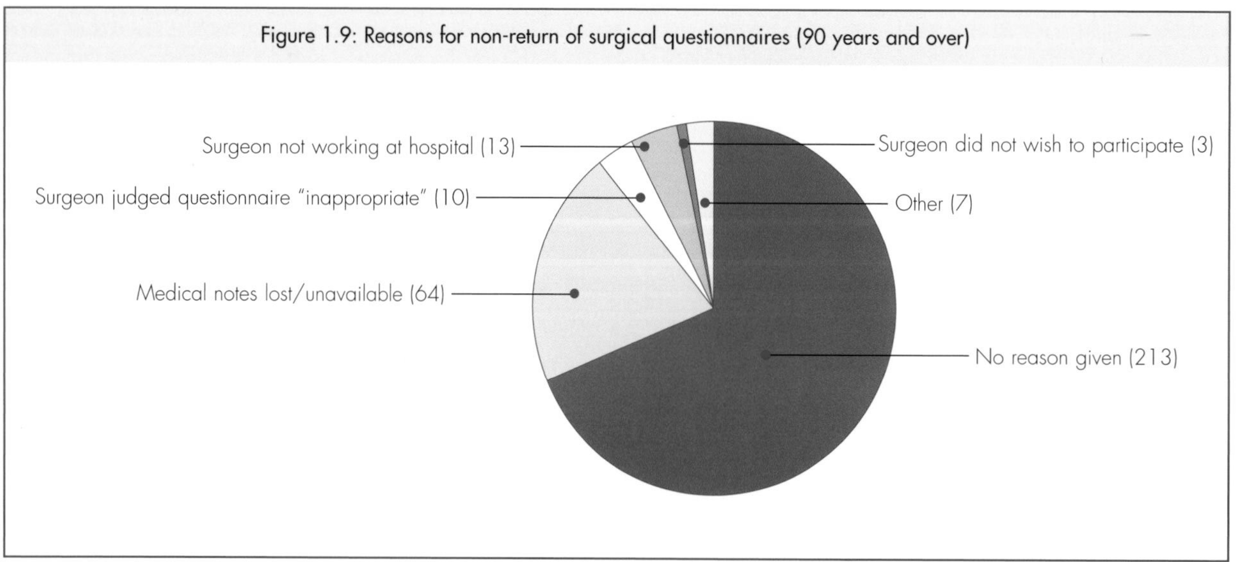

Figure 1.10: Reasons for non-return of anaesthetic questionnaires (90 years and over)

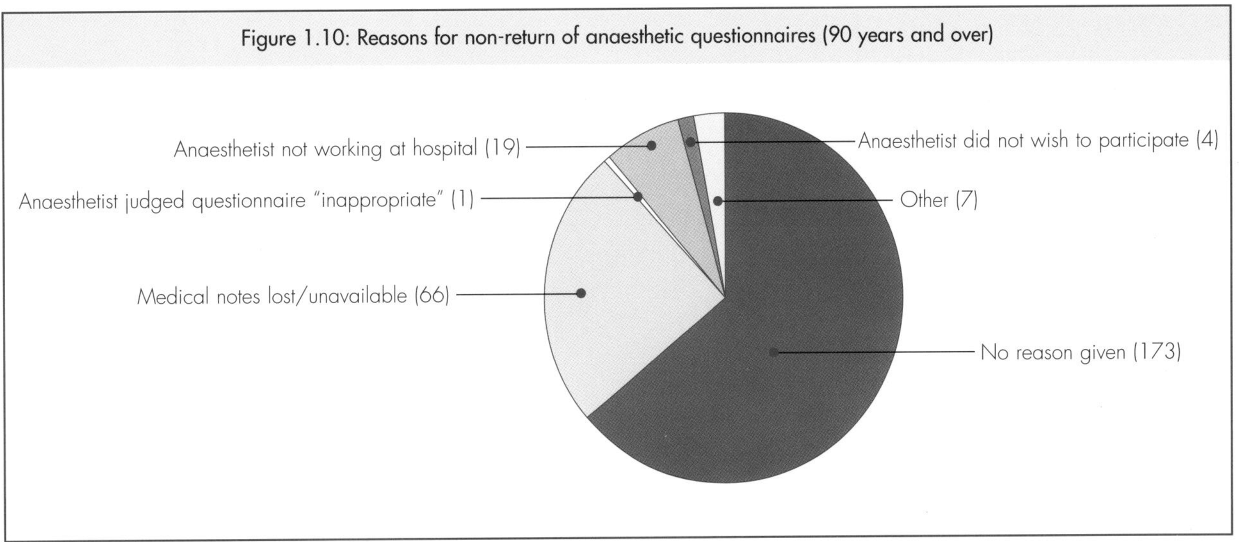

Figures 1.9 and 1.10 show that the reasons for non-return of questionnaires in the elderly sample varied. The largest group (69% of non-returns for surgery and 64% for anaesthesia) failed to return a questionnaire and did not respond to at least two reminders.

The second most common cause for failure to return a questionnaire was the loss or unavailability of the medical notes (21% of the surgical questionnaires and 24% of the anaesthetic questionnaires not returned).

The distribution, return and analysis rate on a regional basis is shown in Table 1.9.

Consultant input was high. Eighty-eight percent of surgical questionnaires (946/1077) and 91% of anaesthetic questionnaires (862/944) were completed, or seen and agreed, by the relevant consultant.

Table 1.9: Distribution, return and analysis of questionnaires by region (90 years and over)

SQ = Surgical Questionnaire AQ = Anaesthetic Questionnaire	Questionnaires distributed		Questionnaires returned		Return rate		Questionnaires analysed	
	SQ	AQ	SQ	AQ	SQ	AQ	SQ	AQ
Anglia & Oxford	144	134	127	115	88%	86%	120	110
North Thames	161	116	118	87	73%	75%	115	85
North West	192	174	148	140	77%	80%	143	136
Northern & Yorkshire	185	159	157	119	85%	75%	146	115
South & West	189	165	162	141	86%	85%	158	134
South Thames	233	206	180	159	77%	77%	176	157
Trent	124	114	93	84	75%	74%	91	83
West Midlands	96	89	61	67	64%	75%	57	66
Wales	73	56	45	38	62%	68%	45	38
Northern Ireland	18	14	15	10	83%	71%	15	10
Guernsey	2	2	2	2	100%	100%	2	2
Jersey	4	4	4	2	100%	50%	3	2
Isle of Man	2	2	2	1	100%	50%	2	1
Defence Secondary Care Agency	0	0	0	0	-	-	0	0
Independent sector	5	5	4	5	80%	100%	4	5
Total	**1428**	**1240**	**1118**	**970**	**78%**	**78%**	**1077**	**944**

LIVERPOOL JOHN MOORES UNIVERSITY LEARNING SERVICES

Distribution and return rates for the total sample group

Key Points

- *The return rate of 78% for surgical and anaesthetic questionnaires is the highest ever recorded by NCEPOD.*
- *The unavailability of medical records remains a problem; 20% of surgeons and 25% of anaesthetists gave this as the reason for not returning questionnaires.*
- *For a total of 242 surgical and 187 anaesthetic questionnaires sent, no reason was given for their non-return.*
- *It is hoped that the mandatory participation in NCEPOD required under clinical governance will result in higher overall reporting figures and improved questionnaire return rates in future years.*

Taking the two sample groups together, the regional distribution, return and analysis rates are shown in Table 1.10.

Over the two sample groups, a total of 1216 (78%) surgical questionnaires were returned. Of the 351 not returned, no reason was given in 242 (69%) cases. The unavailability of medical notes accounted for a further 69 (20%) non-returns (Table 1.11).

Over the two sample groups, a total of 1064 (78%) anaesthetic questionnaires were returned. Of the 296 not returned, no reason was given in 187 (63%) cases. The unavailability of medical notes accounted for a further 73 (25%) non-returns (Table 1.11).

A regional breakdown of the reasons given for the non-return of surgical and anaesthetic questionnaires is given in Tables 1.12 and 1.13.

Table 1.10: Regional distribution, return and analysis rates (total sample)

SQ = Surgical Questionnaire AQ = Anaesthetic Questionnaire	Questionnaires distributed		Questionnaires returned		Return rate		Questionnaires analysed	
	SQ	AQ	SQ	AQ	SQ	AQ	SQ	AQ
Anglia & Oxford	149	138	132	119	89%	86%	125	113
North Thames	197	148	144	118	73%	80%	140	115
North West	209	190	161	153	77%	81%	156	148
Northern & Yorkshire	206	175	170	133	83%	76%	159	128
South & West	201	176	170	145	85%	82%	166	138
South Thames	242	215	185	163	76%	76%	181	161
Trent	147	134	110	97	75%	72%	106	95
West Midlands	105	97	70	75	67%	77%	64	71
Wales	76	56	46	38	61%	68%	46	38
Northern Ireland	22	18	16	13	73%	72%	16	12
Guernsey	2	2	2	2	100%	100%	2	2
Jersey	4	4	4	2	100%	50%	3	2
Isle of Man	2	2	2	1	100%	50%	2	1
Defence Secondary Care Agency	0	0	0	0	-	-	0	0
Independent sector	5	5	4	5	80%	100%	4	5
Total	1567	1360	1216	1064	78%	78%	1170	1029

Table 1.11: Reasons given for non-return of questionnaires (total sample)		
	Surgical Questionnaires	Anaesthetic Questionnaires
No reason given	242	187
Medical notes lost or unavailable	69	73
Surgeon/anaesthetist judged return of questionnaire "inappropriate"	14	1
Surgeon/anaesthetist not working at hospital	14	22
Consultant did not wish to participate	3	4
Other	9	9
Total	**351**	**296**

Table 1.12: Reasons given for non-return of surgical questionnaires by region

	No reason given	Notes lost/ unavailable	Consultant judged return "inappropriate"	Consultant not working at hospital	Did not wish to participate	Other	Total
Anglia & Oxford	9	6	1	1	0	0	**17**
North Thames	42	6	0	3	0	2	**53**
North West	32	8	1	2	1	4	**48**
Northern & Yorkshire	24	9	1	1	0	1	**36**
South & West	18	7	2	2	1	1	**31**
South Thames	44	11	2	0	0	0	**57**
Trent	21	10	5	0	1	0	**37**
West Midlands	27	5	0	2	0	1	**35**
Wales	20	6	1	3	0	0	**30**
N Ireland	5	1	0	0	0	0	**6**
Guernsey	0	0	0	0	0	0	**0**
Jersey	0	0	0	0	0	0	**0**
Isle of Man	0	0	0	0	0	0	**0**
Independent sector	0	0	1	0	0	0	**1**

Table 1.13: Reasons given for non-return of anaesthetic questionnaires by region

	No reason given	Notes lost/ unavailable	Consultant judged return "inappropriate"	Consultant not working at hospital	Did not wish to participate	Other	Total
Anglia & Oxford	16	2	0	1	0	0	**19**
North Thames	16	9	0	4	0	1	**30**
North West	24	6	0	6	1	0	**37**
Northern & Yorkshire	27	10	0	5	0	0	**42**
South & West	18	9	1	2	1	0	**31**
South Thames	30	14	0	2	0	6	**52**
Trent	22	11	0	1	1	2	**37**
West Midlands	17	3	0	1	1	0	**22**
Wales	12	6	0	0	0	0	**18**
N Ireland	3	2	0	0	0	0	**5**
Guernsey	0	0	0	0	0	0	**0**
Jersey	2	0	0	0	0	0	**2**
Isle of Man	0	1	0	0	0	0	**1**
Independent sector	0	0	0	0	0	0	**0**

It must be pointed out that with the advent of clinical governance there will need to be a culture change. NCEPOD has already begun a process of involving medical directors so that they are aware if a questionnaire is not returned or the medical records cannot be traced. As the philosophies and systems encompassed in clinical governance become effective, organisations will demand real commitment from clinicians.

Organisations will need to provide a framework to support the highest quality clinical practice possible. An efficient medical records service underpins clinical practice, audit and risk management. The obligations laid upon all NHS bodies to keep proper records, and guidelines for good practice in managing records, are well-documented[4]. NCEPOD has repeatedly highlighted this problem in the conclusions and recommendations of previous reports:

- 'Hospital notes about dead patients tend to be given a low priority by records staff' [5]
- 'Managers should urgently review the storage and retrieval of medical notes' [6]
- 'Managers need to improve the services provided by medical records departments so that notes are available when required' [7]
- 'Systems should be implemented by Trusts to improve the retention and availability of all notes and records of clinical activity' [8]
- 'Clinical records and data collection still need to be improved' [9]

This service is still failing to support clinicians and we would encourage NHS Trusts and other healthcare providers to address this issue.

The overall percentage return rate of questionnaires in 1997/98 was the highest ever recorded by NCEPOD with 78% of anaesthetic and surgical questionnaires being returned. This compares with 1996/97 return rates of 77% for anaesthetic and 71% for surgical questionnaires. We hope that the trend will continue in years to come, particularly as the requirements of clinical governance begin to be reflected in return rates.

2 CHILDREN

Compiled by: R W Hoile and G S Ingram

RECOMMENDATIONS

- The concentration of children's surgical services (whether at a local or regional level) would increase expertise and further reduce occasional practice.
- A review of manpower planning is required to enable anaesthetists and surgeons in various specialties to train in the management of small children.
- There is a need for a system to assess the severity of surgical illness in children in order to gather meaningful information about outcomes. The ASA grading system is widely used by anaesthetists but, as a comparatively simple system, does have limitations for use in children.
- Anaesthetic and surgical trainees need to know the circumstances in which they should inform their consultants before undertaking an operation on a child. To encourage uniformity during rotational training programmes, national guidelines are required.
- In the management of acute children's surgical cases a regional organisational perspective is required. This particularly applies to the organisation of patient transfer between units. Paediatric units have a responsibility to lead this process.
- All Trusts should address the requirements of the framework document on paediatric intensive care[22]. Most children's hospitals have a good provision but many district general hospitals are deficient.
- The death of any child, occurring within 30 days of an anaesthetic or surgical procedure, should be subject to peer review, irrespective of the place of death.
- The events surrounding the perioperative death of any child should be reviewed in the context of multidisciplinary clinical audit.
- There is a need for central guidance to ensure the uniformity of data collection on surgery in children.

2. Children

Introduction

Most deaths after anaesthesia and surgery in children are associated with congenital anomalies, necrotising enterocolitis (NEC), tumours or trauma (particularly of the central nervous system). These are all conditions with potentially serious implications for the outcome of surgery and the prospects for the child's satisfactory future development. Even from the perspective of an enquiry based on the management of those who died within 30 days of surgery it is clear that anaesthetists and surgeons, despite the problems presented by patients in such parlous medical states, are doing most things well. For example, there were no deaths after the common childhood operations of appendicectomy and tonsillectomy. Many of the children in this study had diseases from which, without surgery, they would certainly have died and even if surgery had been successful many would have been left with permanent disability. Thus, for example, in otorhinolaryngology and head and neck surgery, the operations were an episode in the general deterioration of each of these children who had very serious and ultimately fatal congenital abnormalities or systemic disease.

By comparison with the data from the 1989 NCEPOD report on deaths in children, published in 1990[10], the process and structure of services for the provision of anaesthesia and surgery for children have changed for the better. It is, however, deplorable that there are still little or no data, e.g. numbers of patients who have operations, to enable rates of death to be calculated. A general conclusion of the previous report on children was that the data systems in the NHS in 1989 were inadequate and did not allow the calculation of rates of operations and deaths. Comparisons between centres, which might have influenced clinical practice, could not be made in a timely manner. This situation remains unchanged, despite several voluntary comparative audit projects conducted by the Royal College of Surgeons of England and the British Association of Paediatric Surgeons (BAPS). These studies initially recruited 25% of BAPS members (26/102) in 1993/4[11] and 31% of members (34/109) in 1994/5[12]. In 1997/8 data concerning 50% of neonatal surgical admissions were recorded, which allowed calculation of mortality rates for procedures[13]. However, this does not represent comprehensive national data.

The 1989 NCEPOD report referred to above recommended that 'surgeons and anaesthetists should not undertake occasional paediatric practice'. The information presented here shows that this message has been acted upon; the proportion of anaesthetists not undertaking the care of infants of less than six months has increased from 16% to 58% since the earlier report. Whilst applauding this concentration of practice and the potential benefit to be gained from having fewer but more experienced anaesthetists undertaking the care of infants, it has to be recognised that there is a limit to how far this trend can go unless further changes take place in the staffing and organisation of acute hospital services for the very young.

The sample reviewed in this report includes deaths in children aged from birth to 15 years (i.e. until the day preceding the 16th birthday). All surgical specialties except cardiac surgery are included. A decision was made to exclude cardiac surgery for several reasons. Firstly, an audit of these deaths is already in place and we did not wish to place an additional burden on these clinicians. Secondly, the individual nature of many of the cardiac anomalies makes broad conclusions difficult. Lastly, we wished to revisit the provision of surgery for children and review changes in the ten years since the last report on paediatric anaesthesia and surgery; it was felt that this would be more meaningful within non-cardiac surgical specialties.

General issues

Who anaesthetises and who operates on children?

Key Points

- *There is a lack of uniformity of data collected within the NHS.*
- *The proportion of anaesthetists who do not anaesthetise infants of less than six months old has increased from 16% to 58% when compared with data from ten years ago.*
- *A significant number of anaesthetic consultants giving anaesthesia to children still do a small number of cases each year.*
- *There has been a considerable shift in practice (with more specialisation in children's surgery) within some specialties, for example orthopaedic surgery, whereas in other areas there has been little change, when compared with data from ten years ago.*
- *Very occasional practice in emergency situations persists within surgery on children.*

At the beginning of 1999 a short questionnaire was sent to all consultant anaesthetists and surgeons on the NCEPOD database requesting information on consultants' paediatric practice. Consultants were asked 'Do you ever anaesthetise children aged 15 or under?' or 'Do you, or your junior staff, ever operate on children aged 15 or under?' If an affirmative answer was given to this question, figures were requested on the number of children anaesthetised or operated on each year, in three age groups: birth to less than six months, six months to less than two years and two to 15 years.

The replies indicate that the majority of anaesthetists (66%, 2126/3247) and surgeons (55%, 3580/6513) in all regions treat some children (Tables 2.2 and 2.4). The answers were a mixture of verifiable local data and generous estimates. There are no readily accessible contemporary data with which to check the figures.

Several interesting facts emerged:

- Some anaesthetists and surgeons either could not or would not answer the questions at all. Some did not return the data (28% of anaesthetists and 33% of surgeons) and others replied in a manner which made analysis impossible e.g. 'many', 'rarely', 'all my cases', 'over 1000' etc.

- Trusts throughout the UK are clearly collecting differing sets of data. Returns included: '<6 months, 6 months-$2\frac{1}{2}$ years, $2\frac{1}{2}$-$15\frac{1}{2}$ years'; '<3 months, 3 months-4 years, 5-16 years'; '<6 months, 6 months-2 years, 2-18 years'; 'infants (<1 year), pre-school (<5 years), 5-15 years' and '<1 year, 1-5 years, 5-15 years'.

- Anaesthetists and surgeons who said that they did not treat children aged less than six months wrote that they would only do so in an emergency!

The lack of uniformity of data collected within the NHS is shameful. There is a need for a clearly defined data set, which all Trusts could apply. This is vitally important if any form of comparative audit is to take place, as envisaged as part of clinical governance. Secondly, the worst form of practice, i.e. very occasional practice in emergency situations persists within anaesthesia and surgery on children.

Some departments replied jointly. Whilst the data could not be analysed in the main tables, it was felt that this should be tabulated separately (Table 2.1) in view of the diligent way in which the information was returned. In the future clinical governance may require Trusts to identify individual practitioners within aggregated local data.

The figures in Table 2.1 show a considerable variation in exposure to paediatric practice. Gynaecologists see few children and these cases are usually examinations under anaesthesia or termination of pregnancies. What can be the justification for three neurosurgeons sharing an extremely occasional practice?

Table 2.1: Departmental data

	<6 months	6 months to <2 years	2 to15 years	Total
Paediatric surgery (4 consultants)	Not supplied	Not supplied	Not supplied	**1803**
Anaesthetic (4 consultants)	0	20	825	**845**
Gynaecology (4 consultants)	0	0	10	**10**
Gynaecology (4 consultants)	0	0	8	**8**
Neurosurgery (3 consultants)	1	1	10	**12**
Otorhinolaryngology (2 consultants)	6	40	1000	**1046**
Oral & maxillofacial (4 consultants)	5	100	1600	**1705**
Orthopaedics (4 consultants)	5	50	800	**855**
Orthopaedics (5 consultants)	Not supplied	Not supplied	Not supplied	**300**
Orthopaedics (6 consultants)	11	21	647	**679**
Orthopaedics (5 consultants)	4	20	311	**335**
Orthopaedics (4 consultants)	3	31	349	**383**
Orthopaedics (6 consultants)	1	22	286	**309**
Trauma service (8 consultants)	0	50	700	**750**

Children

Who anaesthetises children?

Table 2.2: Consultant anaesthetists by region: "Do you ever anaesthetise children aged 15 or under?"

	Yes	No	Not returned	Total	Return rate
Anglia & Oxford	229	11	58	**298**	81%
North Thames	251	24	167	**442**	62%
North West	258	53	120	**431**	72%
Northern & Yorkshire	269	22	93	**384**	76%
South & West	263	9	80	**352**	77%
South Thames	237	15	107	**359**	70%
Trent	195	41	74	**310**	76%
West Midlands	195	16	103	**314**	67%
Wales	123	6	58	**187**	69%
Northern Ireland	89	13	33	**135**	76%
Guernsey	5	0	0	**5**	100%
Jersey	3	0	2	**5**	60%
Isle of Man	3	0	1	**4**	75%
Defence Secondary Care Agency	2	0	3	**5**	40%
Independent sector	4	3	9	**16**	44%
Total	2126	213	908	3247	72%

More than a quarter of anaesthetists did not provide answers to these questions. Retirements and other changes in employment are registered slowly and there is inertia in the NCEPOD database. This explanation may partly account for the low figures but some of the return rates are unacceptable (e.g. North Thames).

From this data it appears that 91% of consultant anaesthetists anaesthetise children of 15 years or younger. In the data collected in 1989, 95% of anaesthetists anaesthetised children of ten years or less.

Table 2.3: Number of consultants anaesthetising children in different age groups

Number of cases per annum	<6 months	6 months to <2 years	2 to 15 years
Nil	1135	434	7
1–9	605	573	154
10–19	162	418	222
20–50	119	463	682
>50	94	222	1020
No figures supplied	11	16	41

For the youngest age group, infants under six months, direct comparison can be made with similar data collected in 1989. Expressed in terms of percentages, to facilitate comparison, the respective samples are shown in Figure 2.1.

In the 1989 sample the percentage return of those stating that they gave anaesthetics to children of less than six months but giving no figures that could be included in the analysis was 3%; in the current sample it was less than 1%.

During the period between 1989 and the current sample, the proportion of consultants anaesthetising small numbers of infants has fallen. At the same time, the percentage doing none has increased from 16% to well over half of all anaesthetic consultants. This is evidence of the change that has occurred in anaesthesia for children over the past ten years and perhaps an indication of the influence of the earlier report.

In 1997 the House of Commons Health Committee in their Report 'Hospital Services for Children and Young People'[14] stated that it was 'highly undesirable that some surgeons and anaesthetists should be continuing to undertake occasional paediatric practice'. The evidence that they had received on which to base this recommendation was that an anaesthetist engaged in paediatric practice should have a regular annual caseload of 12 infants under six months, 50 infants and children under two years and 300 children under ten. However, of those consultants who do anaesthetise infants aged under six months, 62% (605/980) do fewer than ten cases a year and for children aged between six months and two years, 34% (573/1676) of anaesthetists also do fewer than ten cases a year.

Figure 2.1: Percentage of consultant anaesthetists (based on returned questionnaires) anaesthetising infants of less than six months grouped by number of cases anaesthetised

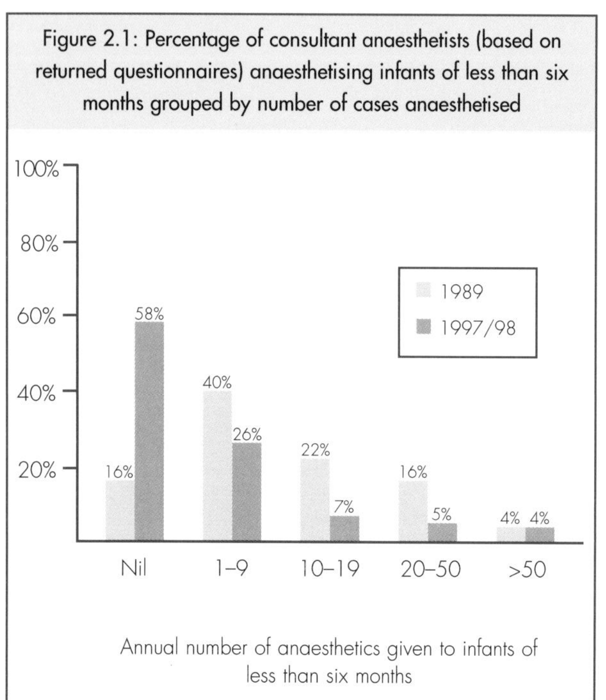

Who operates on children?

Table 2.4: Consultant surgeons by region: "Do you, or your junior staff, ever operate on children aged 15 or under?"

	Yes	No	Not returned	Total	Return rate
Anglia & Oxford	352	41	165	**558**	70%
North Thames	444	107	362	**913**	60%
North West	428	107	329	**864**	62%
Northern & Yorkshire	463	95	260	**818**	68%
South & West	428	62	193	**683**	72%
South Thames	441	74	249	**764**	67%
Trent	301	124	141	**566**	75%
West Midlands	354	72	225	**651**	65%
Wales	204	30	138	**372**	63%
Northern Ireland	127	35	71	**233**	70%
Guernsey	6	1	5	**12**	58%
Jersey	6	0	6	**12**	50%
Isle of Man	8	1	2	**11**	82%
Defence Secondary Care Agency	10	6	4	**20**	80%
Independent sector	8	11	17	**36**	53%
Total	**3580**	**766**	**2167**	**6513**	**67%**

Consultant surgeons by specialty

ACCIDENT & EMERGENCY

Question 2.1: A&E consultants (and teams) who operate on children

- Yes 26
- No 62
- Not answered 64
- **Total 152**

Forty-two percent of consultants in this specialty failed to return the questionnaire to NCEPOD. The calculations below are based on the 88 returned questionnaires.

In 1989 the majority of A&E consultants operated on children (110/134, 82%)[10], whereas this figure is now 30% (26/88). Those dealing with babies aged under six months has fallen from 30% (40/134) in 1989 to 10% (9/88). The advent of trauma teams and better provision of paediatric services probably means that A&E consultants and their teams are less likely to treat surgical conditions in children. However, initiating resuscitation in children is appropriate pending the arrival of specialist teams.

Figure 2.2: Percentage of A&E consultants and teams (based on returned questionnaires) operating on infants of less than six months grouped by number of cases treated

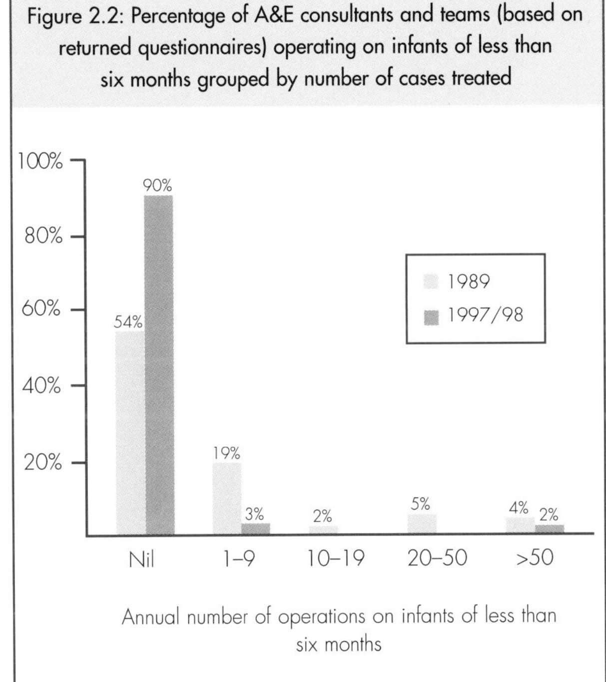

Table 2.5: Number of A&E consultants (and teams) operating on children in different age groups

Number of cases per annum	<6 months	6 months to <2 years	2 to 15 years
Nil	17	13	0
1–9	3	5	2
10–19	0	1	6
20–50	0	0	6
>50	2	3	7
No figures supplied	4	4	5

Children

Children

Orthopaedic surgery

Question 2.2: Consultant orthopaedic surgeons (and teams) who operate on children

Yes	803
No	108
Not answered	437
Total	**1348**

Thirty-two percent of consultants in this specialty failed to return the questionnaire to NCEPOD. The calculations below are based on the 911 returned questionnaires.

Table 2.6: Number of consultant orthopaedic surgeons (and teams) operating on children in different age groups

Number of cases per annum	<6 months	6 months to <2 years	2 to 15 years
Nil	562	245	5
1–9	176	344	82
10–19	23	104	177
20–50	17	68	335
>50	1	12	162
No figures supplied	24	30	42

Figure 2.3: Percentage of consultant orthopaedic surgeons and teams (based on returned questionnaires) operating on infants of less than six months grouped by number of cases treated

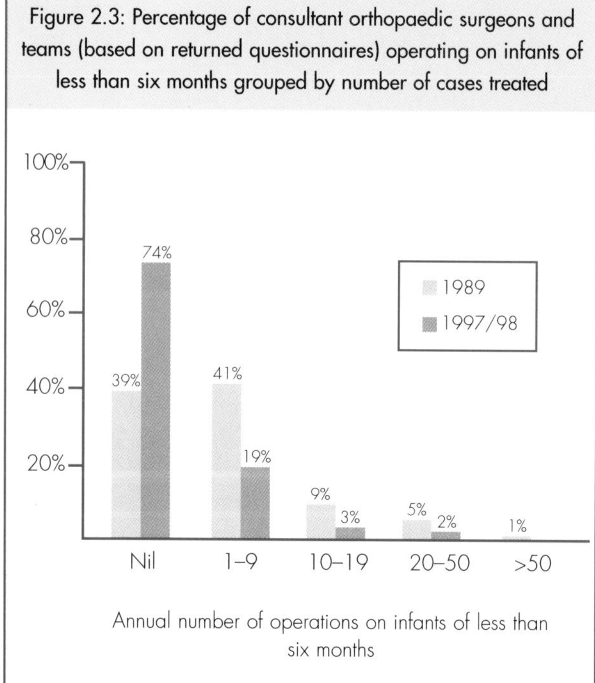

One hundred and eight (108/911, 12%) orthopaedic surgeons do not operate on children at all; a total of 670 (670/911, 74%) do not operate on children under six months old. There appears to be further subspecialisation in childhood orthopaedic surgery compared to 1989[10]. Although 176 (19%) surgeons operate on the occasional child under six months old this is a considerable fall from the figure of 41% in 1989. Until there is further expansion and rationalisation in orthopaedic services the need to manage trauma in district general hospitals may make this occasional practice inevitable.

General surgery

Question 2.3: Consultant general surgeons (and teams) who operate on children

Yes	816
No	207
Not answered	498
Total	**1521**

Thirty-three percent of consultants in this specialty failed to return the questionnaire to NCEPOD. The calculations below are based on the 1023 returned questionnaires.

Table 2.7: Number of consultant general surgeons (and teams) operating on children in different age groups

Number of cases per annum	<6 months	6 months to <2 years	2 to 15 years
Nil	523	335	0
1–9	220	237	104
10–19	37	127	145
20–50	16	85	369
>50	2	11	157
No figures supplied	18	21	41

Two hundred and seven (207/1023, 20%) general surgeons do not operate on children at all; a total of 730 (730/1023, 71%) do not operate on children aged under six months. This compares with a figure of 32% in 1989[10] and suggests further subspecialisation. However, 220 (220/1023, 22%) general surgeons stated that they do operate on infants less than six months old but undertake fewer than ten operations in this age group per annum. This represents a decrease from the percentage of surgeons who reported occasional practice ten years ago[10]. This suggests that recommendations aimed at reorganising the provision of 'general surgery' services for children have had an overall effect, but occasional practice is still occurring.

Figure 2.4: Percentage of consultant general surgeons and teams (based on returned questionnaires) operating on infants of less than six months grouped by number of cases treated

Annual number of operations on infants of less than six months

Figure 2.5: Percentage of consultant oral/maxillofacial surgeons and teams (based on returned questionnaires) operating on infants of less than six months grouped by number of cases treated

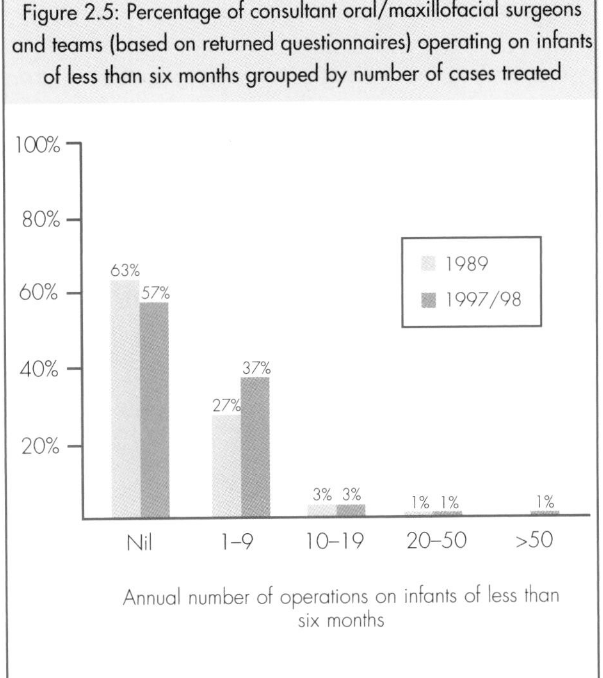

Oral/Maxillofacial surgery

Question 2.4: Consultant oral/maxillofacial surgeons (and teams) who operate on children

Yes	156
No	5
Not answered	97
Total	**258**

Thirty-eight percent of consultants in this specialty failed to return the questionnaire to NCEPOD. The calculations below are based on the 161 returned questionnaires.

Table 2.8: Number of consultant oral/maxillofacial surgeons (and teams) operating on children in different age groups

Number of cases per annum	<6 months	6 months to <2 years	2 to 15 years
Nil	86	22	2
1–9	60	70	2
10–19	5	37	14
20–50	2	20	42
>50	1	4	90
No figures supplied	2	3	6

Dental surgery

Question 2.5: Consultant dental surgeons (and teams) who operate on children

Yes	12
No	3
Not answered	12
Total	**27**

Forty-four percent of consultants in this specialty failed to return the questionnaire to NCEPOD.

Table 2.9: Number of consultant dental surgeons (and teams) operating on children in different age groups

Number of cases per annum	<6 months	6 months to <2 years	2 to 15 years
Nil	7	3	0
1–9	5	2	1
10–19	0	4	0
20–50	0	2	0
>50	0	1	10
No figures supplied	0	0	1

Otorhinolaryngology

Question 2.6: Consultant otorhinolaryngologists (and teams) who operate on children

Yes	320
No	4
Not answered	207
Total	**531**

Thirty-nine percent of consultants in this specialty failed to return the questionnaire to NCEPOD. The calculations below are based on the 324 returned questionnaires.

Table 2.10: Number of consultant otorhinolaryngologists (and teams) operating on children in different age groups

Number of cases per annum	<6 months	6 months to <2 years	2 to 15 years
Nil	156	25	3
1-9	110	82	1
10-19	19	67	2
20-50	17	99	16
>50	6	32	280
No figures supplied	12	15	18

Figure 2.6: Percentage of consultant otorhinolaryngologists and teams (based on returned questionnaires) operating on infants of less than six months grouped by number of cases treated

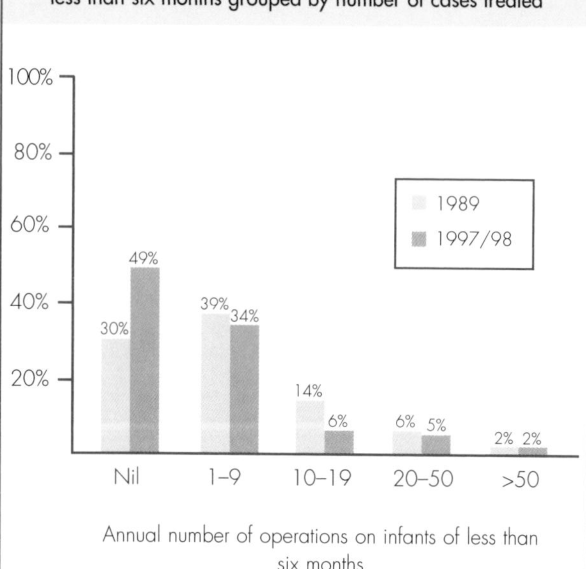

Gynaecology

Question 2.7: Consultant gynaecologists (and teams) who operate on children

Yes	556
No	215
Not answered	324
Total	**1095**

Thirty percent of consultants in this specialty failed to return the questionnaire to NCEPOD. The calculations below are based on the 771 returned questionnaires.

Table 2.11: Number of consultant gynaecologists (and teams) operating on children in different age groups

Number of cases per annum	<6 months	6 months to <2 years	2 to 15 years
Nil	516	429	13
1-9	26	109	444
10-19	0	1	56
20-50	0	0	7
>50	0	0	3
No figures supplied	14	17	33

Figure 2.7: Percentage of consultant gynaecologists and teams (based on returned questionnaires) operating on infants of less than six months grouped by number of cases treated

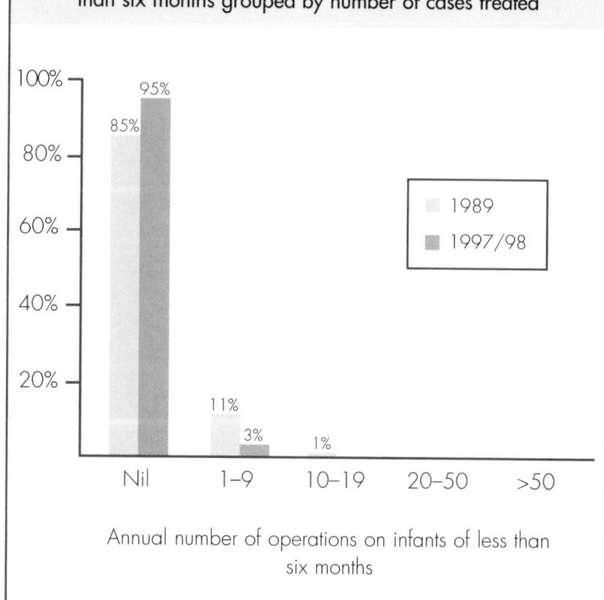

Most gynaecologists do not operate on small children. The percentage of gynaecologists who occasionally operate on infants aged under six months has dropped from 11% in 1989[10] to 3% in 1997/98. The amount of children's surgery in general is small and often consists of a diagnostic examination under anaesthesia or, in older children, termination of pregnancy.

Neurosurgery

Question 2.8: Consultant neurosurgeons (and teams) who operate on children

Yes	88
No	27
Not answered	55
Total	**170**

Thirty-two percent of consultants in this specialty failed to return the questionaire to NCEPOD. The calculations below are based on the 115 returned questionnaires.

Table 2.12: Number of consultant neurosurgeons (and teams) operating on children in different age groups

Number of cases per annum	<6 months	6 months to <2 years	2 to 15 years
Nil	30	20	0
1–9	41	42	37
10–19	2	9	25
20–50	7	8	13
>50	4	5	9
No figures supplied	4	4	4

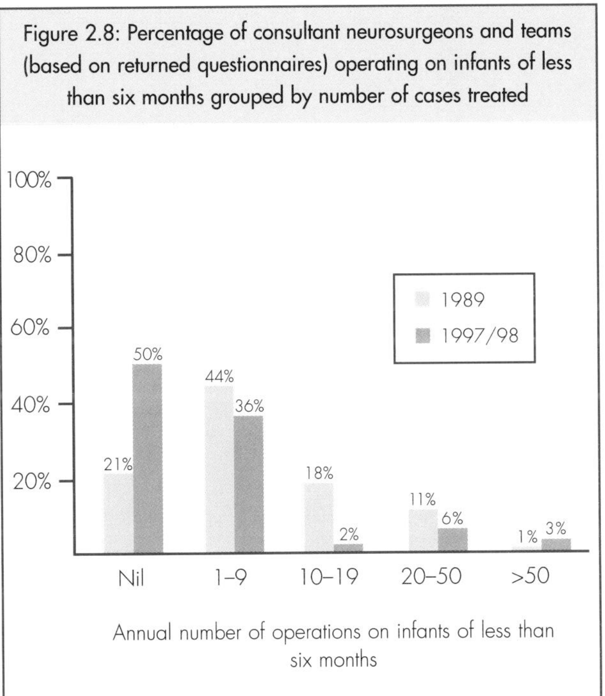

Figure 2.8: Percentage of consultant neurosurgeons and teams (based on returned questionnaires) operating on infants of less than six months grouped by number of cases treated

Twenty-three percent of neurosurgeons (27/115) never operate on children and 50% (57/115) do not operate on babies under six months old. This is a change from the data published in 1989[10] when all neurosurgeons reported operating on children. There is still a considerable amount of surgery on children aged under six months which is done by neurosurgeons with an infrequent practice in children of this age.

Ophthalmology

Question 2.9: Consultant ophthalmic surgeons (and teams) who operate on children

Yes	351
No	26
Not answered	219
Total	**596**

Thirty-seven percent of consultants in this specialty failed to return the questionnaire to NCEPOD. The calculations below are based on the 377 returned questionnaires.

Table 2.13: Number of consultant ophthalmic surgeons (and teams) operating on children in different age groups

Number of cases per annum	<6 months	6 months to <2 years	2 to 15 years
Nil	233	45	4
1–9	92	183	88
10–19	13	65	89
20–50	5	44	120
>50	3	8	43
No figures supplied	5	6	7

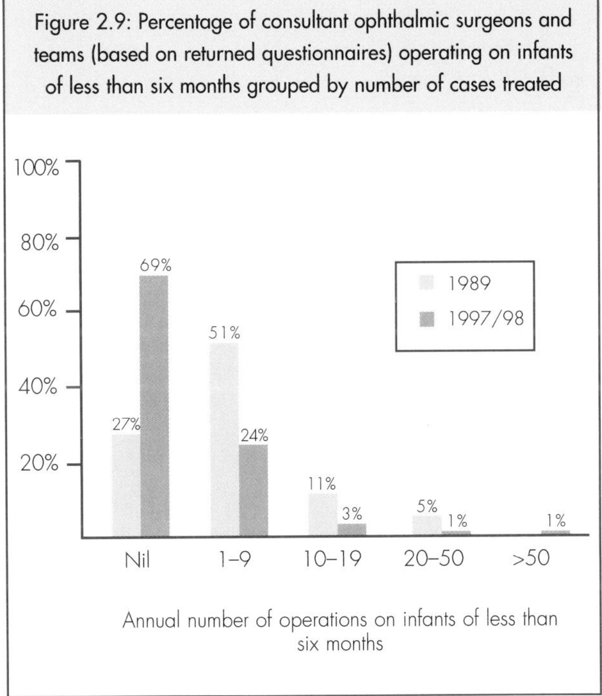

Figure 2.9: Percentage of consultant ophthalmic surgeons and teams (based on returned questionnaires) operating on infants of less than six months grouped by number of cases treated

Most ophthalmic surgeons operate on children but 259 (259/377, 69%) do not operate on babies under six months old. Occasional practice (less than ten cases per annum) in children aged less than six months has halved in the last ten years, from 51% (210/411) of surgeons in 1989[10] to 24% (92/377).

Paediatric surgery

Question 2.10: Consultant paediatric surgeons (and teams) who operate on children

Yes	54
No	0
Not answered	22
Total	**76**

Twenty-nine percent (22/76) of consultants in this specialty failed to return the questionnaire to NCEPOD.

Table 2.14: Number of consultant paediatric surgeons (and teams) operating on children in different age groups

Number of cases per annum	<6 months	6 months to <2 years	2 to 15 years
Nil	0	0	0
1-9	0	0	0
10-19	3	0	0
20-50	5	4	0
>50	38	42	46
No figures supplied	8	8	8

The specialist paediatric surgeons are operating on large numbers of children in all age groups. Those listed as operating on 10-19 and 20-50 cases per annum are probably general surgeons with a specific interest in paediatric surgery.

Urology

Question 2.11: Consultant urologists (and teams) who operate on children

Yes	232
No	76
Not answered	128
Total	**436**

Twenty-nine percent (128/436) of consultants in this specialty failed to return the questionnaire to NCEPOD. The calculations below are based on the 308 returned questionnaires. The practice of a small number of specialised paediatric urologists is included in these figures.

Two hundred and sixty-eight (268/308, 87%) urologists do not operate on children aged under six months (Figure 2.10). This is an increase compared with the situation in 1989[10] (125/251, 50%). The incidence of occasional practice (less than ten cases) in babies aged under six months has fallen from 32% of surgeons in 1989[10] (80/251) to 10% in this report (31/308). This is further evidence of the impact made by guidelines on the provision of surgical services for children[15].

Table 2.15: Number of consultant urologists (and teams) operating on children in different age groups

Number of cases per annum	<6 months	6 months to <2 years	2 to 15 years
Nil	192	99	0
1-9	31	76	44
10-19	3	32	57
20-50	2	15	89
>50	1	2	29
No figures supplied	3	8	13

Figure 2.10: Percentage of consultant urologists and teams (based on returned questionnaires) operating on infants of less than six months grouped by number of cases treated

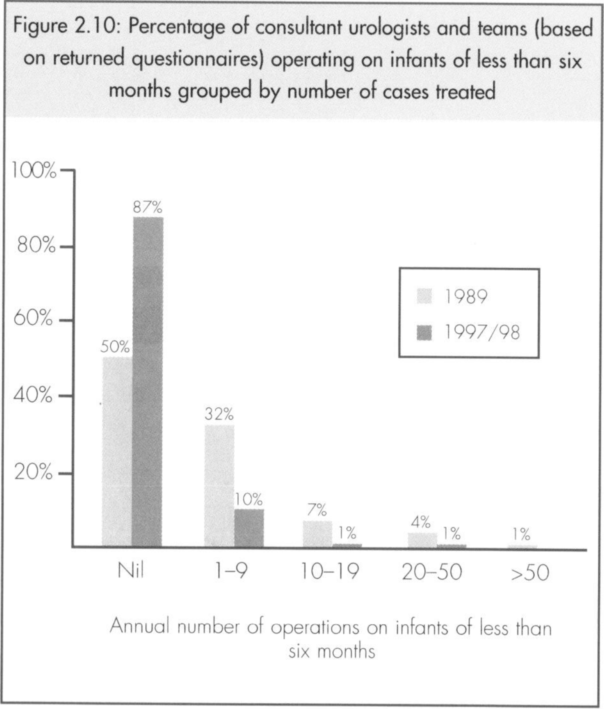

Plastic surgery

Question 2.12: Consultant plastic surgeons (and teams) who operate on children

Yes	102
No	1
Not answered	68
Total	**171**

Forty percent (68/171) of consultants in this specialty failed to return the questionnaire to NCEPOD.

Most plastic surgeons operate on children although for some age groups the practice is infrequent (Table 2.16).

Table 2.16: Number of consultant plastic surgeons (and teams) operating on children in different age groups			
Number of cases per annum	<6 months	6 months to <2 years	2 to 15 years
Nil	25	5	1
1–9	33	21	1
10–19	13	18	9
20–50	21	34	26
>50	5	19	59
No figures supplied	5	5	6

THORACIC SURGERY

Question 2.13: Consultant thoracic surgeons (and teams) who operate on children

Yes 22
No 3
Not answered 8
Total **33**

Twenty-four percent (8/33) of consultants in this specialty failed to return the questionnaire to NCEPOD.

Table 2.17: Number of consultant thoracic surgeons (and teams) operating on children in different age groups			
Number of cases per annum	<6 months	6 months to <2 years	2 to 15 years
Nil	16	8	0
1–9	6	11	16
10–19	0	3	5
20–50	0	0	0
>50	0	0	1
No figures supplied	0	0	0

VASCULAR SURGERY

Question 2.14: Consultant vascular surgeons (and teams) who operate on children

Yes 26
No 24
Not answered 18
Total **68**

Twenty-six percent (18/68) of consultants in this specialty failed to return the questionnaire to NCEPOD.

Table 2.18: Number of consultant vascular surgeons (and teams) operating on children in different age groups			
Number of cases per annum	<6 months	6 months to <2 years	2 to 15 years
Nil	19	13	0
1–9	7	11	13
10–19	0	2	4
20–50	0	0	8
>50	0	0	1
No figures supplied	0	0	0

TRANSPLANT SURGERY

Question 2.15: Consultant transplant surgeons (and teams) who operate on children

Yes 7
No 3
Not answered 6
Total **16**

Thirty-eight percent (6/16) of consultants in this specialty failed to return the questionnaire to NCEPOD.

Table 2.19: Number of consultant transplant surgeons (and teams) operating on children in different age groups			
Number of cases per annum	<6 months	6 months to <2 years	2 to 15 years
Nil	5	2	0
1–9	1	2	3
10–19	0	2	1
20–50	0	0	2
>50	0	0	0
No figures supplied	1	1	1

SPINAL SURGERY

Question 2.16: Consultant spinal surgeons (and teams) who operate on children

Yes 6
No 2
Not answered 3
Total **11**

Twenty-seven percent (3/11) of consultants in this specialty failed to return the questionnaire to NCEPOD.

Table 2.20: Number of consultant spinal surgeons (and teams) operating on children in different age groups			
Number of cases per annum	<6 months	6 months to <2 years	2 to 15 years
Nil	4	2	0
1–9	2	4	5
10–19	0	0	0
20–50	0	0	1
>50	0	0	0
No figures supplied	0	0	0

HAND SURGERY

Question 2.17: Consultant hand surgeons (and teams) who operate on children

Yes	3
No	0
Not answered	1
Total	**4**

Twenty-five percent (1/4) of consultants in this specialty failed to return the questionnaire to NCEPOD.

Table 2.21: Number of consultant hand surgeons (and teams) operating on children in different age groups			
Number of cases per annum	<6 months	6 months to <2 years	2 to 15 years
Nil	1	0	0
1–9	1	0	0
10–19	0	1	0
20–50	1	2	1
>50	0	0	2
No figures supplied	0	0	0

Occasional practice in surgery on children under six months

The figures in Table 2.22 must be seen in the context of the specialty and hospital type. Surgeons may be operating on these small numbers of patients because of local demand and the inability to specialise within the specialty because of a lack of resources. Alternatively the total number of cases may be small and the presenting conditions rare (in which case there should be referral to a centre with adequate experience of these conditions). The precise age which delineates whether a child is treated by a general surgeon with a paediatric interest or a specialist paediatric surgeon has yet to be defined. The important factor is the appropriateness of the procedures done, bearing in mind the expertise and support services available. This is particularly important with regard to anaesthesia. Anaesthetists should not find themselves pressured to maintain a local service, particularly for infants, when there are insufficient cases for them to be able to maintain their expertise. Similar concerns may also be relevant to specialist nursing.

This demand for local provision of healthcare for these young patients may be at variance with the need for rationalisation of specialist services. Recommendations concerning the training of general surgeons were published in 1998[15] but the authors are not aware of much change since then. A review of manpower planning is required to enable surgeons in various specialties to train in the management of small children. This would allow safe local services for those children who do not require major or complex surgery and support the dedicated paediatric surgeons in regional centres.

Table 2.22: Number of surgeons by specialty who operate on small numbers (one to nine) of children per annum aged under six months		
Specialty	Number of surgeons	%
Accident & Emergency	3/88	3%
Orthopaedic surgery	176/911	19%
General surgery	220/1023	22%
Oral/maxillofacial surgery	60/161	37%
Dental surgery	5/15	33%
Otorhinolaryngology	110/324	34%
Gynaecology	26/771	3%
Neurosurgery	41/115	36%
Ophthalmic surgery	92/377	24%
Urology	31/308	10%
Plastic surgery	33/103	32%
Thoracic surgery	6/25	24%
Vascular surgery	7/50	14%
Transplant surgery	1/10	10%
Spinal surgery	2/8	25%
Hand surgery	1/3	33%

PATIENT PROFILE

Key Points

- *Most deaths were associated with congenital anomalies, necrotising enterocolitis, tumours or trauma.*
- *There were no reported deaths after the common childhood operations of appendicectomy and tonsillectomy.*

Age

Table 2.23: Age of patient at time of final operation

Age	Number
Less than one month	28
One month to less than six months	21
Six months to less than one year	6
One year to less than two years	7
Two years to less than four years	7
Four years to less than 11 years	19
11 years to less than 16 years	24
Total*	112

* *total number of cases covered by the 93 surgical questionnaires and 85 anaesthetic questionnaires returned to NCEPOD and included in the analysis*

Early deaths were mostly due to congenital anomalies and neonatal problems such as necrotising enterocolitis, and the later deaths mainly resulted from trauma.

Birthweight and perinatal mortality

The survival rate for infants born weighing less than 1500g (very low birthweight, VLBW) is approximately 80% whereas for those born weighing less than 1000g (extremely low birthweight, ELBW) survival is about 63%. A baby who is premature (birth before 37 completed weeks of gestation) and small for gestational age (less than the 10th centile in weight expected for gestation) is in a high-risk group[16]. If the need for surgery arises then the risks of non-survival are increased. In addition, the survivors of combined prematurity and surgery may not have a good quality of life. There is a relatively high incidence of cerebral palsy, impaired vision and hearing, school failure and behaviour problems in these children. Bearing in mind this increased risk, the gestational age and weights of the children who were less than six months old at the time of surgery were analysed.

Figure 2.11: Gestational age at birth (when under six months old at the time of surgery) by weight at operation

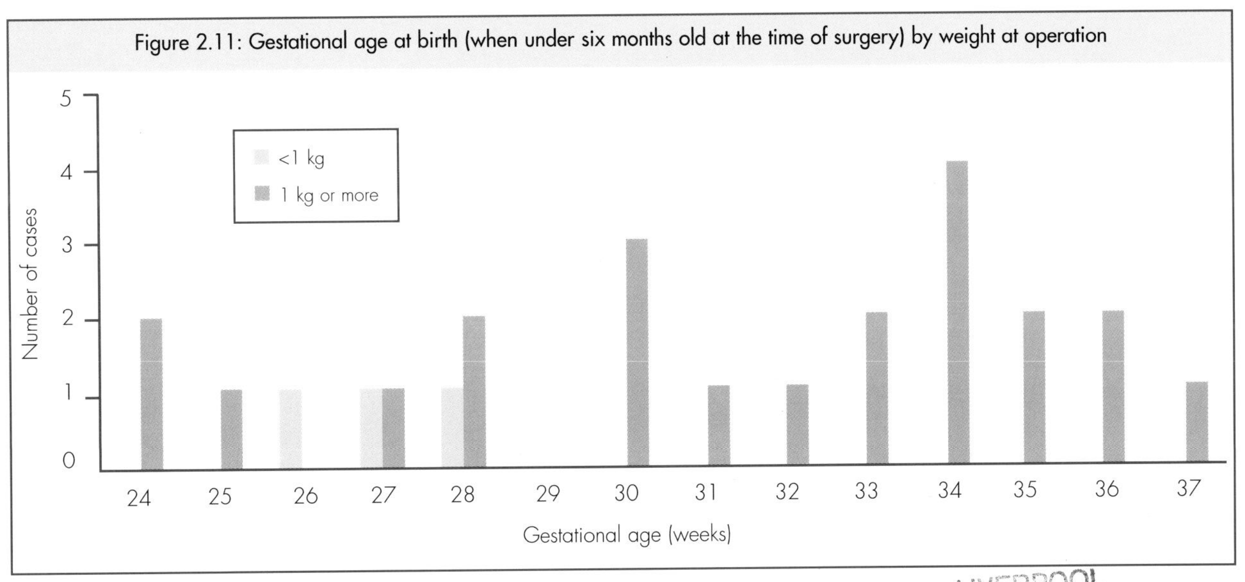

LIVERPOOL
JOHN MOORES UNIVERSITY
AVRIL ROBARTS LRC
TEL. 0151 231 4022

Sex

Question 2.18: Sex of child (SQ5)

Male	53
Female	40
Total	**93**

Overall there was an equal distribution of the sexes in this sample. However, amongst the children who were less than six months old at the time of surgery there were twice as many boys as girls (Figure 2.12).

Figure 2.12: Age at time of surgery for infants under six months by sex (SQs 1 and 5)

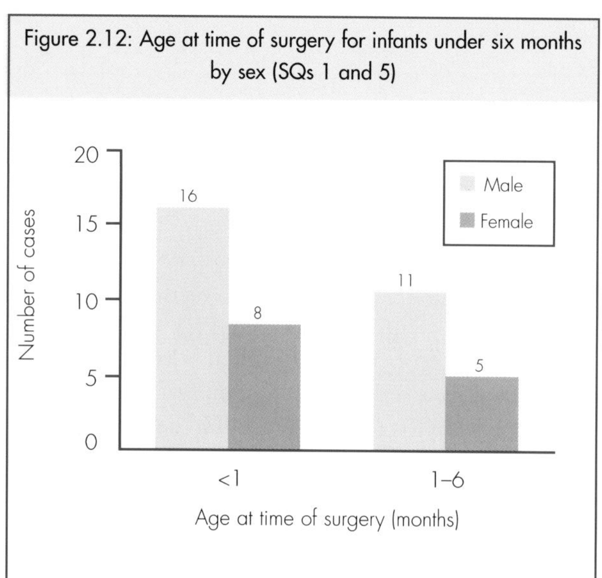

Procedures

Table 2.24 details the procedures done in the 112 cases where the child died. This list is compiled from both anaesthetic and surgical questionnaires. The procedures are grouped by the declared specialty (and subspecialty if known) of the consultant surgeon in charge of the case. There were 58 procedures done by paediatric surgeons, 52% (58/112) of the total. Neurosurgery accounted for 31 procedures, 28% (31/112). Of these neurosurgical operations, 45% (14/31) were done by specialist paediatric neurosurgeons, 26% (8/31) by surgeons with a mixed paediatric and adult practice, 10% (3/31) by neurosurgeons who said they had a mainly adult practice and 19% (6/31) by neurosurgeons who did not specify their type of practice (see page 48 for further discussion on neurosurgery).

In one case (Case 7, page 39) a laparotomy was done under the supervision of a plastic surgeon. This might seem inappropriate but the information returned was incomplete. The patient had undergone reconstructive surgery six days prior to the laparotomy, developed intra-abdominal bleeding and the laparotomy was done by an SpR 4 with a consultant plastic surgeon in theatre. It is not known from which specialty the registrar came. Death from renal failure was unrelated to the surgery.

The management of abdominal trauma in some children was of concern; this is discussed further on page 49.

Table 2.24: Specialty of consultant surgeons and operations performed

Specialty of consultant surgeon	Operation performed
Neurosurgery – Paediatric	Resection of choroid plexus tumour
Neurosurgery – Paediatric	Insertion of intracranial pressure monitor
Neurosurgery – Paediatric	Craniotomy and evacuation of acute subdural haematoma
Neurosurgery – Paediatric	Insertion of intracranial pressure monitor
Neurosurgery – Paediatric	Ventricular drainage and evacuation of cerebellar haematoma
Neurosurgery – Paediatric	Craniotomy and evacuation of haematoma
Neurosurgery – Paediatric	Craniotomy and evacuation of acute extradural haematoma
Neurosurgery – Paediatric	Craniotomy and evacuation of fungal abscess
Neurosurgery – Paediatric	Craniotomy and evacuation of acute subdural haematoma
Neurosurgery – Paediatric	Insertion of intracranial pressure monitor
Neurosurgery – Paediatric	Insertion of ventriculoperitoneal shunt
Neurosurgery – Paediatric	Stereotactic biopsy of brainstem mass
Neurosurgery – Paediatric	Frontoparietal craniotomy (acute subdural empyema). Bilateral antral lavage
Neurosurgery – Paediatric	Cranial expansion surgery
Neurosurgery – Mixed	Posterior fossa craniectomy and debulking of cerebellar tumour (medulloblastoma)
Neurosurgery – Mixed	Craniotomy, evacuation of subdural haematoma, and insertion of intracranial pressure monitor
Neurosurgery – Mixed	Craniotomy and evacuation of acute subdural haematoma

Specialty of consultant surgeon	Operation performed
Neurosurgery – Mixed	Insertion of external ventricular drain and revision of ventriculoperitoneal shunt
Neurosurgery – Mixed	Insertion of intracranial pressure monitor
Neurosurgery – Mixed	Revision of ventriculoperitoneal shunt
Neurosurgery – Mixed	Posterior fossa craniectomy and debulking of cerebellum
Neurosurgery – Mixed	Occipitocervical fixation using lateral mass plates and removal of posterior arch C1
Neurosurgery – Adult	Posterior fossa decompression and C1 - C2 laminectomy
Neurosurgery – Adult	Craniotomy and insertion of external ventricular drain
Neurosurgery – Adult	Evacuation of acute subdural haematoma
Neurosurgery	Craniotomy and evacuation of acute subdural haematoma
Neurosurgery	Insertion of intracranial pressure monitor
Neurosurgery	Endoscopic ventriculoscopy
Neurosurgery	Craniotomy for tumour
Neurosurgery	Craniotomy, evacuation of haematoma and temporal lobectomy
Neurosurgery	Ventriculoperitoneal shunt
Paediatric	Upper GI endoscopy and sclerotherapy to bleeding ulcer in oesophagus. Insertion of Sengstaken tube
Paediatric	Exploration of abdomen and external biliary drain
Paediatric	Exteriorisation of PD catheter cuff site and excision of granulation tissue. Insertion of femoral arterial and venous lines (open technique)
Paediatric	Thoracotomy and repair of aortic fistula
Paediatric	Second look laparotomy (in moribund patient to clarify appropriateness or not of continued active care on PICU)
Paediatric	Laparotomy
Paediatric	Oesophagoscopy
Paediatric	Attempted PEG, converted to open Stamm gastrostomy
Paediatric	Repair tracheo-oesophageal fistula and oesophageal atresia
Paediatric	Left mini-thoracotomy; aspiration of fluid. Bilateral chest drain insertion. Open drainage hip joint
Paediatric	Laparotomy, splenectomy and packing of liver laceration
Paediatric	Laparotomy
Paediatric	Silastic silo construction for gastroschisis
Paediatric	Laparotomy, ileal resection, ileoanal anastomosis and jejunostomy
Paediatric	Muscle and skin biopsy
Paediatric	Right hemicolectomy and insertion of Broviac catheter
Paediatric	Insertion of Hickman catheter
Paediatric	Rectal biopsy and insertion of Hickman catheter
Paediatric	Open muscle biopsy
Paediatric	Repair of intestinal perforations and ileostomy
Paediatric	Laparotomy, small bowel resection and primary anastomosis
Paediatric	Laparotomy, resection of ileum and split ileostomy
Paediatric	Second look laparotomy, ligation of bleeding vessels from liver surface and retroperitoneum, packing of abdominal cavity
Paediatric	Laparotomy, excision and closure of perforated gastric ulcer, peritoneal lavage
Paediatric	Laparotomy
Paediatric	Laparotomy, peritoneal lavage and closure of small bowel perforation
Paediatric	Laparotomy extended to thoracotomy and exposure of thoracoabdominal aorta
Paediatric	Laparotomy and ileostomy
Paediatric	Insertion of peritoneal drain under local anaesthetic
Paediatric	Abdominal drain insertion
Paediatric	Trucut biopsy and central venous catheter insertion
Paediatric	Laparotomy
Paediatric	Laparotomy, Ladd's procedure, ileostomy and insertion of central venous catheter
Paediatric	Second look laparotomy, loop jejunostomy and insertion of Hickman catheter
Paediatric	Laparotomy, division of adhesions, small bowel resection and primary anastomosis, revision of stoma
Paediatric	Anal cut back

Specialty of consultant surgeon	Operation performed
Paediatric	Division of adhesions, ileostomy and mucous fistula
Paediatric	Repair of recurrent inguinal hernia
Paediatric	Laparotomy, small bowel resection and ileostomy
Paediatric	Laparotomy, small bowel resection and jejunostomy
Paediatric	Laparotomy and ileostomy
Paediatric	Laparotomy, splenectomy and packing of abdominal wound
Paediatric	Proposed closure of gastroschisis; baby died at induction
Paediatric	Laparotomy, open and close
Paediatric	Laparotomy, suture of mesenteric vessel and irrigation
Paediatric	Resection small bowel and ileostomy
Paediatric	Laparotomy
Paediatric	Laparotomy
Paediatric	Laparotomy and colectomy
Paediatric	Incision and drainage of perianal abscess
Paediatric	Laparoscopy, laparotomy, division of adhesions and repair of right ureter
Paediatric	Duhamel pull through
Paediatric	Open liver biopsy
Paediatric	Inguinal herniotomy
Paediatric	Laparotomy, biopsy of retroperitoneal mass and gastrojejunostomy
Paediatric	Laparotomy and ileostomy
Paediatric	Insertion of Broviac catheter
Paediatric	Laparotomy and ileostomy
Transplantation	Liver transplantation
Transplantation	Liver transplantation
Vascular	Insertion of Hickman line
Plastic	Fascial excision of full thickness burns to upper trunk and excision of necrotic muscles in both upper limbs
Plastic	Escharotomy
Plastic	Laparotomy
Plastic	Bilateral cleft lip repair
Plastic	Tracheostomy and right upper limb escharotomy
Otorhinolaryngology	Unilateral choanal atresia correction
Otorhinolaryngology	Removal of tracheal stent, reintubation and packing of trachea with adrenaline soaked swabs
Otorhinolaryngology	Microlaryngobronchoscopy and tracheostomy
Otorhinolaryngology	Tracheostomy
Otorhinolaryngology	Repair choanal atresia. Insertion of nasal stent
Otorhinolaryngology	Microlaryngobronchoscopy
Otorhinolaryngology	Bronchoscopy and laser to granulations
Otorhinolaryngology	Tracheostomy and bronchoscopy
Otorhinolaryngology	Drainage of periorbital abscess and insertion of intracranial pressure monitor
Thoracic/Cardiothoracic (Paediatric)	Open lung biopsy
Thoracic	Open lung biopsy
Thoracic	Resection of recurrent sarcoma neck and mediastinum. Repair subclavian and innominate veins
Orthopaedic	Through hip amputation
General + Paediatric	Needle biopsy of mediastinal tumour (closed)
General + Paediatric	Laparotomy; packing to prevent haemorrhage from liver

Preoperative status

Key Points

- *The great majority of children in this sample were very severely ill with associated respiratory and cardiovascular disease in addition to their primary surgical diagnosis.*
- *If surgical outcomes are to be objectively assessed, appropriate weighting of comorbidities is essential. The American Society of Anesthesiologists' (ASA) grading system is widely used by anaesthetists but, as a comparatively simple system, it does have limitations.*

Table 2.25: Coexisting medical disorders (AQ13)
(85 cases; answers may be multiple)

Coexisting medical disorder	Number
None	6
Not answered	2
Respiratory	50
Cardiac	31
Neurological	26
Endocrine	5
Alimentary	27
Renal	25
Hepatic	18
Musculoskeletal	8
Vascular	4
Haematological	24
Genetic abnormality/recognised syndrome	19
Obesity	1
Sepsis	25

Question 2.19: Were any respiratory therapies in use before the operation? (AQ19)

Yes	60
No	24
Not answered	1
Total	**85**

If yes, please indicate which:
(60 cases; answers may be multiple)

Oxygen therapy	33
Artificial airway	25
Ventilatory support (including CPAP, IMV, IPPV etc.)	50

Question 2.20: Were other intensive treatments in progress? (AQ20)

Yes	25
No	54
Not answered	6
Total	**85**

If yes, please indicate which:
(25 cases; answers may be multiple)

Inotropic support	21
Renal support	7

Question 2.21: Was it necessary to delay the anaesthetic to improve the child's state before the operation? (AQ23)

Yes	13
No	69
Not answered	3
Total	**85**

If yes, please indicate which system(s) needed attention:
(13 cases; answers may be multiple)

Cardiac	6
Respiratory	4
Metabolic	3
Not answered	2

The responses to the questions set out above relating to the child's preoperative condition show the extreme problems posed for their anaesthetic management. Fifty-eight percent were on ventilatory support and 25% were receiving inotropic support.

ASA grade

Key Point

- *Surgeons, particularly neurosurgeons, need to understand and adhere to the ASA system or define an acceptable alternative.*

Table 2.26: ASA status prior to the final operation (AQ14 and SQ37)

	Anaesthetic questionnaire		Surgical questionnaire	
ASA 1	3	4%	14	15%
ASA 2	3	4%	6	6%
ASA 3	17	20%	8	9%
ASA 4	35	41%	46	49%
ASA 5	27	32%	18	19%
Not answered	0	-	1	1%
Total	85		93	

Agreement between the disciplines is not good.

In the anaesthetic questionnaires returned, three cases were graded ASA 1, in two of which death occurred at home and was sudden.

CASE 1 • *A male infant was diagnosed in the antenatal period as having a bilateral cleft lip and palate. At birth following a full term delivery he weighed 2.8 kg and was transferred to a specialist centre where he was operated on two days later and all went well. Three days following the operation he was discharged from hospital and died 11 days later at home. Following a postmortem the cause of death was given as sudden infant death syndrome.*

CASE 2 • *Thirty-eight days after delivery at 39 weeks gestation, a 4 kg male child developed a perianal abscess. This was incised and drained by the registrar in paediatric surgery. The child was discharged home. Seven days later he died suddenly and the cause of death given following a postmortem was unexpected death in infancy.*

These deaths are disquieting. There may be no association with their hospital admission and surgery but the occurrence of two such deaths in otherwise fit children must require explanation. The local reporting system to NCEPOD has been developed to identify those deaths following surgery that occur in hospital. The reporting of these deaths that occurred out of hospital is therefore fortuitous. Conceivably there could be others. It is also of note that in the previous examination of paediatric deaths published by NCEPOD in 1990[10] there were two such 'cot deaths' that occurred at home. One followed 18 days after an uneventful Ramstedt's operation in a mature six-week-old who weighed 4 kg and the other was a four-month-old infant born at 30 weeks gestation who had had a bilateral herniotomy.

The Confidential Enquiry into Stillbirths and Deaths in Infancy (CESDI) in its 3rd Report drew attention to the association between previous hospital admission and sudden infant death[17]. Cot deaths occur in approximately 1:700 babies and they are more common in babies who have been born prematurely or have had illnesses requiring hospital treatment. There is, however, no evidence of any causal relationship between either hospital admission or surgery and cot death. Only an effective national scheme, perhaps based on death certification, could identify all such deaths that occurred following surgery and anaesthesia.

The third case, graded ASA 1, was a neurosurgical procedure.

CASE 3 • *A two-year-old child weighing 14 kg had a frontal craniotomy for a tumour. The blood loss of 4.5 litres occurred in 50 minutes and there was some difficulty in obtaining blood products in this single specialty hospital. The anaesthetist stated that the surgeons were unable to control the haemorrhage and surgery was abandoned. No surgical questionnaire was returned on this case.*

The anaesthetist is to be congratulated for keeping up with such a catastrophic blood loss, which amounted to a four-fold exchange transfusion in 50 minutes. The presence of a brain tumour was potentially life threatening and an ASA grade of 3 would therefore seem to have been more appropriate.

Of the 14 patients graded ASA 1 by surgeons, two were also graded ASA 1 by the anaesthetists and are described above. For six others no anaesthetic questionnaire was returned and for the final six the anaesthetist gave a much higher grade. Brief details are given in Tables 2.27 and 2.28.

It would appear that, particularly amongst neurosurgeons, the concept of grading the fitness of patients according to their state of health at the time they undergo surgery and anaesthesia is not properly understood. Surgeons, being less familiar with ASA grading than anaesthetists, are grading on

Table 2.27: Patients graded ASA 1 by surgeons and where no anaesthetic questionnaire was returned		
	Age at death	Details
Case 4	9 days	Jejunal atresia, laparotomy, partial jejunectomy, end to end jejuno-jejunal anastomosis. Complicated by meconium peritonitis due to perforated gangrenous jejunal segment and cardiac tamponade with extravasation of TPN fluid, probably due to myocardial necrosis at the site of cardiac perforation.
Case 5	7 days	Intracranial haemorrhage resulting from haemophilia and minor trauma. Craniotomy and evacuation of acute subdural haematoma.
Case 6	14 years	Head injury with brain oedema. Intracranial pressure monitoring.
Case 7	13 years	Crush injury to abdomen, pelvis and legs. Laparotomy for intra-abdominal bleeding (see also page 39).
Case 8	14 years	Hydrocephalus, blocked ventriculoperitoneal shunt.
Case 9	12 years	Head injury. Evacuation of acute subdural haematoma. Uncontrollable raised intracranial pressure (see also page 39).

Table 2.28: Patients graded ASA 1 by surgeons and where an anaesthetic questionnaire was returned			
	Anaesthetic ASA	Age at death	Details
Case 10	4	10 years	Major head injury, ICP bolt.
Case 11	5	7 years	Massive haemorrhage, ruptured aorta and common iliac artery (see also page 49).
Case 12	3	18 months	Hydrocephalus secondary to cerebellar primitive neuroectodermal tumour, insertion of shunt.
Case 13	4	11 years	Severe head injury, craniotomy and evacuation of acute subdural haematoma.
Case 14	5	14 years	Multiple injuries including head injury, laparotomy.
Case 15	5	13 years	Severe head injury, craniotomy and evacuation of acute subdural haematoma.

Table 2.29: Classification of final operation by ASA status (AQs14 and 27)									
	Emergency		Urgent		Scheduled		Elective		Total
ASA 1	0	-	1	2%	2	12%	0	-	3
ASA 2	0	-	1	2%	2	12%	0	-	3
ASA 3	1	4%	11	25%	5	29%	0	-	17
ASA 4	7	29%	20	46%	8	47%	0	-	35
ASA 5	16	67%	11	25%	0	-	0	-	27
Total	24		44		17		0		85

the child's premorbid state rather than the child's condition at the time of surgery. Any method for comparison of surgical outcomes that is to be of value will require a much more coherent use of such grading systems.

TIME OF DEATH

The pattern of time from operation to death is almost identical to that seen in any age group and sample and has been demonstrated in previous NCEPOD reports[5,9]. Most deaths occur within three days of surgery; a small number of deaths then occur for many days after surgery and presumably continue to occur beyond the chosen, and purely arbitrary, cut-off period of 30 days.

Figure 2.13: Calendar days from operation to death

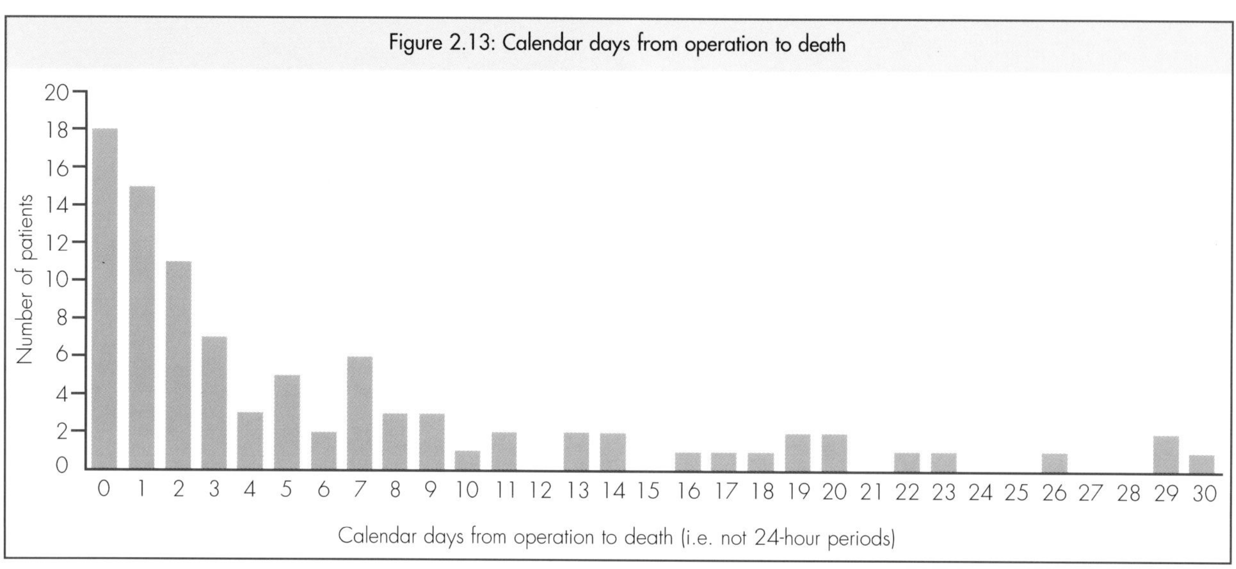

HOSPITALS, FACILITIES AND STAFFING

Key Points

- *Specialist paediatric surgeons carried out 91% of children's surgery.*
- *Consultants anaesthetised 84% of patients. Senior trainees anaesthetised a further 14%.*
- *The recommendations as to the seniority and experience of anaesthetists taking responsibility for particular patients as set out by the Royal College of Anaesthetists[21], and NCEPOD[6,7] in previous reports, are being complied with in the management of these patients.*
- *Suitably experienced assistance was available to anaesthetists for these cases.*

Type of hospital

Table 2.30: Type of hospital in which the final operation took place (AQ2 and SQ9)

Type of hospital	1997/98		1989	
District general (or equivalent)	7	6%	20	22%
University/teaching	45	40%	35	39%
Children's	53	47%	28	31%
Single surgical specialty	7	6%	4	4%
Other	0	-	3	3%
Total	112		90	

Figure 2.14: Comparison of the type of hospitals in which surgery took place in 1997/98 and 1989 (percentage of final operations)

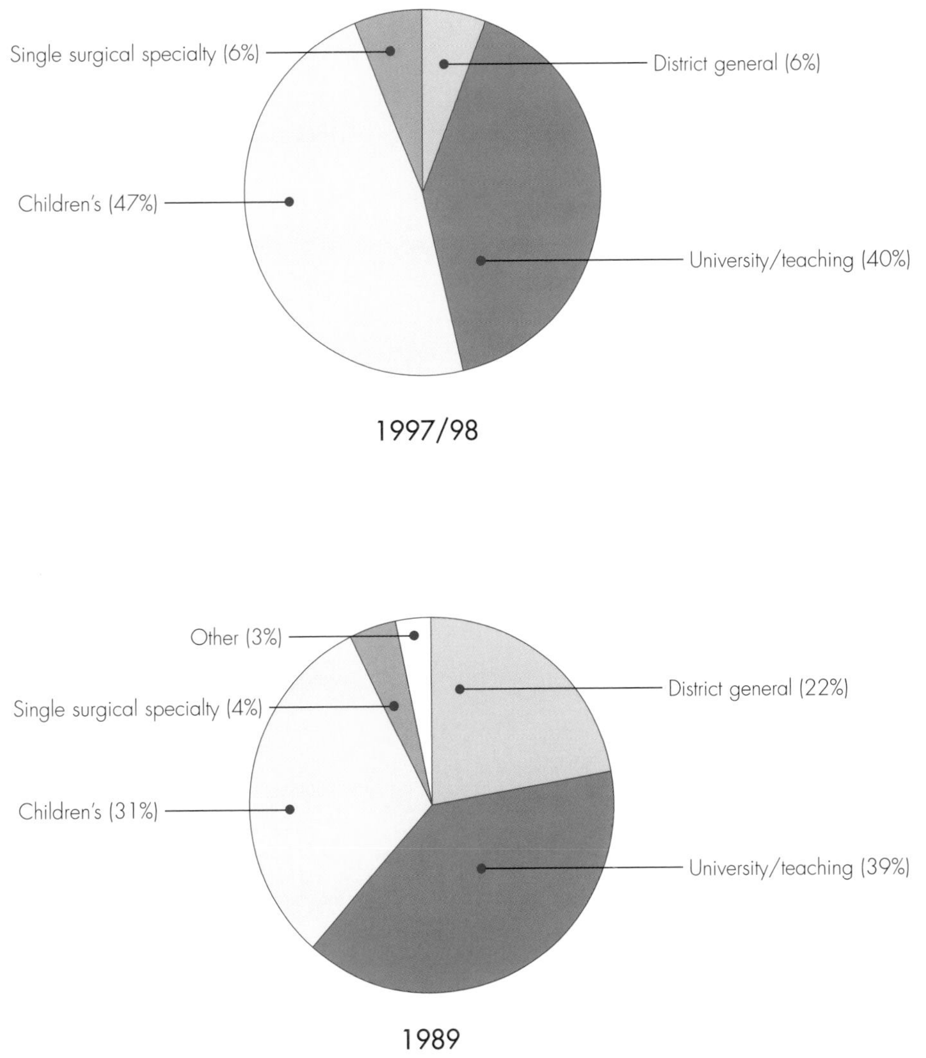

The shift in paediatric practice over the past ten years, such that operations on sick children increasingly take place in specialist paediatric hospitals, is shown in Table 2.30 and Figure 2.14. These compare information collected from anaesthetic questionnaires on deaths in children under ten years in 1989 and the current data taken from both anaesthetic and surgical returns.

Facilities

Table 2.31 shows the provision of special care areas and the out-of-hours availability of CT, MRI and angiography in the 30 hospitals represented. In 66 of the 112 cases both anaesthetic and surgical questionnaires were available, for 19 only the anaesthetic questionnaire had been returned and for 27 only the surgical questionnaire was received.

There were occasionally significant discrepancies in answers given by different clinicians in the same hospital. For this reason, in all cases where there was a conflict between answers or where data was missing altogether, a member of NCEPOD administrative staff contacted the hospital by telephone to ascertain the availability of facilities.

Hospital type	Number of cases	SCBU/ NICU	HDU (C)	HDU (C&A)	ICU (C)	ICU (C&A)	Ward (C)	CT	MRI	Angio
C	7	✓	✓		✓		✓	✓	✓	✓
C	8	✓			✓		✓	✓	✓	✓
C	23	✓	✓		✓		✓	✓	✓	✓
C	2	✓	✓		✓		✓			
C	2	✓	✓		✓		✓	✓	✓	✓
C	7		✓		✓		✓	✓	✓	✓
C	4	✓	✓		✓		✓	✓		
DGH	1	✓	✓			✓	✓	✓	✓	✓
DGH	1	✓		✓		✓	✓	✓		✓
DGH	1	✓	✓	✓	✓		✓	✓	✓	✓
DGH	1			✓		✓	✓	✓	✓	✓
DGH	2	✓		✓		✓	✓	✓		✓
DGH	1	✓				✓	✓	✓	✓	✓
SSS	6					✓	✓	✓	✓	✓
SSS	1	✓	✓		✓		✓			
U/T	5	✓	✓			✓	✓	✓	✓	✓
U/T	2	✓	✓		✓	✓	✓	✓	✓	✓
U/T	3	✓	✓		✓		✓	✓	✓	✓
U/T	1	✓	✓		✓		✓	✓	✓	✓
U/T	2	✓	✓		✓		✓	✓	✓	✓
U/T	2		✓			✓	✓	✓	✓	✓
U/T	2	✓	✓			✓	✓	✓	✓	
U/T	9	✓			✓		✓	✓	✓	✓
U/T	1		✓				✓	✓	✓	✓
U/T	1			✓		✓	✓	✓		✓
U/T	5	✓	✓		✓		✓	✓	✓	✓
U/T	6	✓		✓	✓		✓	✓	✓	✓
U/T	2	✓	✓		✓		✓	✓	✓	✓
U/T	2	✓		✓		✓	✓	✓	✓	✓
U/T	2	✓	✓		✓		✓	✓	✓	✓

Table 2.31: Availability of special care areas and out-of-hours imaging facilities (AQ3 and SQ40)

Total hospitals = 30 Total cases = 112. This table is based on answers given on questionnaires, supplemented by information provided by telephone to NCEPOD staff.

Key	
Angio	Angiography facility
C	Children's
CT	CT scanner
DGH	District general hospital
HDU (C)	Children's high dependency unit
HDU (C&A)	Combined adult and children's high dependency unit
ICU (C)	Children's intensive care unit
ICU (C&A)	Combined adult and children's intensive care unit
MRI	MRI scanner
SCBU/NICU	Special care baby unit and/or neonatal intensive care unit
SSS	Single surgical specialty
U/T	Undergraduate/teaching hospital
Ward (C)	Children's ward

Question 2.22: Does the hospital have a specific separate consultant anaesthetic paediatric on-call rota? (AQ6)

Yes	64
No	13
Not answered	8
Total	**85**

Two of the six anaesthetic questionnaires returned from district general hospitals and 23 of the 29 returned from university hospitals indicated that there was a specific separate consultant anaesthetic on-call rota for paediatric surgery. In 1989 the respective figures were two of 20 questionnaires for district general hospitals and 18 of 35 for university hospitals.

Question 2.23: Where is this paediatric surgical service provided? (SQ9a)

A stand-alone unit	30
Situated within a larger hospital with paediatric medicine on-site	63
Total	**93**

One third of the paediatric deaths occurred in centres that might appear to be isolated, with less than ideal arrangements for dealing with sick children. However, a specific question was asked about paediatric medical cover in the ward at the hospital where the final operation took place (SQ23) and, for 91% (85/93) of the cases, this appeared satisfactory.

Staffing

Question 2.24: Was experienced medical paediatric cover available for this ward/area? (i.e. a resident on-call team of paediatricians, one of whom has more than 12 months experience in acute paediatrics, including neonatal care) (SQ23)

Yes	85
No	6
Not answered	2
Total	**93**

In six instances children were treated in surgical units without experienced medical paediatric support. These were one case of severe burns and five neurosurgical patients.

Improvement is needed in units where it is necessary to provide specialist services, e.g. neurosurgery, for children and where there is currently no medical paediatric cover and no paediatric critical care service. Managers and specialists should work together and make local arrangements which will provide, at a minimum, high dependency care (level 1) facilities for postoperative care, and respiratory support, if necessary, in the context of a level 2 paediatric intensive care unit[18].

Seven children died after surgery or procedures in a district general hospital. These procedures were:

CASE 16 INSERTION OF HICKMAN LINE • *A 15-year-old with acute lymphoblastic leukaemia (ASA 3). Treatment was being given on a medical paediatric ward in a district general hospital with no paediatric oncology provision. An experienced vascular surgeon, with no regular paediatric commitment, inserted a Hickman line. The anaesthetist was a first year SHO. There was a pneumothorax postoperatively and the patient was admitted to the ICU. Death occurred 20 days later due to complications of the underlying disease.*

Should this 15-year-old with acute lymphoblastic leukaemia have been in a paediatric oncology unit?

CASE 17 ESCHAROTOMY • *A one-year-old in a burns unit situated within a district general hospital. The child was graded ASA 5. There was no on-site paediatric cover. Death occurred one day after surgery due to the severity of the burns.*

This child was treated in the correct hospital for the management of the burns but it was an unsuitable unit for a child.

CASE 18 CRANIOTOMY AND EVACUATION OF ACUTE SUBDURAL HAEMATOMA • *A four-year-old with a head injury was treated in a neurosurgical unit (with paediatric facilities) within a district general hospital. Intubated, CT scanned and operated on by a neurosurgeon with paediatric experience. A craniotomy and evacuation of an acute subdural haematoma was undertaken. Massive brain damage was confirmed at postmortem examination.*

There was expert assessment and management in a properly equipped hospital.

CASE 19 BOWEL RESECTION • *A very premature baby with severe necrotising enterocolitis (NEC) and septicaemia (see also page 50).*

CASE 20 LAPAROTOMY • *A premature child with NEC. The findings at laparotomy were incompatible with life and support was withdrawn.*

CASE 21 POSTERIOR FOSSA DECOMPRESSION AND C1 – C2 LAMINECTOMY • *A fifteen-year-old had high-risk neurosurgery in a unit with very little paediatric expertise on hand.*

It appears that the team failed to appreciate the risks (see page 39 for more details on this case).

CASE 22 LAPAROTOMY – PACKING TO PREVENT BLEEDING FROM LIVER • *A 14-year-old with multiple trauma. There was a severe head injury and intra-abdominal bleeding. The patient died the same day, after the laparotomy.*

This was appropriate emergency surgery in a moribund child.

Children

There is little disagreement with the policy of providing surgical treatment for neonates in specialist neonatal surgical centres. Most such centres are based in larger specialist regional centres supported by specialist anaesthetists, critical care services, specialist nurses, physiotherapists, oncologists, radiologists, dieticians etc. Anaesthetists and general surgeons at a local level in district general hospitals satisfactorily undertake most elective general paediatric surgery. This type of anaesthesia and surgery tends to be low risk, high volume work and does not require on-site specialist paediatric services. These anaesthetists and surgeons, who wish to treat children, are required to maintain an appropriate level of practice in line with current guidelines[15, 19]. Paediatric anaesthesia and surgery can, however, be associated with considerable morbidity or mortality if things go wrong. Correct decision-making and the ability to identify the severity of disease are vital. In the acute situation, if appropriate expertise is not available when urgent, but not necessarily immediate, surgical treatment is required in a district general hospital, then the child should be transferred to a specialist centre (see page 43).

Shared care

Question 2.25: Was the care of the child undertaken on a formal shared basis with paediatric physicians? (SQ25)

Yes	69
No	23
Not answered	1
Total	**93**

There was no formal shared care in a quarter of the cases (23/93, 25%). This is an improvement when compared with the 1989 NCEPOD report[10], which showed that 44% of the children who died after non-cardiac surgery were not managed in a collaborative manner. Input from specialists in paediatric medicine is not necessary in all cases but is strongly advised for preterm neonates, oncology patients and others in critical situations. Teamwork is the ideal but in some instances, particularly if an emergency occurs quickly, there may not be time for formal consultation. Paediatric surgeons who are familiar with drugs (and their dosages) and intravenous fluid requirements in childhood, do not always share care with paediatricians in an emergency situation. Systems should be put in place to assist this situation and ensure paediatric medical input into perioperative management. If this does not happen then children in some units, especially those with incomplete paediatric medical cover, are likely be treated by doctors who are unfamiliar with the intravenous regimens and drug dosages appropriate for children (see Questions 2.23 and 2.24 on page 37).

The surgeon

Table 2.32: Specialty of consultant surgeon in charge at the time of the final operation (SQ27)

Specialty	Number
Paediatric	48
General with a subspecialty interest in paediatric surgery	2
Neurosurgery – paediatric	14
Neurosurgery – adult	3
Neurosurgery – mixed	8
Orthopaedic	1
Otorhinolaryngology	8
Plastic	5
Thoracic/cardiothoracic – paediatric	1
Transplantation	2
Vascular	1
Total	93

The answers given in Questions 2.26 to 2.30 below all refer to the consultant surgeon in charge at the time of the final operation.

Question 2.26: What type of surgery does this consultant provide for children? (SQ28)

General (or non-specialist) paediatric surgery *(i.e. relatively common disorders which do not usually require a major or complex operation or perioperative care)*	7
Specialist or tertiary paediatric surgery	85
Other	1
Total	**93**

The figures above are very encouraging. In 91% (85/93) of cases, the care was delivered by surgeons with a specialist practice in paediatric surgery.

Question 2.27: Does this consultant manage neonates (i.e. children under one month old)? (SQ29)

Yes	89
No	3
Not answered	1
Total	**93**

This subspecialisation confirms that the surgeons were appropriately specialised to deal with the children who were aged less than one month.

Question 2.28: Has this consultant had specialist training in surgery on children? (SQ30)

Yes	87
No	6
Total	**93**

The answers to this question do not marry with the previous answers. Where the answer was negative, the surgeons' specialties were given as neurosurgery (in four cases), plastic surgery and otorhinolaryngology (in one case each). Neurosurgeons who are essentially familiar with adult practice are required to operate on children. Some teenage children might be considered adults by clinicians. Details of the clinical situations where the consultant had no specialist training in children's surgery are given below. One neurosurgical procedure (Case 21) was elective. Why was the patient not transferred to a unit with paediatric expertise (see also page 43)?

CASE 7 • *A 13-year-old had a laparotomy done by an experienced registrar (with CCST). The indication was intra-abdominal bleeding a week after reconstructive surgery following an RTA and major injuries, including a crush injury to the abdomen, pelvis and legs. A consultant plastic surgeon, with no specific paediatric training, supervised.*

CASE 9 • *A neurosurgical registrar (SpR 4) operated on a 12-year-old patient following a head injury and raised intracranial pressure. The assistant was a consultant neurosurgeon (with an adult practice). An acute subdural haematoma was evacuated and considerable cerebral contusion noted. The raised intracranial pressure was uncontrollable.*

CASE 21 • *A fifteen-year-old had high-risk neurosurgery (an elective posterior fossa decompression and C1 – C2 laminectomy) in a unit with very little paediatric expertise on hand. Surgery was by a registrar (SpR 4) supervised by a consultant neurosurgeon with an adult practice. The anaesthetist was a trainee. Death occurred eight days after surgery due to respiratory complications.*

CASE 23 • *A four-year-old child with a closed head injury. A registrar (SpR 4) inserted an intracranial pressure monitor under the direct supervision of a consultant neurosurgeon with no formal training in paediatrics but a declared special interest in paediatric neurosurgery.*

CASE 24 • *A seven-year-old child, with known cardiac anomalies, suffered a cervical cord injury. A consultant gave the anaesthetic. A consultant neurosurgeon (with a mixed practice) did an urgent occipitocervical fixation using lateral mass plates, together with the removal of the posterior arch of the first cervical vertebra.*

CASE 25 • *A one-year-old child required revision of a tracheostomy and bronchoscopy because of bleeding from the tracheostomy stoma. A consultant anaesthetist gave the anaesthetic. There were multiple cardiac and tracheo-oesophageal congenital anomalies. Neither the registrar who operated nor the supervising consultant (otorhinolaryngology) had any formal paediatric training.*

Question 2.29: What is this consultant's regular sessional commitment for surgery in children (i.e. operating sessions)? (SQ31)

No regular sessional commitment	10
More than one per week	75
Weekly	7
Not answered	1
Total	**93**

Question 2.30: What is the surgical specialty of consultants with no regular sessional commitment? (SQs 27 and 31)

Neurosurgery – mixed	5
Neurosurgery – adult	3
Transplantation	1
Vascular	1
Total	**10**

Question 2.31: In the hospital in which the final surgery took place, is there an identified consultant surgeon who leads the provision of surgical services for children? (SQ32)

Yes	62
No	22
Not answered	9
Total	**93**

If yes, was this the consultant in charge of this case?

Yes	33
No	26
Not answered	3
Total	**62**

It is recommended that a hospital providing general paediatric surgical services should ensure that at least one surgeon is responsible for these services (a lead clinician, if not a clinical director)[15]. This may not be happening in all centres.

Surgical consultant involvement

Table 2.33: Overall surgical consultant involvement (SQs 44, 53, 54 and 63)

Consultant involvement	Number
Operating	62
Assisting	2
Present in operating room	9
Present in operating suite	3
Elsewhere in hospital	2
Consulted before operation	14
No involvement detailed*	1
Total	93

**SpR 2 was most senior involved.*

In all but one case (1%, 1/93) consultant surgeons were aware and involved in the care of these children. This is a commendable performance and an improvement on the situation NCEPOD identified in 1989[10] when there was no consultant involvement in 4% (4/98) of the cases where children died. Also, in 1989, 14% of non-cardiac index operations (those not associated with death) were undertaken without the knowledge of a consultant. Whenever a child is about to undergo a surgical procedure in theatre, the relevant consultant must be informed.

Table 2.34: Grade of the surgeon who signed the consent form (SQ45)	
Grade of surgeon	Number
Consultant	28
Locum appointment – service (consultant)	1
Locum appointment – training (grade not specified)	1
Specialist registrar	35
Senior house officer	13
House officer	1
Other	10
Not answered	3
Not known	1
Total	93

Consultants were usually the most senior operating surgeons (67%, 62/93) but at the time of this survey (1997/98) consultants took the consent in 31% (29/93) of cases. It is generally recommended that the operating surgeon should deal with the process of obtaining consent[20]. The surgeon and members of the surgical team should give an honest, realistic and sensitive account of the options for treatment. For children, this will usually be followed by obtaining explicit consent from the person with parental responsibility for the child[20]. Children under 16 may be competent to consent to treatment[20]. They should be involved in decisions about their surgical treatment. Realistically it will be the consultant who has the knowledge and experience to lead this process. Obtaining consent should not be delegated to trainees unless there has been a thorough, documented discussion on a prior occasion.

The anaesthetist

Table 2.35: Grade of most senior anaesthetist present at the start of the anaesthetic (AQ32)	
Grade of anaesthetist	Number
Consultant	71
SpR – Accredited/CCST	3
SpR 4	7
SpR 3	2
SHO 1	1
Not answered	1
Total	85

Table 2.36: Grade of most senior anaesthetist present at the start of the anaesthetic, by classification of operation (AQs 32 and 27)

	Emergency	Urgent	Scheduled	Elective	Total
Consultant	19	37	15	0	71
SpR – Accredited/CCST	3	0	0	0	3
SpR 4	1	6	0	0	7
SpR 3	0	1	1	0	2
SHO 1	0	0	1	0	1
Not answered	1	0	0	0	1
Total	24	44	17	0	85

Table 2.37: Grade of most senior anaesthetist present at the start of the anaesthetic, by ASA status (AQs 32 and 14)

	ASA 1	ASA 2	ASA 3	ASA 4	ASA 5	Total
Consultant	2	2	12	32	23	71
SpR – Accredited/CCST	0	0	0	1	2	3
SpR 4	1	0	3	2	1	7
SpR 3	0	1	1	0	0	2
SHO 1	0	0	1	0	0	1
Not answered	0	0	0	0	1	1
Total	3	3	17	35	27	85

Question 2.32: If the most senior anaesthetist present at the start of the anaesthetic was not a consultant, when was a consultant anaesthetist informed about this case? (AQ36)

Before the anaesthetic	8
After the anaesthetic	2
Consultant not informed	3
Not answered	1
Total	**14**

Two of the three cases where the anaesthetic consultant was not informed were neurosurgical cases in older children and the anaesthetist was a trainee in their final year. The third case was 15 years old but ASA 3 and was anaesthetised by a first year SHO. Further details are given in Case 16 on page 37.

Question 2.33: If the most senior anaesthetist at the start of the anaesthetic was not a consultant, where was consultant help available? (AQ37)

A consultant came to the theatre before the end of the anaesthetic	1
A consultant was available in the operating suite but not directly involved	1
A consultant was available in the hospital but was not present in the operating suite	2
A consultant was available by telephone	9
Not answered	1
Total	**14**

The information set out in the preceding tables indicates clearly the very high level of direct involvement that consultant anaesthetists had with the management of these very sick children. Paediatric anaesthesia is a consultant-run specialty. Involvement of trainees was appropriate in almost all cases and it may be noteworthy that consultants and trainees were exclusively involved with these anaesthetics.

Both the Royal College of Anaesthetists[21], and NCEPOD[6, 7] in previous reports, have made specific recommendations as to the seniority and experience of anaesthetists taking responsibility for particular patients. These recommendations can be set out against the paediatric patients in this sample to test compliance.

Royal College of Anaesthetists' recommendations

"A consultant should always accompany SHO1 grades who are anaesthetising children under the age of ten."[21]
No SHO 1 was required, accompanied or otherwise, to anaesthetise a child under the age of ten.

"SHOs and SpR 1 grades should always be supervised at neurosurgery and cardiothoracic operations."[21]
Five SHOs or SpR 1s were present at such operations. All were accompanying more senior anaesthetists.

NCEPOD recommendations

"Very sick patients should be anaesthetised in the knowledge and (or) presence of senior registrar (SpR 3 or 4) or consultant."[7]
In 61/62 children of ASA grade 4 or 5 the anaesthetic was given by a consultant or senior specialist registrar. In one case the question was unanswered (see Table 2.37).

"Many operations, particularly those of long duration, will require two anaesthetists at least for part of the time."[6]
Seventeen anaesthetics took three hours or longer. There were two anaesthetists present in sixteen.

"Anaesthesia for emergency or life-saving operations should ideally be managed by a team of anaesthetists."[6]
The NCEPOD classification was stated as 'Emergency' (immediate life-saving operation) for 24 children. There were at least two anaesthetists present in 23. In one report the question asking whether there was more than one anaesthetist present was not answered.

This analysis shows that paediatric anaesthetic practice conforms very closely indeed to the recommendations from both the Royal College of Anaesthetists and from NCEPOD.

Question 2.34: Was advice sought, at any time, from another anaesthetist who was not present during the anaesthetic? (AQ38)

Yes	12
No	61
Not answered	12
Total	**85**

If yes, from what grade of anaesthetist was advice sought?

Consultant	10
Not answered	2
Total	**12**

In eight of the ten cases where advice was sought from a consultant, another consultant sought the advice. Given the nature and complexity of procedures such as posterior cervico-occipital fixation and craniotomy for resection of large choroid plexus tumour with raised ICP, this is a very positive comment on consultant anaesthetic practice.

Assistance for the anaesthetist

Question 2.35: Was there a trained anaesthetist's assistant (i.e. ODP, anaesthetic nurse) present for this case? (AQ44)

Yes	81
No	1
Not answered	3
Total	**85**

If yes, does the assistant work regularly with children?

Yes	77
No	1
Not answered	3
Total	**81**

The single case where it is recorded that the anaesthetist had no trained assistant is almost certainly an error as in the subsequent question it is noted that the assistant works regularly with children. Similarly, the single case where it is recorded that the assistant does not work regularly with children may be incorrect. The patient was a premature baby with NEC and the operation took place in a single specialty hospital.

It seems therefore that trained assistance was available to the anaesthetist for all these cases and that assistants worked regularly with children. In 1989 a single case was recorded amongst the 89 non-cardiac deaths in which non-medical help was not available.

Anaesthetic monitoring

Question 2.36: Were monitoring devices used during the management of this anaesthetic? (AQ50)

Yes	84
Not answered	1
Total	**85**

If yes, were monitoring instruments already attached to the patient (i.e. from ICU or A&E)?

Yes	58
No	25
Not answered	1
Total	**84**

Table 2.38: Monitoring devices used during the operation (AQ50) (*84 cases; answers may be multiple*)

Monitoring device	Number of cases
ECG	84
Pulse oximeter	84
Indirect BP	61
Oesophageal or precordial stethoscope	23
O_2 analyser	78
Inspired anaesthetic vapour analyser	64
Expired CO_2 analyser	80
Airway pressure gauge	73
Ventilation volume	40
Ventilation disconnect device	68
Peripheral nerve stimulator	14
Temperature	54
Urine output	31
CVP	25
Direct arterial BP (invasive)	39
Intracranial pressure	6

ECG and pulse oximetry were used in all cases. In 1989, 80% of patients were monitored with an ECG and 77% with oximetry.

Six patients did not have their blood pressure monitored by either an indirect or direct method. In three cases, all premature babies with NEC, access for direct measurement could not be achieved and indirect measurement was not used. Two were short anaesthetics for anal surgery and the final case was for bronchoscopy and laser treatment in an infant of one month.

Question 2.37: Did anything hinder full monitoring? (AQ51)

Yes	15
No	67
Not answered	3
Total	**85**

Problems with either obtaining or maintaining arterial access were noted in six cases and in two others there were difficulties with central venous access. Other difficulties which were noted with monitoring included the lack of a suitable temperature probe, the lack of a capnograph in the anaesthetic room, problems related to maintaining satisfactory monitoring during the transfer to various sites in the hospital and obtaining access in a patient with extensive burns.

Admission and transfer

Key Points

- *There should be increased provision for retrieval teams from the specialist hospital with the appropriate paediatric skills and experience.*
- *Whenever possible acute paediatric surgical admissions should go directly to specialist paediatric beds.*
- *Every opportunity should be taken for the transfer before birth of those identified as having potential problems that may require postnatal surgical intervention.*

Admission category and pathway

Information on the admission category and pathway was available for the 93 cases for which surgical questionnaires were returned. In particular, information about an acute transfer was available for 58 of these patients. In addition, information about transfer was available from the anaesthetic questionnaires on 53 of 85 children.

Table 2.39: Admission category (SQ10) (NCEPOD definitions)

Admission category	Number
Elective	10
Urgent	11
Emergency	69
Born in the hospital in which the final operation took place	2
Not known	1
Total	93

Table 2.40: Pathway for admission (SQ11)

Admission pathway	Number
Transfer as an inpatient from another acute surgical hospital	58
Transfer from another non-acute hospital	6
Referral from a general medical or general dental practitioner	4
Admission following a previous outpatient consultation	2
Admission via A&E department	14
Other	9
Total	93

The majority of children who died after anaesthesia and surgery were critically ill, requiring urgent or emergency admission (86%, 80/93); many were transferred from another acute hospital.

Transfer

Questions relating to the transfer of patients were asked in both the anaesthetic and surgical questionnaires. In addition, both the anaesthetic and surgical advisors were asked when they examined the questionnaires and associated information to indicate if, on the information available to them, transfer was performed satisfactorily.

Question 2.38: Was the child transferred as an inpatient from another hospital? (AQ11)

Yes	53
No	31
Not answered	1
Total	**85**

If yes, had the child's condition apparently deteriorated during transfer?

Yes	2
No	47
Not answered	3
Not known	1
Total	**53**

From the responses to this question in the anaesthetic questionnaire it can be seen that 62% of these patients were transferred as inpatients.

A similar question was asked in the surgical questionnaire.

Question 2.39: Did the child's condition deteriorate during transfer? (SQ19)

Yes	4
No	49
Not answered	3
Not known	2
Total	**58**

Of those that deteriorated, only one patient appeared in both anaesthetic and surgical responses. The anaesthetic and surgical advisors also considered this transfer to have been unsatisfactory.

CASE 11 • *A seven-year-old boy was admitted to a DGH following a crush injury to the lower abdomen. A period of one-and-a-half to two hours elapsed during which an abdominal CT scan was performed before transfer to a specialist paediatric unit was commenced. Massive haemorrhage, ruptured aorta and common iliac artery (see also page 49).*

The other transfer identified in an anaesthetic questionnaire in which deterioration occurred was also regarded by advisors as unsatisfactory.

CASE 26 • *An infant was born prematurely at 33 weeks weighing 1.92 kg. He had a severe gastroschisis which the paediatric surgeon who operated described as the "worst gut seen in more than 30 cases". Following a transfer of about 12 miles undertaken by staff from the referring hospital, the consultant anaesthetist at the receiving hospital noted "infant reported to be stable and in good condition on leaving referring unit. Infant acidotic, cardiovascularly unstable and in respiratory difficulty on arrival". It was also noted that the gastroschisis had been diagnosed antenatally at 22 weeks.*

Should the baby have been delivered in a unit with on-site, or at least readily accessible, paediatric surgical facilities? Given the severity of this particular case the outcome was almost certainly inevitable but consideration of better transfer options, including a retrieval team, could be beneficial in the future.

This issue of antenatal diagnosis has been studied in considerable detail. The most important factor is good neonatal care when the baby is born to ensure that it is stabilised and in optimum condition before transfer to a surgical unit.

The other cases stated in a surgical questionnaire to have deteriorated are listed below:

- *Age 7 years. Cerebellar haematoma.*
  Continued deterioration, transfer satisfactory.
- *Age 14 years. Posterior fossa haematoma.*
  Continued deterioration, transfer satisfactory.
- *Age 4 months; weight 5.35 kg. Tracheal stenosis.*
  Difficult transfer but no evidence of deterioration.

Question 2.40: Was the child accompanied by a medical/nursing team during transfer? (SQ18)

Yes	50
No	2
Not answered	5
Not known	1
Total	**58**

If yes, where did the team come from?

Transferring hospital	33
Receiving hospital	14
Not answered	2
Not known	1
Total	**50**

Two patients were identified as being unaccompanied during transfer. One was a 15-year-old referred to a neurosurgical specialist centre for decompression of a Chiari malformation; this patient is described in more detail elsewhere (Case 21, page 39). The other was referred to a specialist children's unit aged five months with respiratory symptoms including apnoeic attacks having had multiple problems since her birth at 24 weeks.

Figure 2.15 shows whether the team came from the transferring or receiving hospital broken down into three age groups.

For those aged under six months it can be seen that 12 were retrieved by the receiving hospital but 16 were transferred by medical staff from the hospital in which the infant was already a patient. By contrast for the older children, many of whom were neurosurgical cases, the transferring hospital was nearly always responsible.

Question 2.41: What was the condition of the child on admission to the receiving hospital? (SQ20)

Satisfactory	37
Unsatisfactory	19
Not answered	2
Total	**58**

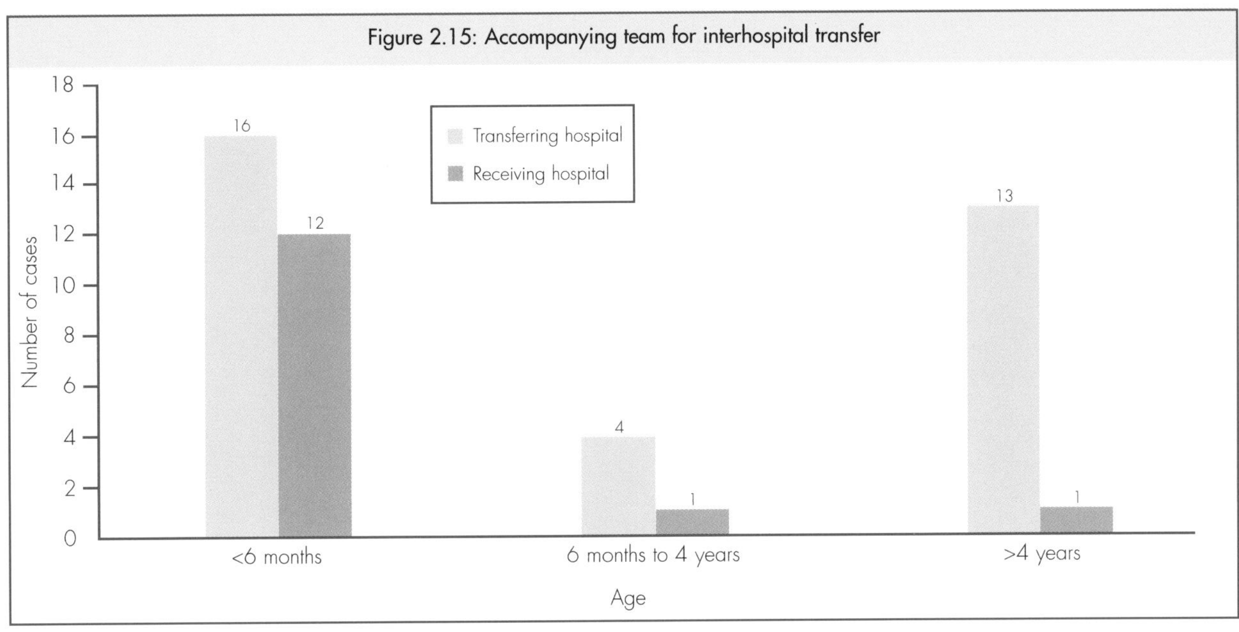

Table 2.41 gives details of the age, weight, gestational age and diagnosis for the 19 children whose condition was unsatisfactory on admission to the receiving hospital. It also gives the reason stated by the surgeon completing the questionnaire as to why the condition of the child was deemed to be unsatisfactory.

Table 2.41: Cases where condition was deemed unsatisfactory on arrival at receiving hospital (SQ20)

Age	Weight	Gestational age	Diagnosis	Reason given as to why unsatisfactory
1 month	0.8 kg	28 weeks	NEC	Metabolic acidosis, coagulation disorder, DIC
25 days	1 kg	27 weeks	NEC	On ventilator, tender distended abdomen with X-ray evidence of perforation, thrombocytopaenia, tachycardia etc.
9 days	1.3 kg	30 weeks	NEC	Very sick because of underlying disease
14 days	1.6 kg	30 weeks	NEC	Poorly perfused, acidotic, clotting derangement but function of disease probably rather than care.
1 month	1.86 kg	28 weeks	NEC	Requiring inotrope support and high ventilatory pressures
24 days	0.91 kg	26 weeks	Bowel perforation	–
7 days	0.62 kg	24 weeks	Bowel perforation	Moribund
1 month	1.47 kg	28 weeks	Bowel perforation	Very sick
2 days	1.48 kg	34 weeks	Bowel perforation	Severely acidotic
6 months	5 kg	–	GI bleeding post cardiac surgery	Critically ill infant brought by retrieval team from receiving hospital
0 days	1.9 kg	33 weeks	Gastroschisis	Poor state of bowel, hypovolaemia, acidotic
14 years	–	–	Posterior fossa haematoma	Despite all attempts at resuscitation
7 years	–	–	Pontine tumour	O_2 because of bradycardia and agitation (for transfer)
4 days	2.72 kg	40 weeks	Intracranial haemorrhage	Unconscious, floppy, poor respiratory effort, signs of intracranial hypertension
7 years	–	–	Head injury	Low blood pressure
9 years	30 kg	–	Head injury	Patient in poor neurological state, GCS 6
7 years	22 kg	–	Intra-abdominal arterial rupture	Continuing haemorrhage
4 months	5.35 kg	39 weeks	Tracheal stenosis	Critical airway narrowing
5 months	4.4 kg	40 weeks	Mitochondrial myopathy	Very poorly

From Table 2.41 it can be seen that the reason for the unsatisfactory condition of these children on admission to the receiving hospital was related to the severity of the underlying disease and their continuing deterioration.

The organisation of paediatric care into specialist centres has the consequence that transfer of sick children is more frequent. The result of this concentration of paediatric practice, although beneficial for overall patient care, is that the skills and experience for paediatric care, particularly of neonates, becomes increasingly limited in many of the hospitals which first admit them. The ability of the staff in these hospitals to handle transfers therefore diminishes.

In this sample of paediatric deaths, transfers that were unsatisfactory were limited to isolated examples. However, the number of patients being transferred as a proportion of the whole group was high. The rigorous auditing of paediatric transfers must be maintained and the responsibility for this, particularly for those of less than six months of age, lies with regional paediatric specialist units.

Site and appropriateness of admission

Table 2.42: Type of area to which the child was first admitted in the hospital in which the final operation took place (SQ22)

Area	Number
Paediatric surgical ward	11
Specialist surgical ward	4
Paediatric medical ward	13
A&E holding area (or other emergency admission ward)	3
Paediatric ICU/HDU	23
Neonatal ICU/SCBU	27
Adult ICU/HDU	3
Direct to theatre	8
Other	1
Total	93

Cases that went into A&E holding area

CASE 6 • *Head injury with brain oedema. Intracranial pressure monitoring. (University/teaching hospital).*

CASE 18 • *Head injury. Craniotomy and evacuation of acute subdural haematoma. (District general hospital). (See also page 37).*

CASE 27 • *Trucut biopsy. Central venous line insertion. (Children's hospital).*

These children may have been admitted to an A&E holding area as a necessity pending the identification of an appropriate bed. The situation does not seem ideal but no further details are available.

Cases that went into adult ICU

CASE 23 • *Insertion of ICP monitor following closed head injury in a four-year-old. (Surgical specialty: neurosurgery) (See also page 39).*

CASE 28 • *Revision of ventriculoperitoneal shunt. (Surgical specialty: neurosurgery).*

CASE 29 • *Posterior fossa craniectomy and debulking of cerebellar tumour. (Surgical specialty: neurosurgery).*

Immediate access to paediatric intensive care beds is crucial; the provision of very high intensity care is known to be beneficial to these critically ill children[22]. An adult ICU can no longer be considered as a satisfactory location in which to manage children and, as a minimum, there should be dedicated paediatric beds available linked with appropriate staffing.

It appears from this sample that, in 1997/98, the standards of the framework document on the provision of paediatric intensive care were not being met[22]. This document was published in 1997; partial compliance was required by July 1998 and full compliance by the year 2000.

Delay in referral or admission

Questions were asked about delays.

Question 2.42: Was there any delay in either the referral or the admission of this child? (SQ26)

Yes	8
No	83
Not answered	1
Not known	1
Total	**93**

There were eight cases where the surgeon replied that there had been a delay. The reasons for the perceived delay were not always clear from the returned questionnaires. The cases are as follows:

CASE 5 • *Intracranial haemorrhage resulting from haemophilia and minor trauma. Craniotomy and evacuation of acute subdural haematoma. (University/teaching hospital).*

CASE 26 • *Severe gastroschisis. Silo construction following transfer to children's hospital. (See also page 44).*

CASE 30 • *Head injury. Craniotomy and evacuation of haematoma after transfer to children's hospital.*

CASE 31 • *Laparotomy, jejunostomy and ileal resection with ileo-ileal anastomosis. (Children's hospital).*

CASE 32 • *Through-hip amputation. (Children's hospital).*

CASE 33 • *Occipital burrhole and insertion of external ventricular drain. (University/teaching hospital).*

CASE 34 • *Laparotomy, suture of mesenteric vessel and irrigation. (Children's hospital).*

CASE 35 • *Laparoscopy, laparotomy, freeing of adhesions and anastomosis right ureter. (Children's hospital).*

Audit

Key Point

- *Audit of deaths in children was not universal practice.*

There were questions concerning audit in both anaesthetic and surgical questionnaires. In order to maintain a good standard of professional practice when treating children (although the same is true for any age group) anaesthetists and surgeons must participate in both internal and external medical and clinical audit[23] and be prepared, as individuals, to undergo regular review of their practice. In particular, any general surgeon who wishes to provide general paediatric surgery in a district general hospital is advised to fulfil a series of criteria including participation in audit and the maintenance of continuing education in paediatric surgery[15]. Similar criteria are laid down by the Royal College of Anaesthetists[24].

Anaesthetic responses

Question 2.43: Do you have morbidity/mortality review meetings in your anaesthetic department? (AQ86)

Yes	78
No	7
Total	**85**

If yes, will this case be, or has it been, discussed at your departmental meeting?

Yes	26
No	51
Not known	1
Total	**78**

Thus seven deaths took place following anaesthesia by an anaesthetist working in a department that does not hold morbidity/mortality review meetings. A total of 65% (51/78) of cases where children died were not discussed in a review/audit meeting by anaesthetists. It is possible that these deaths were not perceived as occurring as a direct result of anaesthesia but, given that the care of children involves teamwork, it is surprising that there was not more involvement in audit by anaesthetists.

Surgical responses

Question 2.44: Has this death been considered, or will it be considered, at a local surgical audit/quality control meeting? (SQ92)

Yes	71
No	19
Not answered	3
Total	93

In surgery, 20% (19/93) of deaths were not discussed at an audit meeting. In which specialties did these deaths occur?

Table 2.43: Specialty of surgeon where cases not considered at a local audit/quality control meeting

Specialty	Number
Neurosurgery – paediatric	6
Neurosurgery – adult	1
Neurosurgery – mixed	5
Paediatric	3
Plastic	3
Otorhinolaryngology	1
Total	19

The majority of deaths where there was no audit took place in neurosurgical units (63%, 12/19). Neurosurgeons will argue that there is little to be gained from repeated audit of common conditions such as extradural and subdural haematomas.

Whatever the special pleading of individual specialties, it is not unreasonable to consider each case and review the events surrounding the death of a child. This should be done in the context of multidisciplinary clinical audit. At present, this process is not universal.

LIVERPOOL JOHN MOORES UNIVERSITY
LEARNING SERVICES

Specific Issues

Neurosurgery

Key Point

- *The organisation of paediatric neurosurgery is complex. There is, however, scope for more shared care.*

The issues around neurosurgery are difficult in that it is a surgical specialty where complex procedures for rare conditions are done on small numbers of children and yet, at the same time, a comprehensive emergency service has to be provided for equally small numbers.

There were 31 deaths in this survey which occurred in neurosurgical patients; this was 28% of the total. There were six cases where no surgical questionnaire was returned and the information available is limited to that in the anaesthetic questionnaire. The neurosurgical procedures are listed in Table 2.24 on page 28. They can be divided into three groups: trauma, shunt surgery and other generally more major operations. The seniority of the surgeon within these groups is shown in Table 2.44.

The document 'Safe Paediatric Neurosurgery'[25], prepared by the Society of British Neurological Surgeons, recognises that some children suffering from these conditions, where travel or transfer to a unit with a paediatric neurosurgical team would be deemed dangerous, will be treated in units without a major paediatric commitment. This happened on four occasions in this sample (4/31, 13%). At present there are neurosurgery units with a paediatric interest but with no resident medical paediatric support and no PICU. There is guidance about the minimum services required for the care of children[22]. If difficulties arise with emergencies then local arrangements with neighbouring paediatric units are needed.

Particular problems are created for anaesthesia as there are few consultants with requisite skills in both neuro and paediatric anaesthesia and those that do have the appropriate training often have great difficulty in maintaining their paediatric skills based on a limited practice. When problems arise, skilled support may not be immediately at hand. Postoperative intensive care and ventilatory support for children (if required) can create considerable problems in isolated units.

Although problems were seen, and some are described in the case studies in this report, it is not justifiable to make broad recommendations on the basis of a few individual cases. However, those responsible for paediatric neurosurgical services will need to consider carefully arrangements for future provision, since amongst these deaths are indications that all is currently not satisfactory.

Table 2.44: Seniority of surgeon in neurosurgical operations

Condition	Consultant	Trainee	Total
Trauma	2	14	**16**
Shunt surgery	0	4	**4**
Other operations	9	1	**10**
Total	**11**	**19**	**30**

Abdominal trauma

Key Points

- *Medical staff treating trauma in children should be familiar with the Advanced Paediatric Life Support (APLS) guidelines.*
- *Contrast-enhanced CT scanning is the radiological investigation of choice for major blunt abdominal trauma in children. Surgeons who manage such cases must have access to this investigation.*

Staff working in centres that receive children with trauma should be familiar with the Advanced Paediatric Life Support (APLS) guidelines[26]. Courses offering tuition on paediatric life support are widely available and the Advanced Trauma Life Support (ATLS) course also contains guidance on paediatric trauma. Centres receiving children with trauma also require an adequate provision of paediatric intensive care beds.

Inappropriate laparotomies were done on children following abdominal trauma. Undue reliance was placed on diagnostic peritoneal lavage. The problem with diagnostic peritoneal lavage, in a haemodynamically stable child, is that the presence of blood does not dictate the need for a laparotomy. A double contrast CT scan of the abdomen (with intravenous and intragastric contrast) is the radiological investigation of choice for major blunt abdominal trauma in children[26]. Such an investigation must be immediately available in centres receiving such cases, should be performed early and must not delay further treatment.

Case 11 • *A seven-year-old boy was admitted to a DGH following a crush injury to the lower abdomen. He was fully conscious but had abdominal bruising and impaired circulation in one leg. A period of one-and-a-half to two hours elapsed during which an abdominal CT scan was performed before transfer to a specialist paediatric unit was commenced. A surgical senior registrar and anaesthetic registrar accompanied the child on the journey of more than 20 miles (the receiving hospital did not have a retrieval team). Massive transfusion was required during this transfer. On arrival he was found to be poorly perfused with no peripheral pulses present. Consultants in paediatric vascular surgery, paediatric surgery and anaesthesia were present to lead the resuscitation but efforts to cannulate a vessel for arterial monitoring and CVP measurement were unsuccessful due to the complete circulatory shutdown. It was decided to proceed to theatre and cross clamp the aorta via a thoracoabdominal incision. There was a complex tear in the lower aorta and common iliac artery. Bleeding and deterioration continued and resuscitation was abandoned when cardiac arrest occurred two hours after arrival at the receiving hospital. A postmortem examination confirmed the surgical findings.*

This was probably not a case for transfer in the first place. The request for sophisticated scanning delayed surgical intervention. Blood loss continued during transfer; an earlier laparotomy might have enabled control of haemorrhage and stabilisation whilst advice and help were sought. There was also questionable senior involvement at the time of transfer.

NECROTISING ENTEROCOLITIS

Key Point

- *The management of this condition requires close teamwork by experienced clinicians and discussion with the infant's parents.*

This condition is associated with prematurity and has a multifactorial causation. Necrotising enterocolitis (NEC) may improve with expert medical care. In general, 30-40% of babies with NEC require a laparotomy (for the repair of a perforation or resection of necrotic bowel), of whom 70% survive. Ninety percent of the babies with this condition are premature and 50% of the survivors of surgery are left with a handicap related either to prematurity or intestinal function. There is a paucity of denominator data concerning surgery for this condition in the UK; the authors are aware of only one study in recent years[27].

The management of this condition requires close teamwork, an appreciation of the risks and wide discussion about care, including the wishes of the parents. Decisions about these sick children need to be made at consultant level. If a child's condition fails to improve with conservative measures then it is usually right to proceed to laparotomy. This surgery should be done by an experienced paediatric anaesthetist and surgeon in a centre with adequate NICU services. Relative contraindications to surgery include extreme prematurity or additional major conditions associated with a predictable severe handicap. Decisions not to operate raise difficult ethical issues. Such decisions need to be discussed and agreed between professional staff (both medical and nursing) as well as the parents. There may be a need to discontinue supportive care if there is total gut necrosis at laparotomy and again parental acceptance is vital.

CASE 19 • *A very premature 600 g baby developed severe necrotising enterocolitis and septicaemia. It was unlikely that the parents would have another child because of their medical problems. The medical staff advised against surgery and suggested withdrawal of treatment but the nursing staff insisted that surgery was the only appropriate option. The parents were warned of the likely poor outcome but pressed for surgery. A small bowel resection was done and the child died 13 days later. No postmortem examination was done.*

This case raises very difficult issues. At this gestation and weight, overall survival is less than 50% and, had the baby survived, the risk of major neurological handicap would have been greater than 25%. An additional issue here is the need for an identified team leader. This could either be someone in an overall position of authority or someone identified case by case. In this case, the anaesthetic and surgical staff felt under pressure from the nurses, team management broke down and conflict occurred.

Postoperative pain relief

Key Point

- *The importance of effective postoperative pain relief in children would appear to be widely recognised.*

Question 2.45: Is there an acute pain team available for children? (AQ78)

Yes	63
No	21
Not answered	1
Total	85

Question 2.46: Do nursing staff receive training in acute pain techniques? (AQ79)

Yes	80
No	4
Not answered	1
Total	85

The importance of the effective management of postoperative pain in children has been a recent concern[28]. No questions relating to this aspect of patient care were asked in 1989, but it would appear that the problem is being addressed.

The four cases where nursing staff were recorded as not receiving training in acute pain techniques came from university hospitals; two were neurosurgical patients.

Question 2.47: Were drugs given in the first 48 hours after operation for pain? (AQ80)

Yes	70
No	9
Not answered	6
Total	85

If yes, which drug type *(answers may be multiple)*

Opiate/opioid	61
Local analgesic	3
Non-steroidal analgesic	4
Paracetamol	15

Method/route *(answers may be multiple)*

Intramuscular injection	3
Oral	12
Rectal	4
Continuous IV/SC infusion	48
PCA	3
Continuous epidural	1
IV bolus *(including nurse controlled analgesia)*	9

The infrequent use of intramuscular injection was commented on very favourably by the anaesthetic advisors.

Question 2.48: Did complications occur as a result of these analgesic methods? (AQ80c)

Yes	1
No	68
Not answered	1
Total	70

The child noted to have complications was delivered at 27 weeks and had NEC. At three months of age the baby had a further laparotomy. Postoperatively the child experienced hypotension related to the use of local anaesthesia and continuous IV/SC infusion for pain relief.

Good handling of deaths

Key Point

- *The death of a child has an impact on clinical staff as well as on the family and close friends. The emotional consequences for clinical staff may not be acknowledged; help and support should be provided if requested.*

The death of a child is a profoundly disturbing situation for all concerned. On occasions treatment is withheld or withdrawn. Amongst the deaths reported to the Enquiry there were examples of children with brainstem death (mainly following head injuries) and children in the 'no chance' or 'no purpose' situation. These deaths were all handled well, sympathetically and according to the framework for practice published in 1997[29].

Most staff are trained in the support of bereaved parents and the questionnaires returned to NCEPOD contained some excellent examples of support and follow-up for parents and siblings. The emotional impact on the healthcare team can often be overlooked in these situations, leading to a sense of failure, guilt and a quest for understanding of the course of events. When time permits, the creation of an ethical forum may provide an opportunity for all those involved with a severely ill child to talk about their concerns, receive advice and ensure understanding of the issues.

In the case studies given below we highlight good practice. An example of the uncertainty which can occur (Case 19) is discussed on page 50.

Case 36 • *A two-day-old full-term infant was referred for assessment of an oesophageal atresia with a tracheo-oesophageal fistula. Initial oesophagoscopy revealed a very atypical anatomy and the planned repair was not feasible. Discussion took place between paediatric ENT surgeons and the paediatric general surgeon. The result of these discussions was that there was a predicted mortality of over 90% for corrective surgery. These facts were presented to the parents who then declined surgical treatment for their child. The child remained on ventilatory support throughout the day whilst the parents continued to think about the options. However, by the following day the parents had not changed their minds and, following a full discussion with them, it was decided to withdraw support. The child died peacefully that day.*

Case 37 • *A premature newborn baby (32 weeks gestational age at birth) developed a fulminant acute abdomen. A laparotomy was done after appropriate resuscitation. This revealed complete infarction of both small and large bowel. A discussion was held with the parents and treatment was then withdrawn. The baby died in the parents' arms.*

Case 38 • *A premature baby (24 weeks gestational age at birth) was transferred to a regional paediatric surgical unit with a clinical diagnosis of necrotising enterocolitis. A laparotomy showed a hopeless situation and this prognosis was discussed with the parents. The child was then extubated in his mother's arms and died peacefully.*

It is perhaps important to remember that the emotional scars inflicted by the death of a child are not limited to family and friends.

Case 39 • *An experienced paediatric anaesthetist reported the case of a death in the anaesthetic room. A neonate with gastroschisis had a cardiovascular collapse on induction and intubation. Resuscitation was unsuccessful. A very thoughtful and thorough investigation and postmortem examination followed but the postmortem was essentially negative.*

It was apparent from the comments in the anaesthetic questionnaire that the death had a profound psychological effect on the anaesthetist concerned. The psychological impact of deaths in children on clinical staff may not be acknowledged and the need for counselling and support of health professionals is too often disregarded. Help and support should be provided if requested.

PATHOLOGY

Key Points

- *There is a need for pathologists to improve the dissemination of information gained at a postmortem examination.*
- *Postmortem examination rates for children have fallen; this is a national trend. A limited or directed postmortem examination, or possibly a magnetic resonance necropsy, may be the way to improve this situation.*

GENERAL

Postmortem examinations were performed in 41 cases (41/93, 44%), of which 30 were at the request of Her Majesty's Coroner and 11 with consent from the next of kin. This is a considerable decline from the situation reported in 1989[10] when the postmortem rate was 72%. Of the 41 postmortem examinations, less than half (19) were performed by a paediatric pathologist, nine by a neuropathologist, four by a Home Office pathologist and five by a general histopathologist (in four cases the status of the pathologist is unknown).

Postmortem reports were available for only 22 cases (13 Coroner's and nine hospital). In some cases at least this was because of refusal of the Coroner involved to release the report to the Enquiry under Rule 57 of the Coroner's Rules 1984. This goes against a recommendation of The Allitt Inquiry[30] which states *"We recommend that in every case Coroners should send copies of postmortem reports to any consultant who has been involved in the patient's care prior to death whether or not demanded under Rule 57 of the Coroner's Rules 1984 (Para 4.2.9)"*. This statement emphasises the importance of obtaining the results of a Coroner's postmortem examination in paediatric medical practice but could reasonably also be applied to surgical practice. It should be noted, however, that this is only a recommendation and there is no obligation for the Coroner to follow it.

The comments that follow are based on the small sample of 22 postmortem examination reports and so no general conclusions about the overall service can be made but some observations still hold.

THE POSTMORTEM EXAMINATION REPORT

Of the reports received the standard was generally good but there were some lamentable exceptions. All postmortem reports were typewritten but not all conformed to the minimum standards laid down by the Royal College of Pathologists[31]. A history was included in 86% (19/22) of cases. The cases without written histories were performed for Coroners, suggesting that in some areas the Coroner does not permit clinical information to be included in the pathological report. There may be good reasons for this practice as any inaccuracy in the history may cause distress to relatives and general confusion. In two of the cases the amount of information supplied was so brief as to be of no help in reviewing the case. On a more positive note, the advisors were particularly struck by the impressive quality of the neuropathology examinations.

The macroscopic description was, in the main, detailed and appropriate to the case but in four cases no description of the surgical operation site was included. In one case the description of the internal organs was telegraphically brief and not a single organ was weighed, or at least their weight was not recorded in the report.

Samples for histology were not taken in every case. In three Coroner's cases histology was not taken. While this may be explicable, if not excusable, it is more difficult to accept that in two hospital examinations no histology was undertaken. When histology was taken it was not always adequate for the case, such as in a child with myeloproliferative disorder when the bone marrow was not examined.

No postmortem examination report was deemed unacceptably bad but three reports were judged to be poor. These included the above case with myeloproliferative disorder and the case of a child with severe burns in whom the description of the burns and internal organs was perfunctory and no histology or microbiology was taken. Assessing the significance of the reports, no report was found in which there was a discrepancy that would have led to a change of treatment or prognosis but there is no room for complacency.

Communication of the postmortem result to the surgical team

This is a continuing theme and is also commented on in the section on pathology in the elderly (see page 98). Twenty-nine percent of surgeons did not receive a copy of the postmortem findings and of those who did less than half did so within 30 days of the examination. This is clearly unacceptable and all pathologists are urged to improve the dissemination of information gained at postmortem examinations. There may be difficulties here with regard to the report of a Coroner's postmortem examination. Such a report is confidential to the Coroner. Whether or not information from it is disseminated to clinicians is entirely a matter for the Coroner to decide. It would be a breach of trust for a pathologist to pass a report (even informally) to a clinician without the Coroner's consent.

Comment

The postmortem rate for children is still low, even in this group of highly selected cases. Paediatric postmortem rates are traditionally higher than in adults. The figures described above are comparable to those collected by the Confidential Enquiry into Stillbirths and Deaths in Infancy (CESDI)[32].

Postmortem examination is an important part of the medical management of a child and an important part of the audit of that process. A postmortem examination on his or her child is the right of every parent.

Case 40 • *A premature baby died two days after a laparotomy for peritonitis and small bowel obstruction secondary to a milk curd obstruction. A patent ductus arteriosus was also present. There was no postmortem examination. This should have been done to confirm the diagnosis, as there was a possibility of cystic fibrosis, which would have implications for the parents and future offspring.*

Where, for whatever reason, the parents are reluctant to agree to full postmortem examination they may consent to a more targeted examination, for example of a single organ system or body cavity. There were no cases in this group in which a report of a limited postmortem was submitted. However, one surgeon did describe the use of a limited postmortem examination.

Case 26 • *A premature baby had a silo constructed for gastroschisis. The child was very sick and died of multiorgan failure within 24 hours. The surgeon expressed an interest in the state of the bowel, and a limited postmortem examination was undertaken in order to obtain the necessary information (see also page 44).*

A limited or directed postmortem examination may yet prove to be the way to improve the postmortem rate. Magnetic resonance necropsy might offer an alternative in infants who die in the perinatal period, which is the most prognostically important age group for necropsy[33, 34]. Whilst some pathologists may still consider MRI to be supplementary to necropsy, it is becoming increasingly widespread.

Hospital pathologists need to include a clinical history in their reports, they need to take more histology and they need to describe the operation site. It is important that postmortem examinations on children be carried out by pathologists with training and experience in carrying out autopsies on children, as recommended by The Allitt Inquiry[30] and the Royal College of Pathologists[31]. Those responsible for paediatric services should ensure that specialist staffing in paediatric pathology is adequate, and that sufficient numbers of pathologists are trained in these skills, to ensure that there is the minimum of delay in obtaining relevant clinical information and releasing the body to the parents.

No examination, however well performed, will achieve its maximum impact if the results are not communicated to the clinicians in charge of the care of the child and pathologists are strongly urged to improve their systems in this regard. This issue was specifically addressed by the Royal College of Pathologists in 1993 in their guidance on postmortem examinations[31], where they particularly suggested that an audit should be undertaken of the time taken for reports to be issued and delivered. We should perhaps reapply ourselves to that exhortation.

3 The Elderly

Compiled by: K G Callum, A J G Gray, I C Martin and K M Sherry

Recommendations

- Fluid management in the elderly is often poor; it should be accorded the same status as drug prescription. Multidisciplinary reviews to develop good local working practices are required.

- A team of senior surgeons, anaesthetists and physicians needs to be closely involved in the care of elderly patients who have poor physical status and high operative risk.

- The experience of the surgeon and anaesthetist need to be matched to the physical status of the elderly patient, as well as to the technical demands of the procedure.

- If a decision is made to operate on an elderly patient then that must include a decision to provide appropriate postoperative care, which may include high dependency or intensive care support.

- There should be sufficient, fully-staffed, daytime theatre and recovery facilities to ensure that no elderly patient requiring an urgent operation waits for more than 24 hours once fit for surgery. This includes weekends.

- Elderly patients need their pain management to be provided by those with appropriate specialised experience in order that they receive safe and effective pain relief.

- Surgeons need to be more aware that, in the elderly, clinically unsuspected gastrointestinal complications are commonly found at postmortem to be the cause, or contribute to the cause, of death following surgery.

3. The Elderly

Introduction

There are good reasons why the very elderly may die following surgery. The life expectancy of those aged 90 years and over in the UK in 1996 was 3.6 years for males and 4.5 years for females[35], and thus for some death will occur coincidentally with surgery. With advancing age there is a functional deterioration of all body systems and this increases the risk of postoperative complications. Very elderly patients have a high incidence of coexisting diseases that will further increase their operative risk.

NCEPOD advisors and coordinators recognised that, within this group of those aged 90 years and over, many of the deaths following surgery were inevitable but were also conscious that many others of this age survive. In order to minimise mortality and morbidity, and to maximise survival with good quality of life, these patients require excellent care. This sample enabled NCEPOD to review the decision-making and care provided to this group of vulnerable patients.

The benefits of an operation need to be carefully weighed against the risks, and the decision to operate includes the commitment to provide appropriate supportive care. NCEPOD found that senior surgical staff involvement in decision-making was commendably high. The grade of operative surgeon and anaesthetist, however, was not well matched to the physical status of the patient. Aspects of postoperative care that should be addressed include the infrequent use of high dependency units and poor fluid management.

Elderly patients may not do well despite being provided with the best care. Nevertheless, all unfavourable outcomes should be reviewed in order that the lessons that they may provide can be learned.

LIVERPOOL
JOHN MOORES UNIVERSITY
AVRIL ROBARTS LRC
TEL. 0151 231 4022

General Issues

Patient profile

Key Point

- *Elderly patients have a high incidence of coexisting disorders and a high risk of early postoperative death.*

Age

Table 3.1: Age of patient at time of final operation (SQ3)

Age (years)	Number
89*-94	827
95-99	224
100-106	26
Total	1077

* *Seven patients were aged 89 years at the time of operation, but at the time of death were aged 90 years and thus formed part of the sample.*

Procedures

Table 3.2 shows the ten most frequently performed operative procedures in this age group, using information from the 1077 surgical questionnaires returned.

Table 3.2: Most frequently performed operative procedures *(procedures may be multiple in some cases)*

Procedure	Number	
Hemiarthroplasty	258	24%
Sliding hip screw	243	23%
Laparotomy	141	13%
Amputation	48 (36 legs, 10 toes, 1 arm, 1 finger)	
Cystoscopy	30	
Embolectomy	27	
Femoral hernia repair	21	
Femoral nailing	21	
Gastrointestinal endoscopy	20	
Inguinal hernia repair	14	

Orthopaedic and general surgeons were the consultants in charge of 92% of the patients in this sample (Table 3.3).

Table 3.3: Specialty of consultant surgeon in charge at the time of final operation (SQ14)

Specialty	Number	
Orthopaedic	648	60%
General (including special interests)	346	32%
Urology	30	
Vascular	12	
Ophthalmology	11	
Otorhinolaryngology	9	
Plastic	9	
Cardiac/Thoracic/Cardiothoracic	4	
Accident & Emergency	2	
Gynaecology	2	
Neurosurgery	2	
Oral/Maxillofacial	1	
Other	1	
Total	1077	

Preoperative status

Table 3.4: ASA status prior to final operation (AQ10 and SQ20)

	Anaesthetic questionnaire		Surgical questionnaire	
ASA 1	9	1%	8	1%
ASA 2	156	17%	197	18%
ASA 3	478	51%	534	50%
ASA 4	266	28%	299	28%
ASA 5	32	3%	22	2%
Not answered	3		17	
Total	944		1077	

Most patients were of a poor physical status, ASA 3 and greater. In this sample there was good agreement between the anaesthetists and surgeons on the ASA grading of patients.

Table 3.5: Coexisting medical disorders (SQ21) *(1077 cases; answers may be multiple)*		
Coexisting disorders	**Number**	
None	128	
Not answered	17	
Cardiac	609	57%
Respiratory	301	28%
Neurological	193	18%
Psychiatric	136	13%
Renal	126	12%
Musculoskeletal	121	11%
Gastrointestinal	105	
Malignancy	92	
Haematological	92	
Vascular	79	
Sepsis	58	
Diabetes mellitus	57	
Other endocrine	37	
Alcohol-related problems	5	
Other	1	

Surgeons indicated that 87% (932/1077) of patients had coexisting medical problems at the time of operation (Table 3.5).

The form of this question differed between the anaesthetic and surgical questionnaires making direct comparisons difficult. However, both specialties reported a very high incidence of coexisting medical problems. Anaesthetists reported coexisting medical diagnoses in 95% of patients.

Anaesthetists reported dementia in 27% of patients. Surgeons reported neurological disease in 18% and psychiatric disease in 13% of patients. In an elderly patient it is important to distinguish between a remediable confusional state secondary to a medical disorder (e.g. urinary tract infection, chest infection, abdominal sepsis, low cardiac output state, electrolyte disorder etc.) and true dementia.

Only 22% of these patients received shared care on a formal basis. This was surprisingly few in a population with such a high incidence of medical comorbidity. When necessary a medical/rehabilitation opinion should be sought from a physician with an interest in care of the elderly; in many cases this is appropriate preoperatively.

Fifty-four percent of patients were admitted via A&E and 27% following referral by their general practitioner (Table 3.6).

The majority of admissions were classified by surgeons as emergency, i.e. requiring immediate admission regardless of time. Figure 3.1 shows that the emergency and urgent admissions appeared to be skewed towards weekdays and in particular to the beginning of the week.

Table 3.6: Admission category (SQ8) *(NCEPOD definitions)*		
Admission category	**Number**	
Elective	79	
Urgent	74	
Emergency	919	85%
Not answered	4	
Not known	1	
Total	**1077**	

Why was this? Is there a problem with provision of emergency medical care within the health care system? Are the patients themselves, or their carers, reluctant to seek medical advice at the weekend? The vulnerability of the elderly is such that a delay in emergency treatment may result in increased morbidity and mortality.

Figure 3.1: Day of admission for emergency and urgent cases

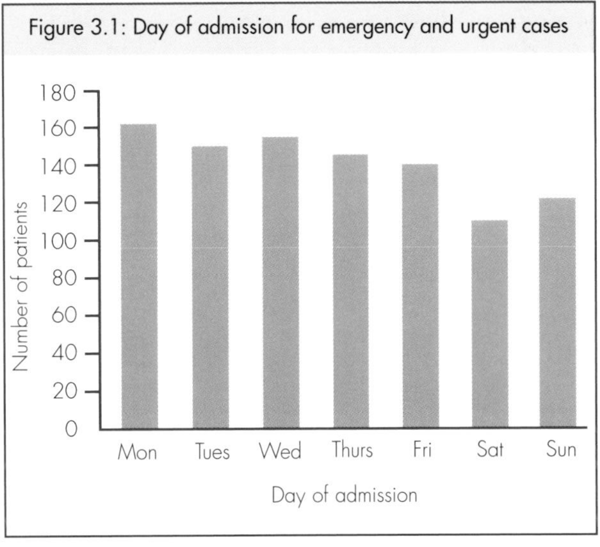

The Elderly

Time of death

Figure 3.2: Calendar days from operation to death

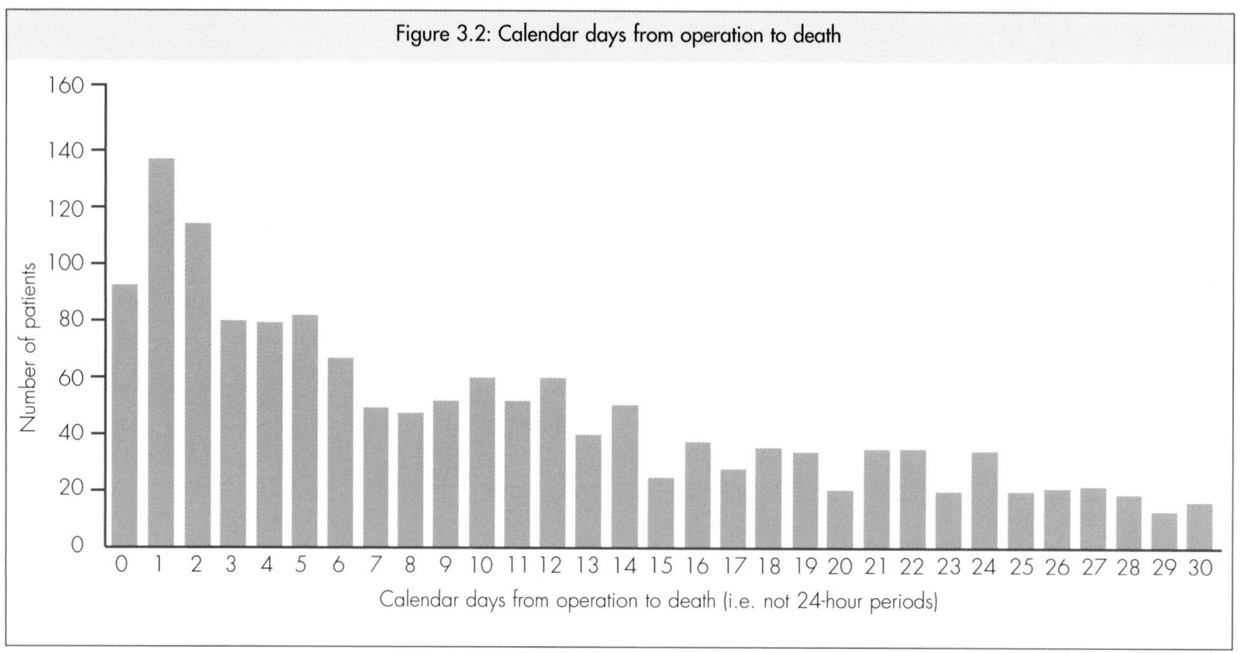

Figure 3.2 is based on the total number of deaths in this age group reported to NCEPOD and shows that one quarter (24%) of patients died on or before the second postoperative day.

Hospitals, facilities and staffing

Key Points

- *Every acute surgical hospital should have a recovery area, staffed and equipped 24 hours a day, and a high dependency unit.*
- *A team of senior surgeons, anaesthetists and physicians needs to be closely involved in the care of elderly patients who have poor physical status and a high operative risk.*
- *There should be adequate daytime operating lists for urgent orthopaedic trauma and general surgical emergencies.*

Type of hospital

Table 3.7: Type of hospital in which the final operation took place (SQ1)

Type of hospital	Number
District general (or equivalent)	875
University/teaching	183
Single surgical specialty	1
Other acute/partly acute	1
Independent	4
Not answered	13
Total	**1077**

Facilities

In both the anaesthetic and surgical questionnaires clinicians were asked about the specialist facilities within the hospital. Table 3.8 summarises responses given by anaesthetists.

Recovery facilities

The surgical questionnaire asked whether recovery facilities were available and staffed 24 hours a day. Of those who responded, 18% (147/813) indicated that they were not.

The operations undertaken in hospitals with recovery facilities that were not available on a 24-hour basis are shown in Table 3.9, and some of these were emergencies.

Intensive care and high dependency units

The percentages quoted in Table 3.8 for high dependency units (HDU) and intensive care units (ICU) are taken from the anaesthetic questionnaires. The surgical response indicated that an HDU existed in the hospital for 53% of cases and an ICU for 97% of patients. Table 3.10 shows the destination of patients on leaving the operating theatre.

The argument for a high dependency unit in all hospitals undertaking acute surgical services has been made by NCEPOD in previous reports[5, 6, 7, 9]. It applies equally forcibly to this very elderly population for the following reasons:

- If a decision is made to operate then that must include a decision to provide appropriate postoperative care that may include HDU/ICU

Table 3.8: Availability of facilities

Facilities available	1997/98	1995/96	1994/95
Recovery area or room equipped and staffed for this purpose (AQ2)	97%	97%	93%
High dependency unit (AQ2)	46%	41%	27%
Intensive care unit (AQ2)	96%	93%	82%
Scheduled emergency lists for urgent general surgical cases (AQ3)	77%		
Scheduled trauma lists for urgent orthopaedic trauma cases (AQ4)	93%		

Table 3.9: Operations in hospitals with recovery facilities not available on a 24-hour basis

Type of surgery	Number
Fractured hip	89
Other orthopaedic trauma	7
Elective orthopaedic surgery	4
Open abdominal surgery including obstruction, perforated viscus, cholecystectomy	17
Endoscopy	11
Other major surgery including leaking abdominal aneurysm, burr holes, above knee amputation, recurrent carcinoma of the breast, postoperative bleeding after rectal prolapse repair	9
Other minor surgery	10
Total	**147**

Table 3.10: Destination of patient on leaving the operating theatre/recovery room (AQs 58 and 62)

Destination	Number	
Ward	787	83%
ICU	52	6%
HDU	34	4%
CCU	3	
Died in theatre/recovery room	27	
Other (including specialised nursing areas)	8	
Not answered	33	
Total	**944**	

Table 3.11: Anaesthetic staffing for general surgical emergency and orthopaedic trauma lists (AQs 3 and 4)

Anaesthetic staffing	General surgical emergency lists	Orthopaedic trauma lists
Consultant/associate specialist	297	507
Trainee	282	148
Staff grade	28	77
Where answers multiple – some consultant sessions	79	103
Where answers multiple – no consultant sessions	34	36
Other/not answered	10	11
Total	**730**	**882**

support. It is accepted that operative findings, e.g. disseminated malignancy, may subsequently influence management.

- Approximately 90% of patients had at least one coexisting medical disorder.
- Eleven percent of patients had received attention to improve their cardiovascular system and 6% to improve their respiratory system preoperatively.
- Postoperative morbidity and mortality are associated with pre-existing disorders and at least 35% of patients had postoperative cardiac and/or ventilatory complications, many of which could be predicted preoperatively.
- Almost one quarter of the patients suffered complications early and died on or before the second postoperative day.

Many clinicians are of the opinion that an HDU can beneficially influence early postoperative patient management and the lack of an HDU results in a lower standard of care. We would suggest that for hospitals without an HDU discussions should take place between clinicians, managers and primary care groups. Why are managers and commissioners of healthcare slow to respond? (See also page 70).

General surgical emergency and orthopaedic trauma lists

NCEPOD has not previously asked about general surgical emergency and orthopaedic trauma lists. From the questionnaires 77% of anaesthetists responded that their hospital provided general surgical emergency lists and 93% indicated that their hospital provided orthopaedic trauma lists (Table 3.8).

It is encouraging that most hospitals have made local arrangements to enable these urgent daytime lists to take place.

Table 3.11 shows the grade of anaesthetist who covered the general surgical emergency and orthopaedic trauma lists most of the time.

Urgent and emergency surgical patients as a group have higher operative risk factors than elective ones. Ideally all daytime emergency lists should come with funding for senior anaesthetic and surgical cover. It appears that trainee or staff grade anaesthetists frequently run them, more often for the general surgical emergency than the orthopaedic trauma lists.

Staffing

Table 3.12 shows that a consultant was the most senior surgeon and anaesthetist present in the operating room in 43% of cases. Importantly a consultant surgeon was involved in the decision-making process in 83% of cases.

Figure 3.3 illustrates that each grade of surgeon operates on a similar percentage of the good and poor ASA patient groups.

The association between the physical status of the patient and the grade of operative surgeon or anaesthetist is poor in this age group.

The care of a patient who is graded as having poor physical status and who requires major surgery should be closely supervised by senior medical staff.

Delays before operation

In a quarter (232/944) of cases the operation was delayed appropriately in order to improve the patient's condition before surgery (AQ20) (see also page 66).

On 175/944 (19%) occasions the operation was delayed for non-medical reasons (AQ21). Included in these were 76 cases (8% of the sample) in which the delay was caused by a lack of theatre time (Table 3.13).

Table 3.12: Grade of most senior surgeon and anaesthetist present in operating room (SQ30 and AQ30)

Grade	Surgeon		Anaesthetist	
Consultant	459	43%	405	43%
Associate specialist	65		52	
Staff grade	96		90	
Clinical assistant	14		7	
SpR – Accredited/CCST	38	37%	11	15%
SpR – 3, 4	171		70	
SpR – 1, 2	98		53	
Visiting SpR or year not stated	92		3	
SHO	41	4%	207	22%
Other	2		39	
Not answered	1		7	
Total	**1077**		**944**	

Figure 3.3: Seniority of surgeon by ASA group

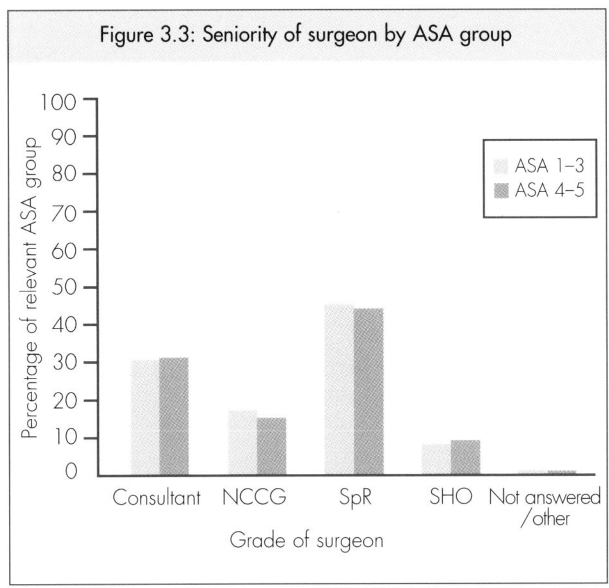

Figure 3.4: Seniority of anaesthetist by ASA group

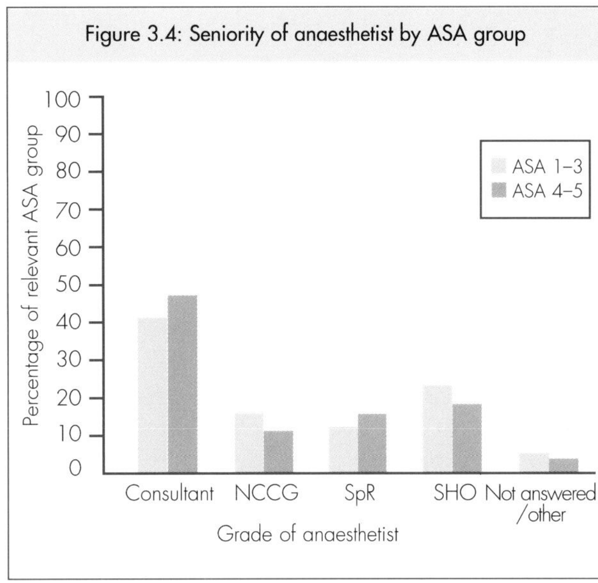

The elderly do not tolerate repeated episodes of preoperative starvation, or prolonged pain, sepsis or immobility, and should be considered as having a high surgical priority. In this sample the number of operations that were delayed because of insufficient theatre time or 'overbooked lists' suggests that the surgical priority of the elderly is low. A fractured hip was cancelled one day because the trauma list was overbooked and cancelled the next after inadvertent feeding in the morning. A laparotomy for an iatrogenic perforated diverticulum that occurred during a barium enema was delayed for five hours for 'patient assessment and correct priority of emergencies'. It was done in the evening by an anaesthetic SHO 1 and a surgical SpR 2.

Some of the non-medical reasons for surgical delay were appropriate, for example, referral to physicians, awaiting consultant operating lists or discussions with patients and relatives. Other reasons were less appropriate. In four cases surgery was delayed for over 24 hours while waiting for the arrival of a relative to give consent. The patients concerned were blind (1) or demented (3). The Association of Anaesthetists' guidance states that a relative cannot legally give consent for operation on an adult, even if the patient is incompetent[36].

In addition there were organisational problems, including lack of surgical or anaesthetic personnel and poor patient preparation. One patient with a fractured hip had surgery delayed for 24 hours because no blood had been crossmatched.

Table 3.13: Operations delayed by lack of theatre time	
Type of surgery	Number
Fractured neck of femur	59
Fractured shaft of femur	2
Screening of hip for suspected fracture, reduction dislocated shoulder and Denham pin	3
Bowel obstruction	5
Perforated abdominal viscus	4
Tibial split skin grafts to lacerations, thyroidectomy and above knee amputation	3
Total	**76**

AUDIT

Key Point

- *All deaths should be reviewed at local audit meetings.*

Question 3.1: Do you have morbidity/mortality review meetings in your anaesthetic department? (AQ79)

Yes	876
No	61
Not answered	7
Total	944

The Royal College of Anaesthetists and Association of Anaesthetists of Great Britain and Ireland recommend a monthly review of deaths[37]. Is it acceptable that some hospitals still have no anaesthetic review of morbidity and mortality?

Question 3.2: Has this death been considered (or will it be considered) at a local audit meeting? (SQ62 and AQ79a)

	Surgical	Anaesthetic
Yes	692	193
No	311	663
Not answered	71	16
Not known	3	4
Total	1077	876

This group of elderly patients has a homogeneous profile; they are urgent cases with a high incidence of comorbidity. The circumstances surrounding such deaths can be educational. They can be used to examine, for example, aspects of the organisation and provision of services for urgent and emergency surgical admissions, as well as the perioperative surgical and anaesthetic management of patients with coexisting medical disorders.

The failure of anaesthetic departments to review deaths has been highlighted by NCEPOD previously[38]. The figure for departments of anaesthesia is again low, with 76% of cases not being considered at a local audit meeting. There was no surgical discussion of circumstances surrounding the death of 29% of patients in this sample.

A lack of review represents a missed learning opportunity, for both disciplines.

The surgical questionnaire asked if problems were encountered in supplying information to NCEPOD.

Question 3.3: Did you have any problems in obtaining the patient's notes (i.e. more than one week)? (SQ63)

Yes	104
No	895
Not answered	75
Not known	3
Total	1077

Question 3.4: Were all the notes available? (SQ64)

Yes	831
No	158
Not answered	88
Total	1077

If no, which part was inadequate/unavailable?
(158 cases; answers may be multiple)

Preoperative notes	11
Operative notes	11
Postoperative notes	19
Death certificate book	99
Nursing notes	15

Anaesthetic notes	18
Postmortem report	62
Other notes	2
Not answered	1

The Audit Commission and NCEPOD have been reporting problems pertaining to the availability of clinical records for many years. It is hoped that the revised NCEPOD systems outlined on page 12 will result in greater assistance from medical record managers and that these problems will diminish.

Question 3.5: Do you have anaesthetic departmental guidelines relating to the care of the elderly? (AQ78)

Yes	51
No	849
Not answered	39
Not known	5
Total	944

The elderly are a group suitable for anaesthetic departmental guidelines. In those few departments (5%) that have them they are based on age, ASA group, coexisting medical conditions, type and urgency of surgery. They trigger discussion with, or referral to, an anaesthetist of specified seniority.

Guidelines need to be appropriately distributed. One anaesthetist commented that the locum junior anaesthetist on duty that weekend did not follow departmental guidelines relating to anaesthetic care of the elderly patient. Were the guidelines available to this locum anaesthetist?

A question about departmental guidelines for the elderly patient was not asked in the surgical questionnaire.

In four cases the most senior surgeon involved in the decision-making process, either before or during surgery, was an SHO (SQs 16, 30, 31 and 35). The cases were as follows:

ASA GRADE 3 • *Laparotomy, division of adhesions, oversew DU. SHO surgeon and SHO anaesthetist. Cardiac and respiratory comorbidity.*

ASA GRADE 3 • *Thompson's hemiarthroplasty. SHO surgeon. Cardiac, renal and vascular comorbidity.*

ASA GRADE NOT KNOWN • *Sliding hip screw. SHO surgeon. Cardiac, respiratory, renal and malignant comorbidity.*

ASA GRADE 3 • *Sliding hip screw. SHO surgeon and SHO anaesthetist. Severe cardiac and respiratory problems. Lengthy procedure.*

Local guidelines on surgical decision-making and management of the elderly patient may also be appropriate.

SPECIAL CLINICAL PROBLEMS

Operative hypotension

Key Points

- *Hypotension is common during anaesthesia in the elderly patient. It requires prompt appropriate treatment.*
- *Hypovolaemia should be corrected before operation whenever possible.*
- *Particular care is required when general anaesthesia combined with epidural analgesia is used during emergency abdominal surgery, especially when there may be sepsis.*
- *When a vasoconstrictor is not effective in repeated dose the anaesthetist should consider alternative drugs and other methods of delivery.*

It was noted that a large number of patients in this sample were hypotensive during surgery.

The precise incidence of operative hypotension was difficult to quantify. Hypotension was reported as a perioperative adverse event in 17% of cases and this may be indicative. However, some of these reports were of transient hypotension or hypotension as part of a terminal event, e.g. during cardiac arrest. Other patients considered to be hypotensive by the advisors did not have it noted as an adverse event in the anaesthetic questionnaire.

The main causes of hypotension in these patients are hypovolaemia and the vasodilator effects of anaesthesia. Hypotension in this age group is poorly tolerated. This opinion is not based on any known association between hypotension and clinical outcome, but on clinical judgement. Myocardial, renal cortical and gastrointestinal blood flow is often at a critical level in the very elderly. Prolonged periods of hypotension may lead to infarction or ischaemic injury to these organs. Perioperative hypotension should, therefore, be treated vigorously and effectively.

The examples described represent a small proportion of patients who were considered to be hypotensive. In these examples the values of systolic arterial pressure cited are the best and worst during the time period. In general the systolic arterial pressure was 85 mmHg or less for most of the time. Many of the examples are patients with a fractured hip. This is not only because they form the largest group in this sample but also because they have more predictable fluid losses than patients with abdominal pathology, and so are easier to evaluate objectively. The problem of hypotension was by no means confined to patients with a fractured hip.

Operative hypotension can be potentiated by hypovolaemia. This should be corrected before operation and for most patients there is time to do this. In this sample anaesthetists indicated that 74% of patients underwent emergency or urgent surgery, but only 12% had an operation on the day of admission and the majority (51%) had an operation within the next two days. It is the surgical trainees who usually supervise the initial preoperative assessment and resuscitation of surgical admissions; they are often the first points of medical contact within the hospital. It is important therefore that surgical trainees are able to detect dehydration and hypovolaemia clinically and understand the management of preoperative fluid resuscitation in the elderly. This should have been learned during their undergraduate and basic postgraduate training. Some patients will require intensive resuscitation with invasive monitoring and for these the early referral to, and involvement of, the anaesthetic department may be valuable.

CASE 1 • *A patient underwent a laparotomy and hemicolectomy for a gangrenous caecum. There was a delay of four days between admission and operation, reportedly for fluid resuscitation. Despite the recognition of, dehydration on admission, the resuscitation was apparently not carefully monitored. There was no CVP monitoring or record of hourly urine output. Over the four preoperative days the haemoglobin increased from 16 to 17 g/dl and urea from 11.9 to 13.5 mmol/l. The creatinine measured on admission was normal. The patient had passed 346 ml of urine on the day before surgery; none had been recorded on the chart for the day of surgery. The anaesthetist first saw the patient at 23.00 and induction of anaesthesia was at 23.30. The patient became hypotensive following the induction of anaesthesia and after 30 minutes had a cardiac arrest and died.*

CASE 2 • *A patient was admitted with cholecystitis and a recent myocardial infarction. After four days he required an operation for a perforated gall bladder from which he made a good recovery. Six weeks later he required a further operation for an ileocaecal intussusception. Before this second surgical intervention he became dehydrated and was transferred to the ICU for insertion of monitoring lines and fluid resuscitation. During the operation he was haemodynamically stable and postoperatively he was managed on the ICU. He died of sepsis six days later.*

The potential for preoperative dehydration in acute admission general surgical and trauma patients is recognised and 73% of patients received intravenous fluids in the 12 hours before surgery. However, for some patients the start of intravenous fluid therapy was delayed and for many their dehydration was inadequately treated.

Fifty-five percent of patients had surgery for a fractured neck of femur. Blood loss with this fracture is concealed, not easy to assess and often underestimated. Nevertheless, some allowance for blood loss should be attempted. There is in general a greater preoperative blood loss from extracapsular than intracapsular fractures.

Increased serum creatinine, urea and sodium preoperatively should trigger a suspicion of dehydration.

CASE 3 • *A patient was admitted with a fractured neck of femur and received no intravenous fluid for the next two days. The total fluid intake over the first two days was 300 ml and urine output was 450 ml. An intravenous infusion was started in the afternoon of the third day. For the third and fourth days the total fluid intake was 1900 ml IV and 635 ml orally, total urine output was 650 ml. Surgery was on the fifth day. Biochemistry on the day of surgery showed* Na^+ *157 mmol/l,* K^+ *5.2 mmol/l, urea 28.8 mmol/l and creatinine 180 micromol/l. Haemoglobin was 13 g/dl and WCC 15.3 x* 10^9*/l. During spinal anaesthesia 700 ml of crystalloid were given. The systolic arterial pressure remained between 70 and 100 mmHg during and after the operation until a cardiac arrest 15 hours postoperatively.*

Operative hypotension is usually a combination of the vasodilator effects of anaesthesia and low circulating volume. Appropriate treatment involves vasoconstrictor and fluid therapy tailored to the needs of the individual. In many patients operative hypotension was appropriately treated. In some patients hypotension was either untreated or treated with large volumes of intravenous fluids or with repeated doses of vasoconstrictors.

CASE 4 • *An ASA 4 patient weighing 46 kg was admitted with sub-acute intestinal obstruction four days before surgery to perform a Hartmann's procedure. At operation a bowel perforation was diagnosed. During three hours of general anaesthesia the systolic arterial pressure was between 55 and 120 mmHg, for 90 minutes it was less than 85 mmHg. No invasive monitoring or vasoconstrictors were used and 5000 ml (109 ml/kg) of crystalloid were transfused.*

In this sample there was an apparently higher incidence of hypotension with spinal anaesthesia than with general anaesthesia, particularly in the presence of hypovolaemia. We are not suggesting that spinal anaesthesia should not be used, but that the requirements of spinal anaesthesia in the elderly include meticulous correction of preoperative and operative hypovolaemia as well as treatment of vasodilatation.

CASE 5 • *A patient with a fractured neck of femur and weighing 60 kg had an operation under a spinal anaesthetic. The operation lasted for 60 minutes during which time the systolic arterial pressure was a maximum of 100 mmHg, and often much lower, and 2500 ml (42 ml/kg) of fluid were given. A vasoconstrictor was not used.*

CASE 6 • *A patient had a sliding hip screw inserted under a spinal anaesthetic. The operation lasted for 1 h 10 min, during which time the systolic arterial pressure was between 80 and 95 mmHg for 60 minutes, and 2500 ml of fluid were given. Intermittent ephedrine IV to a total of 15 mg was given with little apparent effect.*

CASE 7 • *A patient with a fractured neck of femur and weighing 45 kg had an operation under a spinal anaesthetic. The operation lasted for 2 h 15 min. For two hours the systolic arterial pressure was between 85 and 95 mmHg and 1500 ml (33 ml/kg) of clear fluid were given. Ephedrine 3 mg IV was given once at the start of the operation.*

Hypotension was not confined to patients who had spinal anaesthesia.

CASE 8 • *A patient with a fractured neck of femur had a general anaesthetic with mechanical ventilation of the lungs. The operation lasted for 1 h 15 min during which time systolic arterial pressure was between 55 and 75 mmHg and 1500 ml of crystalloid were transfused. Vasoconstrictors were not used.*

CASE 9 • *A patient with a fractured neck of femur had general anaesthesia with mechanical ventilation and a 3 in 1 nerve block. The operation lasted for 60 minutes and during the whole of this time the systolic arterial pressure was between 65 and 90 mmHg and 1000 ml of fluid, and ephedrine in small doses to a total of 33 mg IV, were given.*

Hypotension was common when combined general anaesthesia and epidural analgesia were used during emergency abdominal surgery, particularly in the presence of abdominal sepsis. Would it be better if the use of the epidural was deferred until after completion of the operation?

CASE 10 • *A patient with a four-day history of perforated colon had a Hartmann's procedure under general anaesthesia with epidural analgesia. Operative hypotension was unresponsive to ephedrine 3 mg, increasing doses of dopamine infusion and finally an adrenaline infusion. The patient developed severe acidosis and died the next day.*

Ephedrine in intermittent doses was the most commonly used vasoconstrictor. When ephedrine is ineffective an alternative vasoconstrictor should be tried. It was noticeable that a continuous infusion of vasoconstrictor, as an alternative strategy, was rarely used.

CASE 11 • *A patient with a fractured neck of femur and weighing 60 kg had an operation under a spinal anaesthetic. The operation lasted for 1 h 25 min during which for 55 minutes the systolic arterial pressure was between 45 and 95 mmHg and 1900 ml (32 ml/kg) of clear fluid were given. Ephedrine in doses between 3 and 6 mg IV was given to a total dose of 60 mg with little apparent effect, then methoxamine 5 mg IV was given at the end of the operation.*

Postoperative fluid management

Key Points

- *Fluid imbalance can contribute to serious postoperative morbidity and mortality.*
- *Fluid imbalance is more likely in the elderly who may have renal impairment or other comorbidity.*
- *Accurate monitoring, early recognition and appropriate treatment of fluid balance are essential.*
- *Fluid management should be accorded the same status as drug prescription.*
- *Training in fluid management, for medical and nursing staff, is required to increase awareness and spread good practice.*
- *There is a fundamental need for improved postoperative care facilities.*

The anaesthetic questionnaire requested copies of the fluid balance charts for two days before, the day of, and three days after surgery. In this sample these were returned for about 50% of the patients. Approximately 20% of the charts reviewed were criticised on points of either documentation or management of the patient's fluid therapy. It is from these that the following case studies have been drawn.

CASE 12 • *A patient who was admitted in heart failure developed an ischaemic foot and required an above knee amputation. Preoperative blood tests showed WCC 25.2 x 10^9/l. During anaesthesia a bradycardia of 35/min responded to atropine, and hypotension of 45/30 mmHg responded to ephedrine 6 mg. Fluid balance on the day of operation was 3810 ml positive and on day 1 was 3641 ml positive. Fluid restriction and dopamine were started 27 hours postoperatively when urine output had been less than 10 ml per hour for 12 hours. Fluid intake on day 2 was 1165 ml and urine output 643 ml and fluid intake on day 3 was 1190 ml and urine output 871 ml. The patient died of left ventricular failure on day 3.*

CASE 13 • *A patient with a chest infection and history of previous myocardial infarction was admitted after a hip fracture to be treated by Austin Moore hemiarthroplasty. Preoperative blood tests showed urea 15.8 mmol/l and creatinine 180 micromol/l. The operation was performed during the evening and the patient left recovery at 23.20. On the day of surgery the fluid balance was 2175 ml positive, on day 1 it was 2480 ml positive and on day 2 it was 2156 ml positive. The urine output on day 2 was 108 ml and diclofenac, which had been prescribed on admission, was given on that day. The patient died of pneumonia and renal failure on day 3.*

CASE 14 • *A patient underwent a laparotomy and right hemicolectomy for gastrointestinal bleeding. Concomitant problems were mixed aortic valve disease and mitral regurgitation, ischaemic heart disease and a previous cerebrovascular accident. Haemoglobin was 8.5 g/dl. No ICU bed was available and the hospital had no HDU. An adrenaline infusion was used in theatre. Fluid intake on the day of operation was 6550 ml of clear fluid and 2100 ml of blood and urine output was 250 ml. Fluid intake on day 1 was 3750 ml and urine output 282 ml. On this day the patient was given two doses of frusemide 40 mg IV in the morning without response. The fluid balance charts were discontinued at 15.00 and the patient died 13 hours later.*

CASE 15 • *A patient was admitted with a hip fracture to be treated with a sliding hip screw. The fluid charts were difficult to interpret but the nursing staff had estimated fluid intake on the day of operation as 4850 ml and the urine output was 645 ml. Fluid intake on day 1 was 800 ml and urine output 425 ml. The IV cannula fell out on this day and was not replaced for 34 hours. Fluid intake on day 2 was 460 ml and urine output 325 ml. Fluid balance on day 3 was 330 ml positive. On day 4 the IV infusion tissued and was not replaced, fluid intake was 260 ml and urine output was 1100 ml. On this day diclofenac and frusemide 80 mg IV were given and the fluid balance chart discontinued. The patient died in pulmonary oedema on day 7.*

CASE 16 • *A patient with ischaemic heart disease was admitted with a hip fracture to be treated with a sliding hip screw. Preoperative blood tests showed serum urea 19.5 mmol/l, creatinine was not recorded. The fluid charts were almost unintelligible but a best guess is that on the day of operation fluid intake was 2600 ml and urine output 70 ml. Fluid intake on day 1 (as estimated by the nursing staff) was 1296 ml and urine output 185 ml. There were no records for day 2. Fluid intake on day 3 was 825 ml and urine output 60 ml. The patient died of bronchopneumonia and left ventricular failure on day 26. The quality of recording on the fluid balance charts was such that it is doubtful whether anyone could know what the true fluid balance was.*

CASE 17 • *A patient with a fractured hip was admitted for an Austin Moore prosthesis. She was described as frail and weighed 43 kg. Preoperative blood tests were normal. On the day of operation fluid intake was 4800 ml. There was no urine output. Fluid intake on day 1 was 600 ml and urine output 400 ml. Fluid intake on day 2 was 900 ml and there was no urine output. She had been hypotensive postoperatively and died in heart failure on day 2. Postmortem revealed previously undiagnosed aortic stenosis.*

CASE 18 • *A patient with ischaemic heart disease and hypertension underwent a Hartmann's procedure. Anaesthesia was complicated by atrial fibrillation of 160/min. Fluid intake on the day of operation was*

3560 ml and urine output 945 ml. Fluid intake on day 1 was 6320 ml and urine output 430 ml. Fluid intake for the first six hours of day 2 was 2500 ml and urine output 28 ml when the patient died in left ventricular failure.

CASE 19 • *A patient with small bowel obstruction underwent ileocaecal resection for tumour. She weighed 48 kg and had chronic heart failure causing shortness of breath at 50 yards. She was described as unwell preoperatively. Fluid intake on the day of operation was 5007 ml and urine output 1320 ml. Balances on subsequent days were: day 1 intake 4550 ml and output 1345 ml, day 2 intake 2683 ml and output 576 ml, day 3 intake 3634 ml and output 684 ml, day 4 intake 3062 ml and output 770 ml, day 5 intake 2486 ml and output 240 ml, day 6 intake 3309 ml and output 80 ml. She died of disseminated adenocarcinoma on day 7.*

Fluid imbalance, excessive fluid intake and/or poor urine output, is a symptom of an underlying problem. There are several causes of postoperative fluid imbalance. Each patient in whom postoperative fluid imbalance occurs needs to be clinically evaluated and investigated so that the imbalance can be appropriately treated.

Many patients in this sample had large fluid intake and/or poor urine output postoperatively. A positive fluid balance may be appropriate, for instance if there is dehydration which has not been corrected previously or large concealed fluid losses such as occur following some bowel surgery. However, it may be pathological. Renal function decreases by about 10% for each decade over the age of 40 years and so the elderly are liable to develop postoperative renal failure with fluid retention.

The following coexisting problems make postoperative renal failure more likely:

- Prerenal renal impairment secondary to preoperative dehydration.
- Chronic renal impairment with raised serum creatinine.
- Surgically induced increased secretion of antidiuretic hormone. Hypovolaemia, hypotension, opiates, pain, stress or hypoxia can cause this.
- Low cardiac output states, for example from pre-existing cardiac disease or recent onset arrhythmia.
- Concomitant drug treatment, such as non-steroidal anti-inflammatory drugs.

Postoperative fluid retention increases the likelihood of other postoperative complications, for example left ventricular failure or broncho-pneumonia.

Audit

NCEPOD has estimated that 20% of patients in this sample had either poor documentation of fluid balance or unrecognised/untreated fluid imbalance. Local audit is required to identify where the problems are and what solutions need to be applied.

Patients

Many of the patients who develop low urine output or positive fluid balance postoperatively can be predicted from the severity of their surgical condition or their concomitant medical diseases, for example patients with cardiac, renal or electrolyte disorders. Patients at risk of renal impairment need to be identified, and recorded as such, by clinicians preoperatively on initial assessment and closely monitored postoperatively.

Monitoring

Urinary catheters are used freely by general surgeons. Some orthopaedic surgeons are reluctant to use them for patients with a prosthesis; others will use them routinely if patients are undergoing hip replacement. The association between bladder catheterisation and prosthetic hip infection still needs to be clarified. If urine is not passed within a reasonable time postoperatively, or if there is persistent urinary incontinence, then the benefits of monitoring urine output outweigh the risks associated with a catheter in the bladder (see also page 83).

Most elderly patients should have their serum urea, electrolytes and creatinine monitored daily after operation.

Nine percent of patients in this sample had central venous pressure monitoring. In some situations central venous pressure monitoring can give valuable clinical information and the line can also be used for vasoactive drug infusions. There are many advantages to inserting these in the operating theatre. Further research is required to define the role of more invasive monitoring in this group of patients.

Documentation

Some fluid balance records are poorly completed, making it difficult to identify a problem (see page 71). The importance of accurately recording fluid balance is equal to that of drug administration and the responsibility for this rests primarily with the nursing staff.

In addition to contemporaneous records some hospitals have summary 24-hour fluid balance recorded either on the TPR chart or on a separate sheet. These provide an easy reference for review of the patient.

Management and training

When fluid imbalance was evident from review of the charts it often continued uncorrected. Some doctors and nurses may lack awareness of the central role of good fluid management in these patients. Medical schools may be able to help. Is a high enough priority given to teaching the importance of perioperative fluid management in the medical school curriculum and during preregistration medical training?

Patient fluid management, both preoperatively and postoperatively, should be included as part of the formal surgical SHO training curriculum. In some hospitals surgical SHO training schemes include a rotation through the ICU/HDU. This provides valuable experience in the management of patients undergoing major surgery and should take place early in the rotation. Local guidelines in the management of postoperative fluids could be developed. Is this a situation for national guidelines?

In order to maintain continuity of patient care there is, or should be, a formal handover of patient information between surgical trainees at each change of duty. This handover, and the doctors attending, could be made a matter of record. The most senior trainee on duty and available should attend. Patients' charts and results should be reviewed by the medical staff daily, and daily intravenous fluid prescribing should only be done after clinical evaluation of the patient.

In most hospitals the first line management of postoperative fluid therapy rests with the surgical trainees and the responsibility for supervision rests with their consultants.

In some hospitals this may not be providing the best available care and other clinical input to the patient's postoperative fluid management would be welcomed. Other models of care are possible, including:

- Development of protocols for referral. These would depend on local circumstances, but could possibly be to physicians with an interest in care of the elderly. A strong case can be made for medical preoperative assessment in the very elderly patient, as well as postoperative advice.

- Expansion of the role of the anaesthetic department, the acute pain team, or the acute care team to include advising on postoperative fluid management.

- Some hospitals now have anaesthetic house officers. Could postoperative fluid management be part of their responsibilities?

Such shared care would probably be for a limited time after operation, following which full responsibility would revert to the surgical team.

Patient location

Elderly patients with renal dysfunction, especially with concomitant disorders, need a high level of nursing care. Many wards have a nurse to patient ratio of 1:8 and are ill-equipped to provide this high level of care.

Ideally many of these patients should be nursed in a high dependency unit (see also page 61). In this sample anaesthetists indicated that there was an HDU in the hospital of 46% of patients but only 34/944 (4%) were nursed in one postoperatively. Are the elderly excluded from consideration in prioritising patients for admission to these oversubscribed facilities? Twenty-eight surgical questionnaires indicated that there was an age limit for admission to their HDU or ICU.

A comment was: *"There is no HDU and in my opinion normally all patients over 90 years with a fractured hip should go to HDU."*

There is a need for more properly staffed and equipped high dependency beds.

Most high dependency units plan a nurse to patient ratio of 1:2. There is a large gap between nursing staff to patient ratios on the HDU and the ward. Some hospitals have developed intermediate care facilities for patients whose nursing needs fall between these two. These do not replace the HDU:

- Facilities such as postoperative recovery wards deserve consideration. These specialised postoperative wards have higher nursing staff to patient numbers than general wards. Here patients can receive appropriately monitored specialised pain relief and fluid management following major surgery.

- Monitored beds on the general ward can also be successful. They allow less-well patients to be grouped together in an area where there are nursing staff of appropriate number and experience.

Fluid chart documentation

Key Points

- *The documentation on fluid charts was often poor.*
- *Doctors and nurses of all grades need to understand the clinical importance, and ensure the accurate recording, of fluid intake and output.*
- *Multidisciplinary review of the problem and development of good local working practices is required.*
- *Fluid charts are important documents that need to be retained and appropriately filed for future reference.*

The anaesthetic questionnaire requested copies of the fluid charts for two days before, the day of, and three days after surgery.

Photocopies of fluid charts were returned in approximately 50% of cases. For the majority of the cases when they were not included no reason was given for their absence. Some anaesthetists stated that they had not been filed with the patient case notes; either they were filed separately with ICU notes or had been discarded at the end of the patient's admission. Fluid charts are important patient documents.

Documentation of intake and output on some fluid charts was good. In some hospitals daily summary results are recorded on a separate fluid balance 'flow' chart or on the TPR (temperature, pulse and respiration) chart. These are particularly helpful and make fluid review straightforward.

However, some charts were of poor standard, sufficient to hamper clinical care. The following problems were noted:

POOR IDENTIFICATION • No patient name, no hospital number, no date to which the page referred. This makes review of fluids difficult. In some cases a completely new chart was started postoperatively resulting in two charts for one day. Was this local practice or did it accompany a change of ward? There should be continuity of such important documentation, especially on the critical day of operation.

INACCURATE FLUID INTAKE • Very low oral fluid intake with little or no intravenous supplementation recorded over successive 24-hour periods (i.e. intake compatible with severe dehydration) with the comment "sips" or "sips only". Was the fluid intake in fact greater but being recorded incorrectly? This was probable in those patients who remained well. Or was fluid intake indeed inadequate?

INACCURATE FLUID OUTPUT • Some charts either had no output recorded or only an occasional "wet bed". Some patients had frequent persistent urinary incontinence recorded over several days. Whilst not advising 'routine' urinary catheters in the elderly, in selected patients the benefits of urinary catheterisation outweigh the risks. If no urine is passed postoperatively within a reasonable period of time a urinary catheter can help to differentiate between oliguria and urinary retention. If a patient suffers from persistent 'wet beds' a urinary catheter can help to differentiate between true incontinence and retention with overflow. When there is urinary incontinence a catheter is beneficial both for the patient's dignity and for nursing care. It will reduce the potential for macerated skin and bedsores.

Management of fluid balance is a multidisciplinary exercise involving doctors, nurses and possibly other ward staff responsible for providing oral fluid intake for patients. This is akin to drug therapy where it is the responsibility of doctors to prescribe drugs and the responsibility of nurses to give the drugs and chart their administration. However, it is clear that fluid management is not perceived as having the same importance or status as drug therapy.

Clinical audit and governance should provide a framework for multidisciplinary review of the problem, be responsible for the development of good local working practices and oversee their implementation.

Fluid excess or deficit can contribute to serious postoperative morbidity. Doctors and nurses of all grades need to understand the clinical importance of fluid intake and output and ensure its accurate recording. Its importance is equal to the accurate recording of drug administration and this should be recognised.

LIVERPOOL JOHN MOORES UNIVERSITY ROBARTS LRC 0151 231 4022

Specific Issues

Anaesthesia

Non-training anaesthetic appointments

Key Point

- *There has been an expansion in the number of non-consultant career grade (NCCG) anaesthetists. Their requirements for personal development, continuing medical education and supervision need to be recognised.*

The role of the staff grade anaesthetist

Data from the NCEPOD report of 1993/94[8] indicated that some of the more seriously ill patients were being anaesthetised by staff grade anaesthetists. Less than 50% of the staff grade anaesthetists participating in that report held the FRCA. It was predicted then that staff grade numbers would increase.

Since then the national ceiling on staff grade doctors has been removed[39] and junior doctors' hours have been reduced. The percentage of cases in this sample where the most senior anaesthetist was a staff grade was 10% (90/944). This can be compared to percentages in recent NCEPOD reports as follows: 1994/95, 3%; 1995/96, 5%; 1996/97, 10%. The NCEPOD sample for review has changed annually so that direct comparison year on year has limitations. The 1994/95 sample was of deaths within three days of surgery, the 1995/96 report "Who Operates When?" examined overall surgical activity and the 1996/97 sample reviewed specific types of surgery.

In many hospitals staff grade anaesthetists are contracted to cover trauma and general surgical emergency lists. In this year's sample the high involvement of staff grade anaesthetists may have been due to the large number of patients with a fractured hip operated on during regular trauma lists. The Royal College of Anaesthetists' database records the number of non-consultant career grade anaesthetists in the United Kingdom[40], as shown in Table 3.14.

Table 3.14: Non-consultant career grade anaesthetists

	Total number	Whole time equivalent	Number part-time
Associate specialist	316	295	103
Staff grade	544	533	95
Clinical assistant	342	206	265
Trust anaesthetist	231	221	88
Hospital practitioner	88	78	88
Total	1521	1333	639

Table 3.15: Grade of the most senior anaesthetist by ASA status of the patient (AQs 10 and 30)

	ASA 1	ASA 2	ASA 3	ASA 4	ASA 5	Not answered	Total
Consultant	8	67	190	122	18	0	405
Associate specialist	0	7	32	11	2	0	52
Staff grade	1	14	55	19	1	0	90
Clinical assistant	0	2	4	1	0	0	7
SpR - 3, 4, Accredited/CCST	0	12	36	29	3	1	81
SpR - 1, 2	0	10	26	15	2	0	53
SHO	0	38	113	51	3	2	207
Other	0	4	20	15	3	0	42
Not answered	0	2	2	3	0	0	7
Total	9	156	478	266	32	3	944

Table 3.15 shows that a staff grade anaesthetist, with no anaesthetic qualifications, anaesthetised an ASA 5 patient for a polya gastrectomy.

The requirements of the Royal College of Anaesthetists (RCA) for the appointment of a staff grade anaesthetist include: full registration with the General Medical Council and completion of three years' training in anaesthesia at SHO or higher grade, or comparable overseas training. In addition it is recommended that a staff grade anaesthetist should have the full Fellowship qualification of the Royal College of Anaesthetists of the UK (FRCA) or Ireland (FFARCSI). If not, then the job description should reflect more limited responsibilities[41].

Table 3.16: Highest qualification of staff grade anaesthetists (AQ34)

Qualification	Number
None	6
FRCA	28
Part Fellowship or DA	51
Other	2
Not answered	3
Total	90

Table 3.17: Years in anaesthesia for staff grade anaesthetists without full Fellowship (AQ33)

Years	Number
0-3	5
4-10	14
11-15	20
16-20	9
>21	9
Not known	5
Total	62

Five staff grade anaesthetists indicated that they had not completed more than three years in anaesthetic training. Two had been medically qualified for more than ten years and may have discounted their overseas experience. Another two had been medically qualified for four years in total and it was difficult to understand why they had been appointed to non-consultant career grade posts. Of the five who reported that they had not completed more than three years in anaesthetic training, three had no postgraduate qualifications and two had the DA or part Fellowship.

Staff grade anaesthetists who have been many years in anaesthesia and do not have the full Fellowship qualification are unlikely to sit for it, either because the longer they are in post the less the incentive, or because they have previously tried, failed and have become dispirited. Of those without full Fellowship qualifications there were 19 staff grade anaesthetists with ten years' or less anaesthetic experience and a further 20 with between 11 and 15 years' anaesthetic experience. Accepting the different needs and aspirations of the individual, could more staff grade anaesthetists be encouraged to study for the full Fellowship qualification? Are they getting sufficient access to the final Fellowship courses and do they have a dedicated educational period in their timetables? Training organisations should consider this group more when planning their educational programmes.

The RCA, with the National Health Service Executive, agreed that if the staff grade anaesthetist did not hold the FRCA or FFARCSI then they should work as an SHO equivalent and be closely supervised by senior staff. They should not be involved in the teaching, training or direct supervision of bona fide trainees in the specialty.

In this sample, on 24 occasions, a staff grade anaesthetised a patient with an SHO assisting. Twelve of these staff grade anaesthetists had the FRCA. The other twelve may have been working outside the above recommendation. Nine had part 2 of the Fellowship or the DA, one had the European Diploma, one had no anaesthetic postgraduate qualification and one did not specify a qualification.

Staff grade anaesthetists have an annual appraisal process and review of their job description. This process represents an opportunity to ensure that these non-consultant career grade anaesthetists have access to resources for, and do participate in, continuing professional development and medical education.

Locum anaesthetists

Seventy questionnaires (7%) stated that the most senior anaesthetist present was working as a locum. This percentage is similar to that seen in previous NCEPOD reports[8].

Table 3.18: Locum anaesthetists (AQ30)

Locum grade	Number
Consultant	26
Associate specialist	5
Staff grade	6
Clinical assistant	2
SpR	12
SHO >2	11
SHO 2 and 1	4
LAS	2
Not answered	2
Total	70

The qualifications of the locum anaesthetists varied:

Table 3.19: Qualifications of all locum anaesthetists (AQs 30 and 34)

Qualification	Number
None or Part 1 FRCA only	8
Old Part 1 FRCA, DA or equivalent	21
Fellowship	30
Not answered	11
Total	70

Table 3.20: Qualifications of locum consultant anaesthetists (AQs 30 and 34)

Qualification	Number
None	1
Old Part 1 FRCA, DA or equivalent	3
Fellowship	17
Other	1
Not answered	4
Total	26

The majority of locum consultant anaesthetists did possess the Fellowship of the Royal College of Anaesthetists. Those with part of the FRCA or DA, and particularly the one locum consultant anaesthetist with no anaesthetic qualifications, appear to be inappropriate appointments.

Table 3.21: Years in anaesthesia of locum anaesthetists (AQs 30 and 31)

Year of first full-time anaesthetic post	Number
Before 1973	8
1973 to 1977	6
1978 to 1982	4
1983 to 1987	14
1988 to 1992	9
1993 to 1997	14
Not known	15
Total	70

We do not know the reasons why the 32 anaesthetists who had been practising anaesthesia for over ten years were in locum appointments. However, departments should recognise that those in long term or repeated locum appointments require proper study leave and funding for continuing medical education.

Matching the seniority of the anaesthetist to the patient

Both the Royal College of Anaesthetists[21] and NCEPOD[6, 7] in their previous reports have made specific recommendations as to the seniority and experience of anaesthetists taking responsibility for particular patients. These recommendations can be examined with particular reference to the patients in this sample:

Royal College of Anaesthetists' recommendations

"A consultant should always be available in the operating room when a first-year SHO is anaesthetising patients of ASA grade 3 and over." [21]

First-year SHOs anaesthetised 19 patients of ASA grade 3 and over, without immediate supervision, and for 14 of these no senior advice was sought.

"SHOs and SpR 1 grades should always be supervised at neurosurgery and cardiothoracic operations." [21]

One neurosurgical operation was managed by an SpR 4 anaesthetist and one cardiac operation was managed by a consultant anaesthetist. Both cases therefore complied with the RCA guidance.

NCEPOD recommendations

"Very sick patients should be anaesthetised in the knowledge and (or) presence of senior registrar (SpR 3 or 4) or consultant." [7]

Anaesthetic questionnaires were returned for 298 patients of ASA 4 or 5. An SHO, SpR 1 or SpR 2 was the most senior anaesthetist present for 71 (24%) of these patients. In 36/71 (51%) of these operations, the inexperienced anaesthetist did not seek advice from a senior source before starting the anaesthetic.

"Many operations, particularly those of long duration, will require two anaesthetists, at least for part of the time." [6]

Thirty-nine anaesthetics took longer than three hours. There were two anaesthetists present in 25 (64%) of these.

"Anaesthesia for emergency or life-saving operations should ideally be managed by a team of anaesthetists." [6]

The NCEPOD classification was stated as "Emergency" (immediate life-saving operation) for 35 patients. Of these, there were at least two anaesthetists present in 22 (63%). However, some of the classifications may be suspect. The operation "Left Austin Moore hemiarthroplasty" was one of those classified as an emergency, life-saving operation.

National recommendations might be more closely followed if they were incorporated locally into anaesthetic departmental guidelines.

Pain relief in the elderly

Key Points

- *The majority (81%) of patients were treated in a hospital with an acute pain service.*
- *Only a minority of patients had a pain assessment chart.*
- *The use of a pain assessment chart improves the management of postoperative pain and reduces the chance of complications related to postoperative analgesia.*

Pain service

NCEPOD requested information on several aspects of postoperative pain relief management.

Question 3.6: Does the hospital in which the operation took place have an acute pain service? (AQ68)

Yes	763
No	176
Not answered	5
Total	944

If yes, when is this service available?

24 hours a day, seven days a week	362
Limited times	368
Not answered	33
Total	763

An acute pain service was available to 81% of patients. Unfortunately, in less than half (47%) of the hospitals was this service described as available "24 hours a day".

Question 3.7: Who is on the pain team? (AQ68a)
(763 cases; answers may be multiple)

Anaesthetic consultant(s)	680
Anaesthetic trainee(s)	347
Specialised pain nurse(s)	629
Pharmacist(s)	105
Other	39

Pain teams usually included consultant anaesthetists and specialised pain nurses. Trainees were present in less than half the teams. This represents the loss of a valuable training opportunity. Eleven percent of the questionnaires did not report a consultant anaesthetist as part of the pain team. It is probable that there was no funding for consultant sessions in these hospitals, although presumably there was consultant advice when the service was established, and a facility for consultant referral.

Question 3.8: How many ward nursing staff are specially trained in epidural and/or PCA analgesia? (AQ69)

None	63
Some	725
All	103
Not answered	46
Not known	7
Total	944

Four questionnaires reported continuous intravenous opiate infusion, patient controlled analgesia (PCA) or continuous epidural infusions had been used on general wards although no ward staff had been trained in the management of these techniques.

Pain charts documentation

Two hundred and thirty five (25%) questionnaires reported that the patient had a pain assessment chart. This is disappointing. It is recognised that formal assessment of a patient's pain improves pain management.

Question 3.9: Did this patient have a pain assessment chart? (AQ70)

Yes	235
No	651
Not answered	54
Not known	4
Total	944

In some cases the assessment chart related only to the time the patient spent in recovery. It is disturbing that 37% of those receiving epidural analgesia and 23% of those receiving PCA did not have a pain chart. It is well recognised that these techniques may be accompanied by serious complications such as respiratory depression or hypotension.

Table 3.22: Use of pain assessment charts (AQs 70 and 71b) *(Patients may have received more than one form of analgesia)*		
Type of analgesia	Number of patients	% with pain chart
Epidural	57	63%
PCA	40	77%
IM injection	467	23%
Oral	341	23%
Subcutaneous infusion	22	43%
Rectal	30	17%

Table 3.23: Information recorded on pain assessment charts		
Clinical information recorded	Number	%
Respiratory rate	32	91%
Oxygen saturation	13	37%
Pulse	25	71%
Blood pressure	25	71%
Sedation level	29	83%
Pain score	25	71%
Postoperative nausea and vomiting	25	71%
Total charts reviewed	**35**	

Forty of the questionnaires where pain charts were available were examined. In five cases the pain assessment chart covered only the time in the recovery ward. The information recorded on the remaining 35 charts is shown in Table 3.23.

The charts were examined for completeness. On 20% of occasions when a value should have been entered on the chart, data was absent. This suggests that the patients were not fully monitored at all times and episodes of poor analgesia, hypotension or respiratory depression could have been missed. Recording was carried out for an average of 50 hours, with a range from 12 hours to 7 days. In two-thirds of questionnaires it was not clear why the pain chart had been discontinued.

Most charts recorded pain assessments only. Some charts were designed for specific methods of pain relief only, such as epidural analgesia or subcutaneous opiate infusions. In 12 charts, pain assessment and the side effects of treatment were recorded on the same chart as the regular ward TPR measurements. Greater use of such charts combining these observations may help to promote the recognition that the assessment and treatment of pain is an integral part of patient management.

Non-steroidal anti-inflammatory drugs

Key Points

- *Non-steroidal anti-inflammatory drugs (NSAIDs) should be prescribed with particular caution in elderly patients in the postoperative period.*
- *NSAIDs can contribute to postoperative renal failure in patients with renal impairment and those receiving ACE inhibitors, potassium-sparing diuretics or beta-adrenergic blockade.*
- *Royal College of Anaesthetists' guidelines on the use of NSAIDs need to be more widely consulted.*

In this sample 110 (12%) patients received non-steroidal anti-inflammatory drugs (NSAIDs) post-operatively. Table 3.24 gives examples of these patients.

Table 3.24: Use of non-steroidal anti-inflammatory drugs

Operation	CVS disorder	Renal disorder	GI risk factors	Complication/cause of death
Laparotomy and small bowel resection	None	None	None	ARDS, pulmonary oedema
Austin Moore hemiarthroplasty	Previous MI, on frusemide	Creatinine 180 micromol/l, urea 16 mmol/l	None	Renal failure, pneumonia
Sliding hip screw	Hypertension	None	None	GI bleed
Total hip replacement	Hypertension	None	None	Perforated DU, IHD and CVA
Right hemicolectomy	None	None	None	Respiratory failure, septicaemia, renal failure

Operation	CVS disorder	Renal disorder	GI risk factors	Complication/cause of death
Sliding hip screw	None	Creatinine 132 micromol/l, urea 8.7 mmol/l	None	Heart failure, pulmonary oedema
Debridement hip wound	None	None	Ranitidine	GI bleed
Bilateral femoral hernia repair	Hypertension	Creatinine 137 micromol/l, urea 17.3 mmol/l	None	Cardiac failure, renal failure
Halifax nail	CCF	None	None	GI bleed from diverticular disease
Sliding hip screw	Previous MI, CCF	Creatinine 212 micromol/l	None	CVA and cardiac arrest
Austin Moore hemiarthroplasty	None	Creatinine 146 micromol/l, urea 6.5 mmol/l	None	Cardiorespiratory arrest
Hemiarthroplasty	Hypertension	None	None	Renal impairment, peritonitis, ischaemic bowel, atherosclerosis
Total hip replacement	Previous MI	Creatinine 124 micromol/l, urea 10 mmol/l	Under investigation for melaena, on steroids	Bronchopneumonia
Transurethral resection of bladder tumour and prostate	Previous MI, angina, LVF, AF	None	On steroids	Cardiac failure
Sigmoid colectomy	CCF	None	None	Infarction of the small bowel
Thompson's hemiarthroplasty	None	None	On steroids	Cardiac failure, pulmonary oedema

The following extract from 'Clinical Guidelines for the Use of Non-steroidal Anti-Inflammatory Drugs in the Perioperative Period'[42] published by the Royal College of Anaesthetists, is relevant to patients in this sample:

"Clinical situations

ORTHOPAEDIC SURGERY: *Several studies demonstrated opioid-sparing effects and improved analgesia, although there was little evidence of a reduction in opioid side effects. NSAIDs may be effective alone after some types of orthopaedic surgery.*

GENERAL SURGERY: *There was relatively little information on the use of NSAIDs for general surgery. NSAIDs should not be used as the sole analgesic in the first 24 hours after major surgery. They improve the quality of opioid-based analgesia.*

Adverse effects

GASTROINTESTINAL (GI) BLEEDING: *The risk of bleeding increases with dose and duration, especially in the elderly, and treatment for more than five days markedly increases the risk. NSAIDs should not be given to patients with a history of GI ulceration or bleeding.*

RENAL FUNCTION: *Practising nephrologists recognise that a high proportion of cases of postoperative renal failure are associated with the use of NSAIDs. Rather than being the primary cause, they are usually a contributory factor to the development of acute renal failure, in situations where renal function would otherwise be expected to survive a particular insult, such as sepsis or hypovolaemia. The effects of NSAIDs on renal function postoperatively include decreased urine flow rate, reduced sodium and potassium excretion, a tendency to hyperkalaemia and increased requirement for diuretics.*

NSAIDs should be avoided in the following clinical situations:

a. *renal impairment (plasma creatinine above normal);*
b. *hyperkalaemia;*
c. *hypovolaemia;*
d. *systemic inflammatory response syndrome;*
e. *circulatory failure (hypotension and/or cardiac failure).*

NSAIDs should be used with caution in the following clinical situations:

a. *>65 years (renal impairment likely);*
b. *patients receiving ACE inhibitors, potassium-sparing diuretics, beta-adrenergic blockers."*

These guidelines, the above examples and the problem of low urine output postoperatively described in this report suggest that non-steroidal anti-inflammatory drugs should be used postoperatively for patients of 90 years and older only when there is a strong clinical indication. It is clear that the RCA guidelines are often disregarded.

LIVERPOOL JOHN MOORES UNIVERSITY
LEARNING SERVICES

Postoperative respiratory complications

Key Points

- *Elderly patients need their pain management to be provided by those with appropriate specialised experience in order that they receive safe and effective pain relief.*
- *Postoperative respiratory complications were more serious when patients were anaesthetised by less experienced anaesthetists.*
- *The dose of opioid or sedative drug needs to be titrated to effect.*
- *Elderly patients most at risk of complications are those with concomitant medical disorders, metabolic disorders or electrolyte disturbance.*

In this sample, when compared with previous NCEPOD reports, there was a higher incidence of respiratory complications associated with anaesthesia as evidenced by the use of opiate antagonist or analeptic drugs and the number of patients who required tracheal reintubation. Twenty-four such patients were identified. In some patients respiratory depression occurred despite good clinical management, in some the anaesthetic management could be criticised and in others there was insufficient detail within the questionnaires from which to draw conclusions.

Pharmacokinetics and pharmacodynamics change with age. The initial dose of opioid or sedative is often the same as for a younger person but to achieve an adequate response such drugs need to be titrated to effect. There is, however, a reduction in the ability of the elderly to metabolise and excrete drugs and this results in a longer drug half-life. It is more likely that some drugs, for example opioids, will accumulate when given in repeated doses at frequent intervals or when given as infusions. Elderly patients most at risk of drug accumulation are those with concomitant medical disorders (cardiovascular, respiratory or cerebrovascular disease, renal, hepatic or endocrine impairment), metabolic disorders (acidosis, sepsis) or electrolyte disturbance. All patients who were reported as having respiratory depression were ASA 3 or more and, for these patients, a drug dose which would be considered normal or moderate in a younger, fitter patient may have been excessive.

Some of the cases are summarised and illustrate the wide range of clinical circumstances.

CASE 20 • *An SHO 1 anaesthetised an ASA 4 patient with cardiac and renal disease for a sliding hip screw starting at 20.30. General anaesthesia included morphine 4 mg IV. In recovery the administration of morphine 10 mg IM was followed by respiratory depression and the $PaCO_2$ increased to 15.3 kPa. The trachea was reintubated, the lungs were ventilated for 10 minutes and the patient given intravenous doxapram and naloxone. The patient returned to the ward at 00.30 and died of a cardiac arrest later that day.*

CASE 21 • *An SHO 1 anaesthetised an ASA 3 patient with basal lung crepitations and hypothyroidism for amputation of a great toe starting at 18.00. General anaesthesia with a laryngeal mask airway (LMA) included fentanyl 100 micrograms IV. The patient had tracheal aspiration of gastric contents around the LMA in recovery and the trachea was intubated for tracheal toilet. The patient was returned to the ward at 19.00 and died of bronchopneumonia on day 6.*

CASE 22 • *An SHO 2 anaesthetised an ASA 4 patient with myasthenia gravis and hypothyroidism for a laparotomy, hemicolectomy and drainage of subphrenic abscess. Anaesthesia was induced at 19.20. Persistent supraventricular tachycardia and hypotension that were treated with amiodarone and adrenaline followed general anaesthesia and epidural analgesia. Blood gases taken during surgery revealed a base excess of -14 that was treated with sodium bicarbonate. Postoperatively the patient received ventilation of the lungs in recovery for 45 minutes before tracheal extubation. Poor respiratory effort was unresponsive to intravenous naloxone, doxapram and neostigmine and the trachea was reintubated. The patient required 39 ml/hr of adrenaline 5 mg/50 ml to maintain arterial pressure. No ICU bed was available so the patient was transferred to another hospital and died 15 minutes after arrival there.*

CASE 23 • *An SHO of more than two years' experience anaesthetised an ASA 4 patient with dementia and mitral regurgitation for an EUA and screening of a hip prosthesis for a suspected fracture; no fracture was seen. The unexpectedly short general anaesthesia included muscle relaxant and fentanyl 100 micrograms IV. There was hypotension peroperatively and poor respiratory effort postoperatively. The patient was unresponsive to naloxone, was returned to the ward and died shortly after.*

CASE 24 • *An SHO 2 anaesthetised an ASA 3 patient with ischaemic heart disease and dementia for an Austin Moore hemiarthroplasty. Morphine 10 mg IM had been given twice on the day of surgery and the patient was drowsy and hypotensive (arterial pressure 80/40 mmHg) on entering the anaesthetic room at 15.20. General anaesthesia, which included fentanyl 25 micrograms and relaxant,*

The Elderly

was complicated by profound hypotension unresponsive to vasoconstrictors and cardiac arrest occurred after 60 minutes.

CASE 25 • *An SpR 4 anaesthetised an ASA 3 patient with chronic cardiac failure and hypothyroidism for a Hartmann's procedure at midnight. Preoperative blood tests showed* Na^+ *128 mmol/l, creatinine 248 micromol/l, urea 17.8 mmol/l and metabolic acidosis with a* $PaCO_2$ *of 2.64 kPa. During surgery 3000 ml of crystalloid were given without a CVP line in place. Postoperatively the patient received ventilation of the lungs in recovery until tracheal extubation after 90 minutes. Respiratory failure supervened and the patient received ventilation of the lungs in recovery for a further nine hours until an ICU bed became available.*

CASE 26 • *An SHO 1 anaesthetised an ASA 4 patient with ischaemic heart disease, renal impairment and chronic obstructive pulmonary disease for repair of an inguinal hernia. Surgery progressed to a resection of gangrenous and perforated bowel. Preoperative blood tests showed Hb 16.4 g/dl, WCC 19.1 x* 10^9*/l,* Na^+ *129 mmol/l and urea 22 mmol/l. Surgery was at 17.50. Spinal anaesthesia was supplemented with sedation using midazolam to a total of 40 mg IV and ketamine to a total of 50 mg IV. Postoperatively oxygen saturation was 82% on 4 l/min nasal oxygen, doxapram 50 mg IV was given, no flumazanil was used, the patient returned to the ward and died after six hours.*

CASE 27 • *An associate specialist anaesthetised an ASA 3 patient, described as "frail and dry", for a sliding hip screw. General anaesthesia included fentanyl 50 micrograms IV and a 3 in 1 nerve block. Pethidine 50 mg IM in recovery was followed by respiratory depression that responded to naloxone.*

CASE 28 • *An SHO 2 anaesthetised an ASA 4 patient with atrial fibrillation for oversew of a peptic ulcer. Preoperative blood tests showed WCC 31.4 x* 10^9*/l, creatinine 149 micromol/l, urea 15.3 mmol/l. General anaesthesia at 18.55 included fentanyl 100 micrograms IV and relaxant. At 20.00 in recovery the patient had poor respiratory effort unresponsive to naloxone. Arterial blood gases revealed pH 7.194,* PaO_2 *58 kPa,* $PaCO_2$ *5.73 kPa, bicarbonate 15.9, base excess -11.3. The patient became disorientated before apnoea supervened. The trachea was reintubated and the patient went to ICU.*

Postoperative respiratory complications were more serious when patients were anaesthetised by less experienced anaesthetists. These anaesthetists appeared not to anticipate the predictable respiratory failure associated with gross coexisting metabolic abnormalities. Was this a deficit in training or a lack of experience in anaesthesia for the elderly? Eight of the 11 anaesthetic SHOs involved with these 24 patients had asked advice from a more experienced anaesthetist either before the case or when problems supervened, but managed the patient alone.

Most patients who had postoperative respiratory failure also had an early death; 18 of the 24 died within one week of surgery. Undoubtedly this reflected that these patients were amongst the sickest in the sample. In some cases the anaesthetic management may have been implicated in the patient's death.

Management of pain relief in the elderly is of paramount importance. Elderly patients must receive adequate analgesia. It should, however, be recognised that the elderly metabolise drugs differently from the younger patient. The expertise of the acute pain team, use of pain assessment charts by appropriately trained nursing staff, the use of local anaesthetic techniques and careful titration of systemic analgesic drugs to effect will result in safe and effective pain relief for these patients (see also page 75).

Orthopaedic surgery

Perioperative care

Key Points

- *Orthopaedic surgeons need to establish whether there is sufficient expertise available within their team to manage the complex medical problems of these patients, or whether local guidelines for shared care should be developed.*
- *Pressure sores remain a problem in orthopaedic patients. Constant vigilance is required in this high risk group of patients.*

There were 648 cases undertaken by orthopaedic surgeons, of which 258 (40%) were hemiarthroplasties and 243 (38%) were sliding hip screws.

Coexisting medical problems were reported in 90% of the elderly orthopaedic patients. Many of these conditions are aggravated by the physiological disturbance of trauma, anaesthesia and surgery. Eighty-six percent of the sample had postoperative complications. Sixty-six percent had cardiac, respiratory or renal complications. Despite the high incidence of comorbidity, only 25% of patients were managed on a shared care basis.

These patients require complex medical care from experienced clinicians. Orthopaedic surgeons need to determine locally whether that degree of expertise is available within the orthopaedic team, or whether arrangements for formal shared care should be established.

Advisors were concerned about the development of pressure sores. Pressure sores were identified as a postoperative complication in 24 orthopaedic patients.

Case 29 • *A 91-year-old ASA 3 patient underwent an Austin Moore hemiarthroplasty for a fractured neck of femur. He died 28 days later with bronchopneumonia and pressure sores. Should not pressure sores be preventable?*

Training

There were still a significant number of cases which were performed by inappropriately junior trainees, often outside normal working hours.

Case 30 • *An SpR 1 performed an Austin Moore hemiarthroplasty, under spinal anaesthetic administered by an SHO 1, on a 91-year-old ASA 3 patient. The procedure took 1 h 45 min and the patient died of bronchopneumonia 11 days later.*

The advisors were also concerned that a significant number of procedures appeared to be performed, often on elective trauma lists, by consultants without any trainees present in theatre. Managing trauma in the frail and elderly requires considerable expertise and every opportunity should be taken to involve trainees in the management of these cases.

Seniority

Key Points

- *The physical status of the patient, not just the procedure, should determine the seniority of surgeons and anaesthetists involved in perioperative management and undertaking procedures in the elderly.*
- *There is wide variation in the experience and qualifications of non-consultant staff undertaking emergency orthopaedic surgery. Consultants' delegation should be appropriate to the needs of individual patients.*

The overall level of consultant input into the management of orthopaedic patients was commendably high at 88%. For urgent and emergency admissions the level was 555/633 (88%) and for fractures of the neck of femur it was 488/559 (87%).

NCEPOD repeatedly raises concerns about the seniority of surgeons and anaesthetists performing procedures in the elderly. It is difficult to make accurate comments, however, because trainees and non-consultant career grades (NCCG) have very varying degrees of experience.

Comparison with data from 1995/96[43] shows an increasing number (135/633, 21%) of emergency and urgent admissions are having surgery undertaken by NCCGs. Some of these surgeons are relatively inexperienced in emergency surgery, and in 36/135 (27%) cases the surgeon did not possess a post-basic qualification.

In 31/135 (23%) cases NCCGs undertook surgery following emergency or urgent admission without seeking advice from consultants. It is important that consultants follow the guidance from the Royal College of Surgeons regarding appropriate delegation to members of the surgical team: *"The extent to which any invasive procedure can be delegated must depend upon the consultant knowing the ability and experience of the team, whether permanent or locum."*[44]

Of the 559 patients treated for fractures of the neck of femur, in 117 (21%) cases the most senior surgeon present at the procedure was an NCCG. The range of experience was from four months to 30 years (mean six years and six months) in orthopaedics. The number of similar procedures performed in the previous 12 months ranged from two to 400 (mean 46) but these figures should be viewed with caution, since they were almost all multiples of five or ten, and it is possible that some gave the total number of procedures undertaken in that grade, rather than the number for the previous 12 months.

To put the death rate into context, data from Hospital Episode Statistics[45] for the same period indicate that there were 4707 Finished Consultant Episodes (FCEs) in Trauma and Orthopaedics, where the patient was 90 years or over when discharged or at the time of death, following a diagnosis of fractured neck of femur. Of these, 2207 had hemiarthroplasty or total hip replacement, with a 30-day mortality of 272 (12%), and 1640 had a sliding hip screw, with a 30-day mortality of 161 (10%).

It is interesting to note that there were 584 FCEs in which no operation was recorded and the mortality rate was 28% (162/584).

Figure 3.5: Grade of most senior surgeon and anaesthetist in theatre for fractured neck of femur *(414 cases where full data available)*

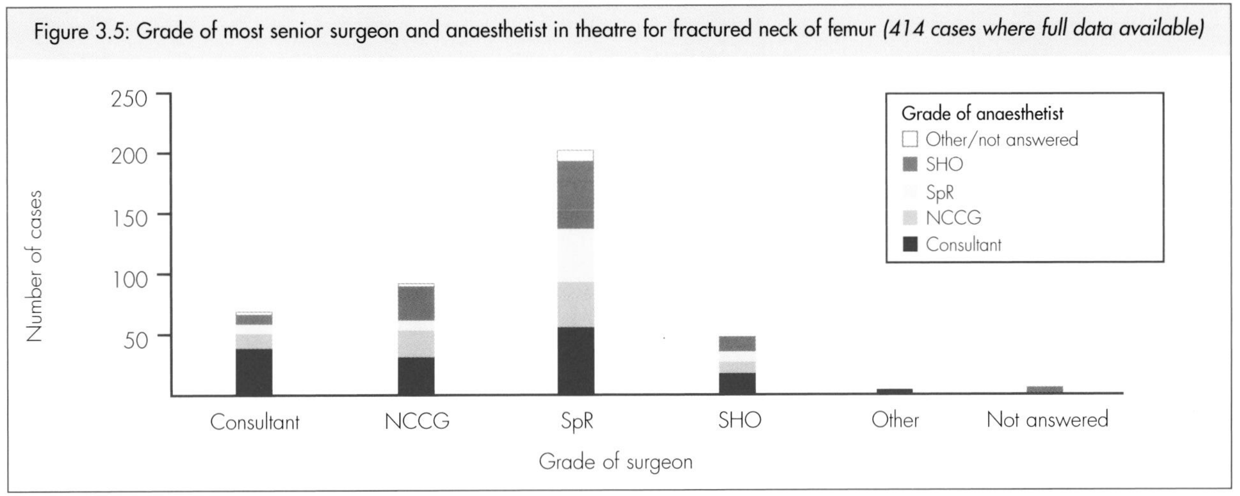

The Elderly

Delay and organisation of trauma lists

Key Point

- *There should be sufficient, fully-staffed, daytime theatre and recovery facilities to ensure that no patient requiring an urgent operation waits for more than 24 hours once fit for surgery. This includes weekends. There will need to be consultant expansion and a modification of job plans to ensure that trauma lists continue to be consultant led.*

The original CEPOD report of 1987[46] highlighted the deficiencies in provision of facilities for the management of trauma nationally, with 66% of cases operated on by non-consultants having had surgery performed out of normal working hours. This state of provision of care was rightly considered to be unacceptable, particularly considering that 73% of trauma cases had ASA grades of three or more. The response to this was the establishment of theatre lists dedicated to trauma - variously called trauma, urgent surgery or CEPOD lists. It is disappointing to note that despite 97% of orthopaedic cases being undertaken in hospitals having established daytime orthopaedic trauma lists, 50% of orthopaedic cases were still treated by non-consultants out of hours.

Whilst the increase in daytime trauma lists is welcomed, there remains a deficiency in service provision, with 87/463 (19%) orthopaedic cases undertaken in hospitals with a daytime orthopaedic trauma list having their surgery delayed for non-medical reasons, usually stated as lack of theatre time.

Most orthopaedic trauma cases are classified as urgent (not emergency) and out of hours surgery is seldom undertaken. As the trauma workload increases due to the ageing population and the increased expectations of patients and their relatives, there will be an increasing demand for dedicated trauma lists. This will be further compounded by the concentration of trauma from smaller units with minimal trauma workload into units serving populations of approximately 500 000 as envisaged in 'Provision of Acute General Hospital Services'[47]. In order to facilitate this rationalisation of services there will need to be considerable expansion of consultant numbers to achieve the optimal level of one consultant orthopaedic surgeon for 30 000 population.

Historically, the provision of trauma resources has been reactive rather than proactive and with long time lags. In the sphere of elective surgery this has not been the case, particularly with up to date information systems which permit accurate tailoring of resources to need within narrow tolerances. In the trauma sphere there is no such organisation since one of the major driving forces for it is missing, namely a waiting list.

Should there be formal trauma waiting lists of patients who are medically optimised for surgery?

Should combined or shared care of elderly patients, with care of the elderly physicians, become the norm rather than being present in only 118/559 (21%) patients with fractured necks of femur as found in this report?

With modern information systems this list of medically optimised patients could be readily monitored against a waiting time standard (24 hours has been recommended by the British Orthopaedic Association[48] with respect to fractured neck of femur). In 289/633 (46%) urgent or emergency orthopaedic admissions, there was a delay of two days or more between the decision to operate and operation. Advisors identified 49/648 (8%) cases in which they were particularly concerned about organisational delays. In a number of cases the delay was attributed to there being no time on the next available trauma list and, since these were usually not performed at weekends, this accounted for a substantial delay in a number of cases. Of necessity there would have to be greater redundancy in provision to allow for peaks, and theatre hours available would have to be based on the statistical mode, not the mean, of workload.

Urinary catheterisation

Key Points

- *Fluid management is often deficient. All clinicians should understand the fluid requirements of the elderly, and ward staff should have robust systems for identifying significant deviations from expected care both pre and postoperatively.*
- *Studies need to be undertaken to establish the relative advantages and disadvantages of using urinary catheters in orthopaedic trauma patients.*

In 59/648 (9%) cases advisors were concerned about fluid management. The general level of record keeping was poor, and in many more cases it was impossible to determine either fluid intakes or outputs in the perioperative period. The fact that record keeping was so poor must raise the suspicion that fluid management was even poorer than in the 9% of cases where records were sufficiently complete to definitely identify deficiencies (see also page 71).

Only 132/633 (21%) patients had a urinary catheter inserted preoperatively in urgent and emergency orthopaedic admissions. Not only did this make the measurement of urinary output difficult but, in a number of cases, patients were noted on the fluid charts to be sitting in wet beds. In 48/501 (10%) patients who did not have a catheter inserted there was known to be pre-existing renal disease.

CASE 31 • *A patient underwent a sliding hip screw for fractured hip following a six day delay during which the bed was noted to be wet and fluid balance could not be adequately assessed.*

CASE 32 • *A patient underwent a sliding hip screw for fractured hip. It was noted that the bed had been wet for three days. There was no fluid chart but the patient was hypokalaemic, incontinent, dehydrated and went into renal failure.*

There appears to be a need to establish guidelines for the use of urinary catheters in the elderly, weighing up the advantages in terms of fluid balance management and the potential disadvantages of postoperative infection, both of the urinary tract and of the orthopaedic prosthesis. Of the 414 patients treated for fractured neck of femur, for whom an anaesthetic questionnaire was returned, only 279 (67%) received a general anaesthetic. Those patients who have undergone epidural anaesthesia, particularly males, are at a greater risk of developing postoperative urinary retention.

There is a paucity of research into the risk of postoperative complications in elderly orthopaedic trauma patients who undergo urinary catheterisation. Such published work as is available is equivocal regarding the risks and benefits of urinary catheterisation in orthopaedic patients. The widespread dogma relating to increased infection rates in prostheses appears to be an extrapolation of work carried out in patients undergoing elective hip replacement to the trauma situation, which may not be valid. What is clear from this enquiry is that perioperative fluid management in orthopaedic trauma patients is deficient and could be improved by the appropriate selective use of urinary catheters.

Management of impacted intracapsular fractures

Minimally displaced subcapital fractures represent a small but important proportion of all proximal femoral fractures.

In a number of cases patients had presented initially with hip pain or a history of a fall and had been falsely reassured:

"It can't be broken if she can walk"

There were cases where doctors had failed to spot the fracture on the radiograph and other cases in which no radiographs had been taken. All clinicians and others involved in the care of the elderly need to be aware of this problem and have a high index of suspicion.

CASE 33 • *A 94-year-old ASA 4 patient attended A&E following a fall at the nursing home. A radiograph did not demonstrate a fracture at that time, but two weeks later she returned because of immobility and increasing pain and was found to have a subcapital fracture of the femur. She died five days after a hemiarthroplasty. Despite the patient's physical status she received treatment in a hospital which did not have an HDU bed.*

Management decisions in this frail group of patients should not be delegated to inexperienced surgeons. A careful evaluation of patient factors and an understanding of the fracture pattern are necessary for a proper decision to be made. The choice of *in situ* fixation or hemiarthroplasty should be made in the knowledge that if fixation of the fracture fails there is a very high mortality rate associated with a second procedure. Conservative management of an impacted fracture in this group of patients should be used with caution. These patients are often unable to comply with an instruction to limit weight bearing and the secondary displacement will require a more major procedure than fixation *in situ*. Inevitably this will give rise to greater morbidity and mortality.

Deaths due to cement reaction

Key Point

- *Cement reactions, whilst infrequent, are often lethal in the elderly. Guidelines should be available for the management of cement related complications.*

Twelve patients suffered a severe intraoperative reaction following insertion of cement into the femoral shaft. There were wide variations in the management of hypotension in these cases. It is recognised that cementation of hemiarthroplasties is sometimes the preferred method of dealing with fractures of the femoral neck. The physical status of the patient in whom cement is to be used should be optimised. Particular care should be taken to correct hypovolaemia and electrolyte imbalance preoperatively. The relative indications and contraindications for the use of cement need to be established.

Thromboembolic prophylaxis

Key Point

- *Studies are still required to determine the place of thromboembolic prophylaxis in orthopaedic patients.*

In only 393/648 (61%) cases were precautions taken to prevent venous thromboembolism.

In the orthopaedic sample, the number of reported cases of definite death from pulmonary embolism established at postmortem was 32, but only 32% of the orthopaedic sample underwent postmortem examination. Of these patients 22/32 (69%) had received some form of thromboembolic prophylaxis.

The debate regarding thromboembolic prophylaxis in orthopaedic surgery continues. Not only does controversy remain over the different methods and duration of thromboembolic prophylaxis, but even the basic question of whether *any* prophylaxis should be given is still unanswered.

The incidence of venous thrombosis is dependent on the assessment method used. An autopsy study[49] reported an incidence of deep venous thrombosis of 83%. Studies using routine venography give incidences of 19-91%[50, 51, 52] and between 10-14% for pulmonary embolism when routine isotope lung scans are used[53]. Summation of studies which report on the incidence as diagnosed in clinical practice, give rates of venous thrombosis of about 3% and pulmonary embolism of about 1%. In summary, the 'pathological' incidence of thrombosis is high, and some degree of venous thrombosis probably occurs in all patients after a hip fracture, but the symptomatic incidence of venous thrombosis is low.

The Cochrane meta-analysis of randomised trials of heparin and physical methods for thromboembolic prophylaxis for hip fracture patients indicated that measures such as heparin will reduce the incidence of venographic thrombi from 39% to 24%, and mechanical devices from 19% to 6%. The overall mortality, however, showed a non-significant increase from 8% to 11% for those patients allocated to receive heparin.

For mechanical devices the trend in mortality was reversed, being lower in those who were allocated to use the devices. This finding of a reduction in the incidence of thromboembolic complication for heparin, but a failure to reduce the overall mortality, has been demonstrated in previous meta-analysis[54].

Consensus statements have given unequivocal recommendation that thromboembolic prophylaxis must be used for hip fracture patients[55, 56, 57]. These are at odds with the more recent Cochrane meta-analysis which, whilst confirming that thromboembolic prophylaxis will reduce the risk of thrombotic events, fails to establish whether this benefit is offset by other adverse events affecting the overall mortality.

For the foreseeable future thromboembolic prophylaxis will remain a controversial topic. The PEP (pulmonary embolism prevention) trial should be able to give information on the possible benefits of aspirin when the results are released.

Until large-scale randomised trials of different methods of prophylaxis are undertaken, with full reporting of all outcomes (not just thromboembolic complications), many questions on the benefits and risks of thromboembolic prophylaxis will remain unanswered.

Audit

Sixty percent (389/648) of cases were considered at an audit meeting. In the era of clinical governance should all deaths be considered?

General surgery

Key Points

- *The decision whether or not to operate on these elderly patients is frequently difficult and should be made at consultant level.*
- *Preoperative resuscitation and optimisation is of paramount importance, especially in terms of fluid balance.*
- *An accurate method of assessing the risk of surgery is required. P-POSSUM is suggested as a possibility.*
- *The experience of the surgeon and anaesthetist should be tailored to the needs of the patient, not just the technical skill required for the procedure.*
- *A number of patients, in whom the initial diagnosis from their symptoms was a hernia, were found at operation to have obstruction or peritonitis from other causes.*
- *More careful investigation might prevent futile major surgery in patients with disseminated malignancy.*

There were 360 questionnaires returned by general, vascular and A&E surgeons. The 81 vascular procedures are described elsewhere (see page 93). The remaining 279 general surgical cases are considered in this section. The most common procedures were laparotomy (141/279, 51%) and hernia repair (35/279, 13%).

Consultant involvement

A consultant was involved in the decision to operate in 242/279 (87%) general surgical cases.

Whilst consultant involvement in decision-making was high, in these very frail and elderly patients the decision as to whether or not an operation should be performed should ideally be made at consultant level in *all* cases.

The consultant surgeon was in theatre in 160/279 (57%) cases.

The presence of the consultant in theatre in only 57% of cases certainly leaves room for improvement. General surgical consultants need to have timetables which leave them free to help with emergencies without other routine commitments, such as outpatients or elective operating lists. The level of availability of daytime emergency theatres for general surgery needs to be increased from the present level of 77%. This is a crude figure, and only indicates that daytime emergency theatres are available some of the time. In order to be effective, daytime emergency theatres should be available every day *including weekends*, and should be fully and appropriately staffed.

Figure 3.6: Grade of most senior surgeon and anaesthetist in theatre for general surgical cases *(185 cases where full data available)*

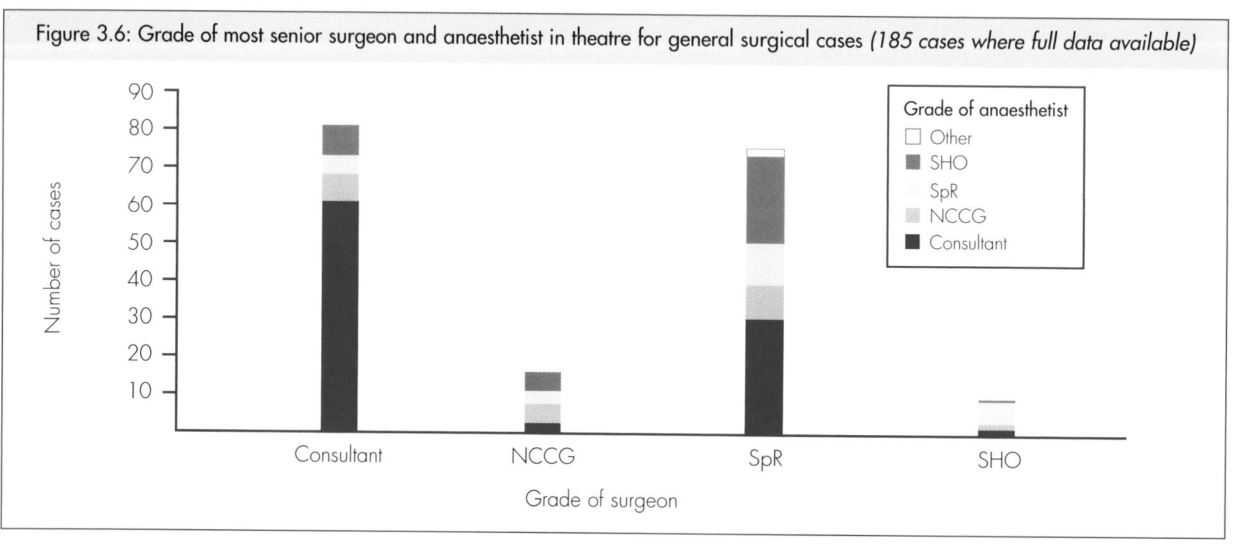

ASA status

Table 3.25: ASA status of general surgical cases	
ASA grade	**Number**
ASA 1	1
ASA 2	38
ASA 3	138
ASA 4	86
ASA 5	14
Not answered	2
Total	279

The majority of the patients were assessed as ASA grades 3 or 4. Whilst this is a useful method of assessing the physical status of a patient it was never intended to predict the likely outcome of surgery. The Physiological and Operative Severity Score for Enumeration of Mortality and Morbidity (POSSUM) provides a possible better tool for risk adjustment[58]. A revised method of prediction of death, the Portsmouth Predictor Equation (P-POSSUM)[59] has also been proposed. This has been found particularly applicable to predicting outcome in vascular surgery[60].

The advisors felt that P-POSSUM is probably the best predictive scoring system available and would be useful for patient information to allow comparisons between individual surgeons and units and to give appropriate weight to case mix considerations.

CASE 34 • *A 92-year-old lady had an anterior resection for carcinoma of the rectum, following which she had a myocardial infarction, atrial fibrillation and hypotension. She developed a respiratory infection, congestive cardiac failure and a low serum albumin when she had an anastomotic leak. She died following a subsequent laparotomy for this.*

P-POSSUM would predict a 99% risk of mortality for this second operation.

CASE 35 • *A 92-year-old man, with no other medical problems (ASA 1), had a palliative right hemicolectomy.*

P-POSSUM would still predict a 37% risk of mortality.

Delays in referral or admission

In 20 general surgical cases there was a perceived delay in either referral or admission (Table 3.26).

Table 3.26: Reasons for delay in referral or admission of general surgical patients	
Reason	**Number**
Delayed diagnosis or referral by medical team	8
Delay in referral by GP	6
Patient intially refused admission	1
Delay in obtaining CT scan	1
No bed available for transfer of patient	1
Insufficient information given	3
Total	20

Preoperative preparation

Preoperative preparation was frequently less than ideal, particularly from the point of view of fluid balance, given that 244/279 (87%) patients were either emergency or urgent admissions.

Of the urgent and emergency admissions, 196/244 (80%) had coexisting medical problems other than the main diagnosis. Only 29/196 (15%) of these patients had formal shared care.

A quarter (14/56) of patients with pre-existing respiratory problems did not have any appropriate preoperative precautions or therapeutic manoeuvres undertaken. The importance of optimising a patient's condition, and in particular ensuring adequate oxygen delivery prior to major surgery, has recently been highlighted[61].

Seven patients admitted as urgent or emergency cases had no preoperative preparation at all. Given their ASA status, the fact that all of these patients had pre-existing medical problems, and the surgical diagnosis and procedure undertaken, some preoperative preparation might have been appropriate in these patients. The cases were as follows:

ASA	*Operation*	*Diagnosis*
3	Removal of skin cancer and skin graft	Squamous cell carcinoma leg
4	Flexible sigmoidoscopy	Pseudo-obstruction
3	Right hemicolectomy for carcinoma	Carcinoma of ascending colon
3	Left groin exploration for obstructed inguinal hernia	Obstructed left inguinal hernia
2	Mastectomy, latissimus dorsi flap and skin graft	Carcinoma right breast

ASA	Operation	Diagnosis
3	Gastroscopy and dilatation	Benign oesophageal stricture
3	Upper GI endoscopy	Oesophageal stricture

The reader is referred particularly to the section on perioperative fluid management on page 65.

Femoral hernia

The 1991/92 NCEPOD report[6] dealt with the surgical management of strangulated hernia. This was defined as a hernia in which the contents of a sac had interrupted the blood supply leading to impaired viability of the contents. At that time 5000 primary femoral hernia repairs were performed on adults over the age of 16 each year. One hundred and twenty deaths occurred in England in 1990 as a result of femoral hernia complications and the comment was made that "despite the fact that these patients were elderly and ill, resuscitation was often inadequate and surgery hasty". Forty-four percent of procedures were performed out of hours and consultants were rarely involved in management.

In the 1991/92 report, 70 questionnaires relating to the management of hernia were analysed. Of these, 39 were femoral, 14 inguinal, 7 umbilical, five incisional and five other.

That report highlighted *inter alia* the need for consultant input, because of the predominantly elderly age group and high incidence of comorbidity, the need for adequate preoperative resuscitation and the need to consider whether surgery is appropriate at all.

Femoral hernia in the elderly today

Twenty-one patients in this sample had operation for repair of femoral hernia. The operative approach was a local femoral incision in ten patients, in two patients a pararectus (McEvedy) approach was used and in nine patients a laparotomy. Twelve of these patients also had resection of small bowel. The details are shown in Table 3.27.

Strangulated femoral hernia is a dangerous condition and is particularly common in elderly females. The sooner the patient is taken to theatre the more likely it is that bowel will be viable and resection avoided. However, this must be balanced against the need to get patients fit for theatre, particularly their fluid and electrolyte balance and the management of heart failure, to maximise their chances of surviving the operation. There is sometimes a place for preoperative admission to the HDU for close supervision of resuscitation.

Table 3.27: Femoral hernia repair

ASA grade	Grade of surgeon	Grade of anaesthetist	Emergency /Urgent	Operative approach	Bowel resection
5	Consultant	SHO 2	Urgent	Femoral	No
5	Consultant	Not known	Urgent	McEvedy	No
5	Clinical assistant	Not known	Urgent	Laparotomy	Not known
4	SpR 1	SHO 2	Urgent	Femoral	Yes
4	Senior SHO	SHO 2	Urgent	Femoral	Yes
4	SpR 4	Consultant	Urgent	Laparotomy	No
4	Associate specialist	SHO 2	Urgent	Femoral	No
4	SpR 3	Consultant	Urgent	Femoral	No
4	Visiting SpR	Staff grade	Urgent	Laparotomy	Yes
3	Visiting SpR	SHO 1	Urgent	Pararectus	Yes
3	SHO 2	Not known	Urgent	Femoral	Yes
3	SpR 2	Consultant	Urgent	Laparotomy	Yes
3	Staff grade	Staff grade	Emergency	Femoral	No
3	Other registrar	Not known	Urgent	Laparotomy	Yes
3	Accredited SpR	Not known	Urgent	Femoral	No
3	SpR 4	Consultant	Urgent	Laparotomy	Yes
3	Consultant	Consultant	Urgent	Laparotomy	Yes
3	Staff grade	Not known	Urgent	Laparotomy	No
3	Staff grade	SpR 1	Urgent	Femoral	Yes
3	Staff grade	SHO 2	Urgent	Laparotomy	Yes
3	Locum consultant	Consultant	Urgent	Femoral	Yes

Incidental hernia

There were ten patients in whom the initial diagnosis of the cause of the symptoms appeared to be a hernia, but who actually had some other pathology with the hernia being merely incidental. Five were femoral, two inguinal, one umbilical, one incisional and one parastomal (Table 3.28).

CASE 36 • *An ASA 4 patient was referred by a general practitioner with a history of abdominal pain and a diagnosis of femoral hernia. The hernia was explored and found to contain omentum only. Twelve days later the obstruction persisted and a left hemicolectomy was performed for a diverticular abscess.*

CASE 37 • *An ASA 3 patient was referred by a general practitioner to the general physicians who made a diagnosis of femoral hernia. A laparotomy demonstrated large bowel obstruction secondary to a rectal carcinoma and a Hartmann's procedure was performed.*

It can be difficult to tell whether or not the hernia is the cause of the problem, as judged by the fact that there was consultant input in the diagnosis of all these patients. Nevertheless, it is worth bearing in mind that a hernia may not always be the cause of a patient's obstruction or peritonitis.

A consultant should be involved in the diagnosis, which may often be misleading, particularly in the elderly.

Diagnosis of intestinal obstruction in the elderly

Full assessment and accurate diagnosis are essential if unnecessary or ultimately futile surgery is to be avoided in the elderly. The importance of hernia has been discussed above. Surgeons should have a high index of suspicion for underlying malignancy in this age group. In suspected large bowel obstruction an unprepared barium enema should be undertaken before surgery, to exclude pseudo-obstruction and confirm mechanical obstruction.

CASE 38 • *An ASA 4 patient in rapid atrial fibrillation underwent decompression of pseudo-obstruction through an appendicectomy approach despite a preoperative potassium level of 2.8 mmol/l. Should the consultant surgeon have resisted pressure, in this case from the physicians, to operate?*

Laparotomy for disseminated malignancy

Forty-five patients underwent laparotomies where disseminated malignancies were found. In the majority the indication for surgery was intestinal or gastric outlet obstruction. In these patients laparotomy was performed to relieve obstruction despite the known presence of metastases. Symptomatic relief of intestinal obstruction in patients with widespread malignancy may sometimes be achieved by non-surgical means and consideration should be given to involving the palliative care team.

There were seven patients in whom the indication for surgery, other than "exploratory" was unclear, and in whom the finding was simply one of widespread metastatic cancer (Table 3.29).

Whilst there was a high proportion of consultant input into the management of these patients, the advisors felt that in most of them an ultrasound

Table 3.28: Incidental hernia and other pathology

Type of hernia	Other pathology	Specialty of consultant	Most senior surgeon consulted	Most senior surgeon in theatre
Femoral	Carcinoma of caecum	General and vascular	Consultant	SHO 2
Femoral	Mesenteric ischaemia and bowel infarction	General and colorectal	Consultant	SpR 4
Femoral	Stenosing carcinoma of upper rectum	General and vascular	Consultant	Accredited SpR
Femoral	Diverticular abscess	General and gastroenterology	Consultant	Consultant
Femoral	Gastric carcinoma	General and vascular	Consultant	Consultant
Incisional	Perforated colonic carcinoma	General and gastroenterology	Consultant	Consultant
Inguinal	Perforated duodenal ulcer	General and vascular	Consultant	Visiting SpR
Inguinal	Perforated sigmoid colon	General	Consultant	SpR 3
Parastomal	Abdominal adhesions	General and gastroenterology	Consultant	Consultant
Umbilical	Mesenteric embolus	General and vascular	Consultant	Consultant

scan, and perhaps in some a CT scan, might have established the diagnosis and prevented an unnecessary laparotomy.

Early involvement of the palliative care team might also have prevented the need for a surgical approach to symptom relief in some patients.

Bowel resection

Of 67 patients undergoing bowel resection only 35 (52%) received preoperative prophylactic antibiotics. There is strong evidence to support the use of antibiotic prophylaxis where bowel resection is planned or probable[62]. Table 3.30 summarises the 32 cases where no antibiotic prophylaxis was used.

Table 3.29: Laparotomy for disseminated malignancy

Finding on laparotomy	Specialty of surgeon	Most senior surgeon consulted	Most senior surgeon in theatre
Metastatic carcinoma of stomach	General and hepatobiliary	SpR 3	SpR 3
Metastatic carcinoma of gall bladder	General and gastroenterology	Consultant	Consultant
Widespread metastases, ? primary	General and breast	Consultant	Consultant
Widespread metastases, ? primary	General and gastroenterology	Consultant	Consultant
Widespread metastases, ? primary	General and gastroenterology	Consultant	Consultant
Advanced carcinoma of colon and other metastases	General and gastroenterology	Consultant	Consultant
Widespread metastases, ? primary	General and vascular	Consultant	Consultant

Table 3.30: Patients undergoing bowel resection without preoperative antibiotic prophylaxis

Diagnosis	Operation
Caecal cancer with abscess	Extended right hemicolectomy (en bloc abdominal wall and bladder), sigmoid colectomy
Sigmoid colon carcinoma	Sigmoid colectomy
Major rectal bleed	Gastroscopy. Proceed to laparotomy with intraoperative colonic irrigation and colonoscopy to identify site of bleeding. Right hemicolectomy.
Strangulated right femoral hernia	Exploration and repair through pararectus approach of strangulated femoral hernia and small bowel resection
Bowel obstruction, near perforation	Extended right hemicolectomy
Bowel obstruction	Limited right hemicolectomy
Carcinoma of caecum	Right hemicolectomy
Peritonitis	Right hemicolectomy, end ileostomy and mucous fistula
Perforated ulcer	Extended right hemicolectomy
Caecal volvulus	Laparotomy, right hemicolectomy
Large bowel obstruction/perforation	Laparotomy, right hemicolectomy
Peritonitis perforated intra-abdominal viscus	Sigmoid colectomy (Hartmann's procedure)
Carcinoma of colon and bowel obstruction	Right hemicolectomy
Small bowel obstruction	Right hemicolectomy
Caecal carcinoma (on barium enema and colonoscopy)	Right hemicolectomy
Intestinal obstruction	Sigmoid colectomy
Intestinal obstruction	Untwisting of volvulus of sigmoid and sigmoid colectomy
Small bowel obstruction	Laparotomy, small bowel resection for strangulated internal hernia secondary to adhesions
Small bowel obstruction	Laparotomy, freeing of band adhesion, small bowel resection and anastomosis
Small bowel obstruction	Laparotomy and freeing of small severe radiation enteritis of small bowel
High intestinal obstruction ? pyloric stenosis	Laparotomy, small bowel resection, repair left femoral hernia
Carcinoma of ascending colon	Right hemicolectomy for carcinoma of ascending colon
Small bowel obstruction due to caecal carcinoma	Right hemicolectomy
Large bowel obstruction with local perforation to caecum	Subtotal colectomy and ileorectal anastomosis
Bowel obstruction	Extended right hemicolectomy, division of adhesions
Sigmoid colon diverticular perforation with abscess formation	Left hemicolectomy for right femoral hernia
Fluid depletion, irreducible right femoral hernia, causing small bowel obstruction	Exploration of right femoral hernia under LA, converted to general anaesthesia. Laparotomy and resection of necrotic Meckel's diverticulum with end-to-end small bowel anastomosis

Diagnosis	Operation
Small bowel obstruction	Division of adhesions, small bowel resection
Carcinoma rectosigmoid	Sigmoid colectomy
Intestinal obstruction pneumonia	Right hemicolectomy
Small bowel obstruction, probably secondary to strangulated right femoral hernia	Laparotomy, small bowel resection and repair right femoral hernia
Right strangulated femoral hernia	Exploration right femoral hernia, resection of small bowel and femoral herniorraphy

Denominator figures

A previous criticism has been the lack of denominator data available for use by NCEPOD. The surgical advisors performed an audit of those patients aged 90 years or over operated on between 1 April 1997 and 31 March 1998 in their own hospitals. The overall 30-day death rate was approximately 20%.

Since this group of vulnerable patients is a small percentage of the total treated in any one unit each year, it is important that local audit is performed over several years, and compared with national standards, to avoid drawing invalid conclusions. Until good quality denominator data are available, any conclusions drawn with regard to comparative study of death rates should be viewed with extreme caution. The heterogeneity of surgical practice in different units means that qualitative peer review remains important in identifying deficiencies in the standard of care.

Thromboembolic prophylaxis

Thromboembolic prophylaxis was used in 212/279 (76%) of the general surgery patients.

These were very elderly patients and should all have had some form of prophylaxis against venous thromboembolism.

Audit

A total of 74% (207/279) of general surgery deaths in this sample were considered in an audit meeting.

This is a commendably high figure but, with the introduction of clinical governance, should all deaths now be considered at an audit meeting?

Pathways of care

The advisors felt that one way of improving postoperative management of patients might be by the use of 'pathways of care', particularly in relation to overcoming difficulties surrounding information handover caused by the limitations on junior doctors' hours.

Could 'pathways of care' help identify deviations from the expected progress of patients and assist in prioritisation of care, particularly where multiple nursing and medical staff changes occur?

Urology

Key Points

- *Consultants were involved in the care of all patients.*
- *Sixty-six percent of patients were operated on by a consultant, but in only half of these were trainees present. Is this a missed training opportunity?*
- *General anaesthesia was used for a number of simple procedures where local anaesthesia might have been preferable in these frail patients.*
- *Check cystoscopy guidelines should take into account the risks due to the high incidence of comorbidity in the elderly.*

Thirty questionnaires were received from urologists. The quality of care was generally high; criticisms are relatively minor. Consultant involvement in care was 100% and only one non-medical delay was reported.

Table 3.31: Urological procedures

Procedure	Number
Cystoscopy, no other procedure	8
TURBT	7
TURP	5
Revision TURP	1
Cystodiathermy	2
Insertion of prostatic stent	1
Urethral dilatation and removal of calculi	1
Clot evacuation	1
Urethroscopy and bladder neck incision	1
Urethrotomy	1
Deflation of catheter balloon	1
Urethroscopy and litholopaxy	1
Total	30

Twenty operations were performed by a consultant, and consultants were involved in decision-making in all 30 cases. There was some concern that in only 50% of cases where a consultant was operating was a trainee present and benefiting from training in the management of this difficult group of elderly patients.

The majority of cases (18/30) were considered at audit meetings.

There was some concern that general anaesthesia was employed too often in the elderly where local anaesthesia might have been more appropriate.

CASE 39 • *A 92-year-old ASA 3 patient underwent general anaesthesia to deflate a catheter balloon. Was this appropriate?*

CASE 40 • *A 90-year-old ASA 3 patient had a general anaesthetic (GA) administered by an SHO 1, for a urethral stricture. The patient died of a post operative MI. Could GA have been avoided here? Was the anaesthetist suitably experienced?*

Bleeding from transitional cell bladder carcinoma was the most common indication (9/30) for surgery closely followed by outflow obstruction (8/30).

The advisors wondered if a policy of check cystoscopy was always appropriate.

CASE 41 • *A 94-year-old ASA 3 patient underwent check cystoscopy and biopsy under general anaesthetic. She had already had radiotherapy and further treatment other than palliation was unlikely to be available.*

In a few cases the diagnosis could probably have been made using non-invasive imaging modalities rather than submitting the patient to procedures under GA or sedation.

CASE 42 • *A 91-year-old ASA 4 patient underwent GA cystoscopy for haematuria and a pelvic mass. The diagnosis could probably have been established without recourse to a general anaesthetic procedure.*

As in the 1994/95 NCEPOD report[9], the most common cause of death was cardiovascular (8/30), with bronchopneumonia and renal failure being the cause in five each. This is not surprising, since 17/30 had pre-existing cardiovascular disease. Perhaps it is a little surprising then that only 7/26 patients with comorbidity enjoyed the benefit of shared care.

Neurosurgery

Key Point

- *In elderly patients with confusion, if the diagnosis is unclear, a CT or MRI scan of the head should be performed promptly, so that surgically remediable intracranial conditions can be identified.*

Two deaths were reported in this specialty; both cases were admitted to medical wards. In one patient there was a delay of eight days between the request and obtaining a CT scan. In the other patient a CT scan was not requested for ten days in an elderly confused patient.

Although this counsel is often recognised by practitioners, the general lack of resources for CT and MRI scanning in many hospitals leads to delays.

Vascular surgery

Key Points

- *The decision whether or not to operate on these elderly patients is frequently difficult and should be made at consultant level.*
- *It is questionable whether any patient of 90 years or over should have a ruptured aortic aneurysm repaired.*
- *It is important for an anaesthetist of suitable experience to be present during embolectomy under local anaesthetic, for appropriate sedation, monitoring and resuscitation.*
- *Embolectomy should be performed by surgeons who have sufficient vascular experience and expertise to be able to perform an arterial bypass operation if required.*

Eighty-one questionnaires were received concerning patients who died following vascular procedures. The full list of procedures is shown in Table 3.32.

Table 3.32: Vascular procedures
(81 cases; procedures may be multiple)

Procedure	Number
Repair of leaking abdominal aortic aneurysm	4
Femoral embolectomy	22
Brachial embolectomy	5
Axillofemoral bypass	1
Femorofemoral crossover graft	1
Femoropopliteal bypass	4
Femorotibial bypass	2
Femoral endarterectomy	1
Above knee amputation	26
Gritti-Stokes (supracondylar) amputation	1

Procedure	Number
Below knee amputation	6
Amputation of toes	6
Debridement of toe wound	1
Debridement of BK amputation stump	1
Debridement of heel ulcer	1
Debridement of leg ulcer	1
Debridement of leg for necrotising fasciitis	1

Leaking abdominal aortic aneurysm

Table 3.33: Repair of leaking abdominal aortic aneurysm

Age	ASA grade	Comorbidity	Grade of surgeon making decision	Grade of most senior surgeon at operation	Grade of most senior anaesthetist	Length of operation	Number of days from surgery to death	Place of death
91	3	Cardiac and renal disease	Consultant	Consultant	Consultant	2 h	0	Operating theatre
92	3	Chest infection	Consultant	Consultant	Consultant	1 h 30 min	3	Ward
90	4	Cardiac disease	Consultant	SpR with CCST	Not known	3 h 30 min	1	ICU
91	4	Renal disease	Consultant	Consultant	SpR 3, consultant came to theatre later	3 h 30 min	5	ICU

There was good consultant input from both surgeons and anaesthetists and no operation was unduly long. However, it is questionable whether any patient of 90 years or over should have a ruptured aortic aneurysm repaired, especially if there is significant comorbidity.

Embolectomy

Nearly all embolectomies were performed under local anaesthetic, with four patients receiving a general anaesthetic and one a plexus block. In only seven out of the 22 local anaesthetic operations was an anaesthetist present (32%). An anaesthetist should always be present during an embolectomy even though the majority in this age group are performed under local anaesthetic. The anaesthetist is needed for proper management of sedation, performance of appropriate monitoring, control of acidosis, particularly at the time of restoration of the circulation when the clamps are released, and for resuscitation.

Success of embolectomy and specialty of surgeon

Five patients had a femoral embolectomy, performed by a surgeon who did not profess to have a special interest in vascular surgery, where the procedure failed to restore the circulation and no further therapeutic manoeuvre was undertaken (Table 3.34).

Table 3.34: Failure of embolectomy to restore circulation

Age	ASA grade	Grade of surgeon making decision	Specialty of surgeon making decision	Grade of surgeon at operation
94	3	Consultant	General and gastroenterology	SpR 3
93	3	Consultant	General, breast and gastroenterology	Consultant
92	4	Consultant	General and gastroenterology	Consultant
93	4	Staff grade	General and urology	Staff grade
93	4	Locum registrar	General and gastroenterology	Locum registrar

In these five patients embolectomy failed to restore the circulation and it is likely that the operation was inappropriate, since the problem was probably an arterial thrombosis rather than an embolus. Whilst there is an argument for trying embolectomy under local anaesthetic in a very frail and elderly patient, the advisors considered that the surgeon should at least have the experience to know when a patient might benefit from a bypass procedure at the same operation, and should have the expertise to be able to proceed to this if necessary. In none of the five cases in Table 3.34 was this done.

Amputation

Amputation was the most common vascular procedure and it is interesting to note that of the lower limb amputations 26 were above the knee while only six were below knee level. This is in contrast to amputations in younger age groups. The Scottish Vascular Audit Group has also shown a higher incidence of above, compared with below, knee amputations in those aged over 80 years, compared with younger patients[63]; it also showed that increasing age was an independent risk factor for 30-day mortality. However, although amputation does carry a high mortality risk, it is frequently the only way of obtaining satisfactory pain relief.

Surgical consultant involvement

In 72/81 (89%) cases a consultant surgeon was involved in the decision to operate. This is highly commendable, but the proportion of patients where the consultant either performed the operation or was present in the operating theatre was only 41/81 (51%); this proportion should have been higher.

Figure 3.7: Grade of most senior surgeon present in theatre for vascular procedures

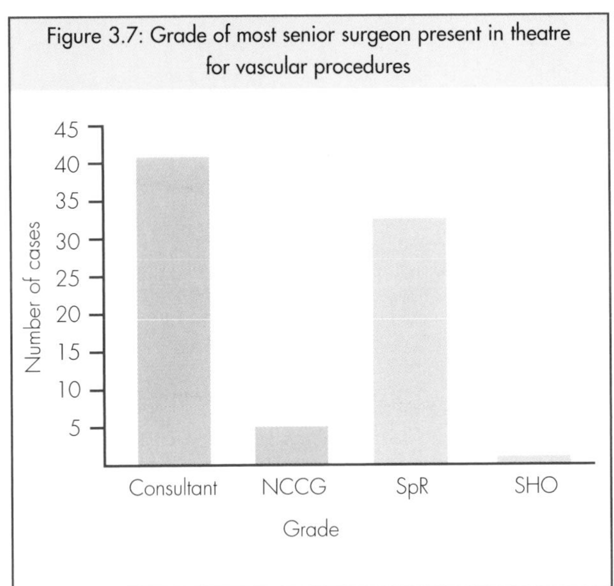

Anaesthetic consultant involvement

In 24/50 (48%) cases where an anaesthetic questionnaire was received the anaesthetic was given by a consultant.

Decision-making

The decision whether or not to operate in these very old and often frail patients is frequently a difficult one, requiring experience, and should therefore be made at consultant level. Further help may be obtained using the Portsmouth Predictor Equation (P-POSSUM), which is particularly applicable for use in vascular surgery[59, 60] (see also page 87).

Thromboembolic prophylaxis

Fifty-five of the 81 patients (68%) were given thromboembolic prophylaxis. The incidence should be 100% in elderly patients having vascular surgery.

High dependency units

Question 3.10: Does your hospital have an age-related policy for admission to HDU/ICU? (SQ41)

Yes	3
No	75
Not answered	3
Total	81

Question 3.11: If the patient's condition warranted an admission to an HDU/ICU, were you at any time unable to transfer the patient into an HDU/ICU within the hospital in which the surgery took place? (SQ45)

Yes	2
No	26
Condition did not warrant admission to HDU/ICU	38
Not answered	15
Total	81

There should be no age limit for admission to an HDU or ICU. HDU care is desirable for patients following treatment for acute limb ischaemia. If it is considered appropriate to perform a major vascular operation then it is usually also appropriate to have HDU care.

Audit

Twenty percent of these patients were not considered at local surgical audit meetings. In these days of clinical governance close to 100% should be considered at such meetings.

OTHER SPECIALTIES

Key Points

- *Consultant involvement in the care of patients in these specialties is uniformly high.*
- *Involvement in audit appears low, and this is unchanged from the 1994/95 NCEPOD report.*

Gynaecology

Two gynaecology cases were reviewed from the total of 1077 surgical questionnaires received in this age group.

Consultants operated in both these cases.

In one case, a laparotomy was undertaken on a 93-year-old ASA 3 patient with known malignant ascites from an ovarian carcinoma. Would paracentesis have been a simpler palliative procedure? This case was not considered at an audit meeting.

Ophthalmology

Eleven ophthalmology cases were reviewed from the total of 1077 surgical questionnaires received in this age group. Consultants were involved in the care of all patients and performed 9/11 procedures. In only one case was a consultant not present in theatre.

Table 3.35: Ophthalmology procedures

Procedure	Number
Unilateral cataract	6
Bilateral cataract	2
Drainage of nasolacrimal duct	1
Evisceration of orbital contents	1
Resuture corneal dehiscence	1
Total	11

In five cases local anaesthesia was administered by the surgeon. In only one case was a general anaesthetic administered, in an ASA 2 patient for drainage of a lacrimal abscess.

Advisors were surprised that one ASA 3 patient, with angina and arrhythmias, underwent bilateral cataract surgery, undertaken by an SpR 1 under local anaesthesia.

In all other cases the level of care was felt to be appropriate.

Only one case was considered at an audit meeting. A low audit rate was also noted in the 1994/95 NCEPOD report.

Oral and maxillofacial surgery

One case was reviewed from the total of 1077 surgical questionnaires received in this age group. This case demonstrated high quality care. The consultant was involved.

CASE 43 • *A 91-year-old ASA 3 patient was admitted via A&E with facial lacerations. Formal shared care was undertaken between the surgeons and the care of the elderly team. The lacerations were repaired under local anaesthetic, but the patient died of a myocardial infarction five days later.*

The case was not, however, considered at an audit meeting. The low involvement in audit of this specialty was highlighted in the 1994/95 NCEPOD report.

Otorhinolaryngology

Nine questionnaires were received from otorhinolaryngologists from the total of 1077 surgical questionnaires received in this age group.

Consultants were involved in the care of 6/9 patients.

Table 3.36: Otorhinolaryngology procedures

Procedure	Number
Laryngoscopy/pharyngoscopy	4
Oesophageal dilatation and insertion Souttar tube	1
Removal of oesophageal foreign body	1
Laser pharyngeal pouch	1
Tracheostomy and repair neck laceration	1
Tru-Cut biopsy parotid gland	1
Total	9

One case was considered at an audit meeting. The low involvement in audit of this specialty was noted in the 1994/95 NCEPOD report.

Plastic surgery

Nine questionnaires were received from plastic surgeons from the total of 1077 surgical questionnaires received in this age group.

Consultants were involved in the care of all patients. Consultants operated in 5/9 cases.

Table 3.37: Plastic surgery procedures

Procedure	Number
Mastectomy, latissimus dorsi flap and skin graft	2
Excision skin tumour	2
Wound/burn debridement	2
Above knee amputation	1
Finger amputation	1
Inguinal node dissection	1
Total	9

In one case there was delay in referring an ASA 3 patient with a wrist wound from the primary sector.

In a further patient undergoing mastectomy and latissimus dorsi flap reconstruction, no ICU/HDU facility was available in the hospital. Is it appropriate to be undertaking major cancer and reconstructive surgery without HDU/ICU facilities?

In all other cases care was felt to be appropriate.

Three cases were considered at audit meetings. The 1994/95 NCEPOD report noted the low involvement in audit of this specialty.

Cardiothoracic surgery

Four questionnaires were received from cardiothoracic surgeons out of the total of 1077 surgical questionnaires received in this age group.

Consultants were involved in the care of all patients.

In all but one patient, undergoing oesophagoscopy and dilatation, operations were performed by consultants.

Table 3.38: Cardiothoracic surgery procedures

Procedure	Number
Aortic valve replacement	1
OGD and insertion NG tube	1
OGD and dilatation	1
Pharyngeal pouch stapling	1
Total	4

Care was felt to be appropriate in all cases. Two out of four cases (50%) were considered at audit meetings.

The Elderly

LIVERPOOL
JOHN MOORES UNIVERSITY
AVRIL ROBARTS LRC
TEL. 0151 231 4022

Pathology

Key Points

- *Systems need to be established to ensure that clinicians always receive copies of Coroner's or hospital postmortem reports.*
- *The patient's medical records should always be available to the pathologist at the time of postmortem.*
- *The Royal College of Pathologists' guidelines may now need expansion and updating, with inclusion of guidance on OPCS formatting for cause of death and examination of the locomotor system.*
- *Clinically unsuspected gastrointestinal complications are commonly found to be the cause, or contribute to the cause, of death following surgery in the elderly.*

General

Of the 1077 surgical questionnaires received, 60% (648/1077) were from orthopaedic surgeons. Two hundred and sixty-four (25%) of the returned questionnaires stated that a postmortem (PM) had been performed. Only 140 (53%) postmortem reports were available for scrutiny (127 Coroner's PMs and 13 hospital/consent PMs). The low postmortem rate is not surprising considering the age of the patient group and is not strictly comparable to PM rates in previous years. Six hundred and sixty-seven (62%) cases were reported to the Coroner and a postmortem was ordered in 244 (37%) cases. A further 20 cases had a hospital postmortem performed. No cases were performed by non-pathologists, but one was undertaken by a haematologist.

The Postmortem Examination Report

Clinical history

A clinical history was provided in 83% of Coroner's PMs and 100% of the hospital cases. In 97% of cases the history was satisfactory or better, with only 3% deemed poor or totally inadequate.

Description of external appearances

Most reports had an adequate description of the external appearances with only five (4%) falling below an acceptable standard. Scars and incisions were measured in 85 (61%) cases.

Gross description of internal organs

The majority of descriptions of the internal organs were deemed satisfactory or better (89%). In 15 cases (11%) the gross description of the internal organs was thought to be poor or inadequate, or inappropriate to the clinical problem. In the majority of cases (87%), five or more organs were weighed (paired organs counting as one). In eight cases (6%) the skull and brain were not examined. The operation site was described in 100/138 (72%) cases where it was applicable.

Description of the operation site

Table 3.39: Description of the operation site

Operation site described	Orthopaedic cases		Other cases		Total	
Yes	73	71%	27	73%	100	72%
No	30	29%	8	22%	38	27%
Not applicable	0	-	2	5%	2	1%
Total	103		37		140	

The operation site was less frequently and adequately described in orthopaedic operations than in operations of other types. A high proportion of the postmortem cases were following orthopaedic operations, the majority of which were for fractured necks of femur. In many cases the pathological cause of the fracture was not commented upon and the method used by pathologists to assess bones for osteoporosis was unclear and inconsistent.

Postmortem histology

Seventeen cases (12%) had postmortem histology performed (13 (10%) of the Coroner's cases and four

(31%) of the hospital cases). In six further Coroner's cases and two hospital cases it was felt by the advisors that histology should have been taken. In only eight (five Coroner's and three hospital) of the 140 cases was a histology report included with the postmortem report. All of these eight reports were graded satisfactory or better. In the majority of the cases histology would have added little or nothing to the value of the postmortem and in only 14 cases was the absence of a histology report thought to detract from the value of the postmortem report.

Summary of lesions

A summary of the lesions was present in 38 (27%) cases, which in 92% (35/38) of cases corresponded with the text report. In the six hospital cases where a summary was included it was an accurate record of the findings of the PM.

Clinicopathological correlation and OPCS cause of death

A clinicopathological correlation was present in only 76 (54%) cases. Eleven percent of these were felt to be poor or inadequate. The majority of the reports (94%) included an OPCS cause of death but in 14% of cases this did not correspond to the text report and in 13% it did not follow OPCS formatting rules. The lack of a list of lesions was not thought by the advisors to be so detrimental to the quality of the report as a lack of a clinicopathological correlation or a well formulated OPCS cause of death.

Table 3.40: Cases where OPCS cause of death given

OPCS cause of death	1997/98		1996/97	1994/95	1993/94*	1992/93
Yes	131	94%	94%	96%	91%	82%
No	9	6%	6%	4%	9%	18%
Total	140					

** The 1993/94 report did not specifically mention an OPCS cause of death but asked "Is a certified cause of death present?"*

In only 64/140 (46%) cases was the operation mentioned in the OPCS cause of death (Table 3.41). Even when death occured within the first week following operation, only 38/85 (45%) pathologists mentioned the operative procedure in the cause of death.

Table 3.41: Record of operation in OPCS cause of death

Day of death	Number of cases		Operation in OPCS cause of death	
Day of operation	15	11%	9	60%
Day 1-7	70	50%	29	41%
Day 8-30	55	39%	26	47%
Total	140		64	46%

Overall score for postmortem examinations

Table 3.42: Quality of postmortem examinations

Quality of postmortem	1997/98		1996/97	1994/95	1993/94	1992/93	1991/92	1990
Unacceptable, laying the pathologist open to serious professional criticism	4	3%	2%	2%	2%	3%	4%	5%
Poor	23	16%	11%	10%	13%	25%	13%	19%
Satisfactory	59	42%	36%	43%	41%	43%	66%*	56%**
Good	44	31%	37%	41%	39%	25%	66%*	56%**
Excellent, meeting all standards set by RCPath guidelines	10	7%	13%	4%	5%	4%	17%	20%
Total	140							

** the 1991/92 report grouped good and satisfactory.*

*** the 1990 report had a grouping of adequate/satisfactory. Good was not a grouping.*

Table 3.43: History, antemortem clinical diagnosis and cause of death compared with postmortem findings (140 cases; answers may be multiple)			
Postmortem findings	Coroner's	Hospital	Total
A discrepancy in the cause of death or in a major diagnosis which, if known, might have affected treatment, outcome or prognosis	5	0	5
A discrepancy in the cause of death or in a major diagnosis which, if known, would probably not have affected treatment, outcome or prognosis	15	1	16
A minor discrepancy	1	0	1
Confirmation of essential clinical findings	99	9	108
An interesting incidental finding	12	0	12
A failure to explain some important aspect of the clinical problem, as a result of a satisfactory autopsy	8	2	10
A failure to explain some important aspect of the clinical problem, as a result of an unsatisfactory autopsy	14	3	17

Table 3.42 shows that only four (3%) of the 1997/8 reports were thought to be of a very low standard, often because of their brevity and lack of correlation with the clinical history. Twenty-three (16%) of the cases had a poor report. One hundred and thirteen (81%) were graded satisfactory or better.

Table 3.43 shows that the detection of unexpected findings at postmortem reiterates the findings of previous years with 21 cases (15%) where a major discrepancy between clinical diagnosis and postmortem examination was found and a further 13 cases (9%) where a minor discrepancy or interesting incidental finding was found. In 27 (19%) cases there was a failure to explain some important aspect of the case, but in ten of these the autopsy was felt to have been conducted satisfactorily.

It was not known whether the full medical records were available to the pathologist at the time of postmortem but is was thought by the advisors that this might improve the clinicopathological correlation, particularly in the more complex cases.

Attendance of the surgical team at the postmortem

An analysis of all 264 questionnaires indicating that a postmortem had taken place showed that only 53 (20%) surgical teams reported that they had been informed of the time and place of the postmortem. Only 14 clinicians indicated attendance at the postmortem. Lack of attendance was mainly due to unavailability of the surgeon or other commitments (47%) or a feeling that nothing was to be gained from the PM as the diagnosis was already known (8%).

Communication of the postmortem result to the surgical team

Table 3.44: Communication of postmortem results to the clinical team							
Communication of PM results	1997/98		1996/97	1994/95	1993/94	1992/93	1990
Yes	191	72%	76%	36%	36%	79%	78%
Informal report/verbal message	10	4%	7%	N/A	N/A	N/A	N/A
No	51	19%	15%	52%	55%	18%	19%
Not answered	11						
Not known	1						
Total	264						

N/A denotes information not available. No information available for 1991/92 or 1995/96.

Days after patient's death	Coroner's		Hospital		Total	
Less than 8 days	51	29%	5	42%	56	29%
8 days to 30 days	33	19%	2	17%	35	18%
31 days to 60 days	11	6%	0	–	11	6%
More than 60 days	12	7%	1	8%	13	7%
Not answered	72		4		76	
Total	179		12		191	

Table 3.45: Time taken for first information to be received by clinical team

In 51 (19%) cases the postmortem result was not communicated to the surgeons (Table 3.44). The majority of those who answered the question (91/115) indicated that the reports were received within one calendar month (Table 3.45). The pathological information was thought by the surgeons to confirm the clinical impression in 201 cases. This data is comparable to previous years.

CAUSE OF DEATH ASSIGNED BY PATHOLOGIST

Table 3.46: Cause of death assigned by pathologist

Cause of death	Number
Cardiovascular disease	62
Pulmonary embolism	7
Pneumonia (excluding aspiration)	39
Aspiration pneumonia	6
Cerebrovascular disease	1
Malignant disease (as cause of death)	3
Gastrointestinal disease	16
Sepsis	2
Other, including old age	4
Total	140

The majority of deaths were due to cardiovascular disease (62) and infective pneumonias (39) which together made up 72% of the causes of death. Pulmonary embolism was uncommon and caused only seven deaths (5%). Two of these were in cases with malignant disease (carcinoma of the colon), three followed procedures for fractured neck of femur, one had a vascular bypass operation and one an amputation for a septic fracture of the arm. Malignant disease was the direct cause of death in only three cases, but was a contributory factor in another seven (Table 3.47). Death was attributed primarily to old age in only two cases, and in one case the term "senile degeneration of the heart" was recorded which was regarded by the advisors as outdated. Only one patient died from a stroke and one was thought to have died from obstructive airways disease.

Table 3.47: Malignant disease as direct or contributory cause of death

Tumour type	Cause of death	Reason for surgery
Carcinoma of ovary	Direct	Large bowel obstruction
Carcinoma of bladder	Direct	Fractured neck of femur
Carcinoma of prostate	Direct	Pathological fractured neck of femur
Carcinoma of stomach	Contributory	Bleeding malignant ulcer
Carcinoma of lung	Contributory	Fractured neck of femur
Carcinoma of lung	Contributory	Fractured neck of femur
Carcinoma of colon	Contributory	Obstructed hernia
Carcinoma of prostate	Contributory	Fractured neck of femur
Carcinoma of colon	Contributory	Large bowel obstruction
Chronic lymphatic leukaemia	Contributory	Fractured neck of femur

GASTROINTESTINAL COMPLICATIONS

Table 3.48: Gastrointestinal complications in patients undergoing orthopaedic procedures

Orthopaedic condition	OPCS cause of death (1)	Contributory cause of death	Clinical suspicion of GI complication
Fractured neck of femur	Perforated duodenal ulcer	-	Suspected
Fractured neck of femur	Intestinal infarction	-	Suspected
Fractured neck of femur	Perforated diverticular disease	-	Suspected
Fractured neck of femur	Perforated duodenal ulcer	-	Suspected
Fractured humerus	Perforated diverticulitis	-	Suspected
Fractured femur/amputation	Infective colitis	-	Suspected
Fractured neck of femur	Bleeding diverticular disease of colon	-	Suspected
Fractured neck of femur	Ischaemic colitis	-	Suspected
Fractured neck of femur	Pseudomembranous colitis	-	Suspected
Fractured neck of femur	Ischaemic heart disease	Perforated sigmoid diverticulitis	Suspected
Fractured neck of femur	Ischaemic heart disease	Bleeding duodenal ulcer	Suspected
Fractured neck of femur	Aspiration pneumonia	Small bowel volvulus	Suspected
Fractured ankle	Perforated duodenal ulcer	-	Unsuspected
Fractured neck of femur	Perforated diverticulitis	-	Unsuspected
Fractured neck of femur	Perforated oesophageal ulcer	-	Unsuspected
Fractured neck of femur	Pneumonia	Pancreatitis	Unsuspected
Fractured neck of femur	Ischaemic heart disease	Peritonitis due to jejunal diverticulitis	Unsuspected
Fractured neck of femur	Aspiration pneumonia	Perforated pseudomembranous colitis	Unsuspected
Fractured neck of femur	Bronchopneumonia	Perforated duodenal ulcer	Unsuspected
Fractured neck of femur	Old age	Antibiotic associated colitis	Unsuspected

Forty patients had operations for gastrointestinal disease, or had gastrointestinal complications postoperatively, causing or contributing to death. Twenty of these operations were orthopaedic procedures and in eight of these the complications were clinically unsuspected. In three cases these were the direct cause of death as indicated in the pathologist's report (Table 3.48).

COMMENT

The Royal College of Pathologists' guidelines[31] are in general being followed, with most postmortem reports being of a good standard. A clinicopathological correlation, however, was not present in almost half of the cases studied.

OPCS formatting rules for cause of death are not always followed and causes of death given in parts 1a, 1b and 1c are sometimes not appropriately related. The recent operation is frequently omitted from the OPCS cause of death. It should be given as part of the cause of death in most cases, usually under 2 (contributory cause not directly causing death). An update of the Royal College of Pathologists' postmortem guidelines with specific attention to OPCS rules may help address this in the future.

The examination of the locomotor system by pathologists is not as well performed as examination of other organ systems. The site of fracture is not always adequately examined and there is no agreed method of assessing osteoporosis.

Histology would often add little information in the types of case covered by this sample. However, histology should be performed in cases of pathological fracture thought to be due to neoplastic disease.

Very few postmortem examinations are attended by the surgical team, but the majority of clinicians are informed of the cause of death in a timely manner.

Pulmonary embolism appears to be an infrequent cause of death, with cardiovascular disease being the most common cause of death assigned by pathologists in this age group.

'Senile degeneration of the heart' is not an acceptable cause of death, whereas 'old age', when there are no other findings, is at least honest and may well be appropriate in this age group when no other cause is found.

Gastrointestinal complications are a common cause, or contribute to the cause, of death after operations in the elderly. Many of these are unsuspected clinically, particularly after orthopaedic procedures.

References

1 *The new NHS Modern Dependable.* Cm 3807. Department of Health, 1997.

2 *A First Class Service: Quality in the new NHS.* Department of Health, 1998.

3 *Clinical Governance: Quality in the new NHS.* NHS Executive, 1999.

4 *For the Record.* HSC, 1998/1999.

5 Campling EA, Devlin HB, Hoile RW, Lunn JN. *The Report of the National Confidential Enquiry into Perioperative Deaths 1990.* London, 1992

6 Campling EA, Devlin HB, Hoile RW, Lunn JN. *The Report of the National Confidential Enquiry into Perioperative Deaths 1991/1992.* London, 1993.

7 Campling EA, Devlin HB, Hoile RW, Lunn JN. *The Report of the National Confidential Enquiry into Perioperative Deaths 1992/1993.* London, 1995.

8 *The Report of the National Confidential Enquiry into Perioperative Deaths 1993/1994.* NCEPOD. London, 1996.

9 Gallimore SC, Hoile RW, Ingram GS, Sherry KM. *The Report of the National Confidential Enquiry into Perioperative Deaths 1994/1995.* London, 1997.

10 Campling EA, Devlin HB, Lunn JN. *The Report of the National Confidential Enquiry into Perioperative Deaths 1989.* London, 1990.

11 *1993/1994 Paediatric Surgery Data.* Comparative Audit Service, Royal College of Surgeons of England. London, 1995.

12 *1994/1995 Paediatric Surgery Data.* Comparative Audit Service, Royal College of Surgeons of England. London, 1996.

13 *1997/1998 Analyses of Neonatal Surgical & Laparoscopic Registers.* Comparative Audit Service, Royal College of Surgeons of England. London, 1998.

14 *Hospital Services for Children and Young People.* House of Commons, Health Committee 5th Report. HMSO. London, 1997.

15 *The provision of general surgical services for children.* The Senate of Surgery of Great Britain and Ireland. London, 1998.

16 Rennie JM. *Neonatal intensive care: perinatal mortality and morbidity.* In: Paediatric Surgery and Urology: Long Term Outcomes. Eds. Stringer MD, Oldham KT, De Mouriquand P and Howard ER. WB Saunders. London, 1998.

17 *Confidential Enquiry into Stillbirths and Deaths in Infancy 3rd Annual Report.* Department of Health. London, 1996.

18 *Standards for paediatric intensive care including standards for the transportation of the critically ill child.* Paediatric Intensive Care Society. Bishop's Stortford, 1996.

19 *Children's Surgical Services.* Royal College of Paediatrics and Child Health. London, 1996.

20 *The Surgeon's Duty of Care.* The Senate of Surgery of Great Britain and Ireland. London, 1997.

21 *Specialist Training in Anaesthesia, Supervision and Assessment.* Royal College of Anaesthetists. London, 1994.

22 *Paediatric intensive care: a framework for the future.* National Coordinating Group on Paediatric Intensive Care, Department of Health. London, 1997.

23 *Maintaining good medical practice.* General Medical Council. London, 1998.

24 *Guidelines for the Provision of Anaesthetic Services.* Royal College of Anaesthetists. London, 1999.

25 *Safe Paediatric Neurosurgery.* Society of British Neurological Surgeons. London, 1998.

26 *Advanced Paediatric Life Support.* 2nd Edition. Advanced Life Support Group, BMJ. London, 1997.

27 *British Paediatric Surveillance Unit, 11th Annual Report.* Royal College of Paediatrics and Child Health. London, 1997.

28 *Ouch! Sort it out.* Royal College of Nursing. London, 1999.

29 *Withholding or Withdrawing Life Saving Treatment in Children.* A Framework for Practice. Royal College of Paediatrics and Child Health. London, 1997.

30 *The Allitt Inquiry.* HMSO. London, 1994.

31 *Guidelines for Postmortem Reports.* The Royal College of Pathologists. London, 1993.

32 *The Confidential Enquiry into Stillbirths and Deaths in Infancy, 5th Annual Report.* Maternal and Child Health Research Consortium. London, 1998.

33 Bisset R. *Magnetic resonance imaging may be an alternative to necropsy.* BMJ 1998; **317**:145.

34 Brokes JAS, Hall-Craggs MA, Sams VR, Lees WR. *Non-invasive perinatal necropsy by MRI.* Lancet 1996; **348**:1139-41.

35 Mortality statistics. Courtesy of Government Actuaries Department, 1999.

36 *Information and Consent for Anaesthesia.* Association of Anaesthetists of Great Britain and Ireland. London, 1999.

37 *Good Practice: A Guide for Departments of Anaesthesia.* Royal College of Anaesthetists and Association of Anaesthetists of Great Britain and Ireland. London, 1998.

38 Gray AJG, Hoile RW, Ingram GS, Sherry KM. *Report of the National Confidential Enquiry into Perioperative Deaths 1996/97.* London, 1998.

39 *The Quality Framework.* EL (97) 25. NHS Executive, 1997.

40 Royal College of Anaesthetists database. Courtesy of Dr W R MacRae, 1999.

41 *Guidance for the Appointment of Staff Grade, Associate Specialist and Hospital Practitioner Grade Anaesthetists.* Royal College of Anaesthetists. London, 1998.

42 *Clinical guidelines for the use of non-steroidal anti-inflammatory drugs in the perioperative period.* Royal College of Anaesthetists. London, 1998.

43 Campling EA, Devlin HB, Hoile RW, Ingram GS, Lunn JN. *Who Operates When?* A report by the National Confidential Enquiry into Perioperative Deaths. London, 1997.

44 *Report of the Working Party on Consultant Responsibility in Invasive Surgical Procedures.* Royal College of Surgeons of England. London, 1990

45 Hospital Episode Statistics, 1997-98 (ungrossed data). Department of Health, 1999.

46 Buck N, Devlin HB, Lunn JN. *The Report of a Confidential Enquiry into Perioperative Deaths.* London, 1987.

47 *Provision of Acute General Hospital Services - Consultation Document.* Joint Working Party of the British Medical Association, the Royal College of Physicians of London and the Royal College of Surgeons of England. London, 1998.

48 *The Management of Skeletal Trauma in the United Kingdom.* British Orthopaedic Association. London, 1992.

49 Sevitt S, Gallagher N. *Venous thrombosis and pulmonary embolism: a clinico-pathological study in injured and burned patients.* Br J Surg 1961; **48**:475-489.

50 Handoll HHG, Farrar MJ, McBirnie J, Tytherleigh-Strong G, Awai KA, Milne AA, Gillespie WJ. *Prophylaxis using heparin, low molecular weight heparin and physical methods against deep vein thrombosis and pulmonary embolism in hip fracture surgery.* Cochrane Database of Systematic Reviews, Update Software. Oxford, 1997.

51 Montrey JS, Kistner RL, Kong AYT, Lindberg RF, Mayfield GW, Jones DA, Mitsunaga MM. *Thromboembolism following hip fracture.* J Trauma 1985; **25**:534-537.

52 Parker MJ, Pryor GA. *Hip Fracture Management.* Blackwell Scientific Publications. Oxford, 1993.

53 Rørbæk-Madsen M, Jakobsen BW, Pedersen J, Sorensen B. *Dihydroergotamine and the thromboprophylactic effect of dextran 70 in emergency hip surgery.* Br J Surg 1988; **75**:364-365.

54 Jørgensen LN, Wille-Jørgensen P, Hauch O. *Prophylaxis of postoperative thromboembolism with low molecular weight heparins.* Br J Surg 1993; **80**:689-704.

55 Clagett GP, Anderson FA, Heit J, Levine MN, Wheeler HB. *Prevention of venous thromboembolism.* 4th ACCP Consensus Conference on Antithrombotic Therapy 1995; **108**:312s-334s.

56 *Management of elderly people with fractured hip.* Scottish Intercollegiate Guidelines Network (SIGN). No. 15, 1997.

57 Thromboembolic risk factors (THRIFT) consensus group. *Risk and prophylaxis for venous thrombosis in hospital patients.* Br Med J 1992; **305**:567-574.

58 Copeland GP, Jones D, Walters M. *POSSUM: a scoring system for surgical audit.* Br J Surg 1991; **78**:355-60.

59 Whiteley MS, Prytherch DR, Higgins B, Weaver PC, Prout WG. *An evaluation of the POSSUM surgical scoring system.* Br J Surg 1996; **83**:812-15.

60 Midwinter MJ, Tytherleigh M and Ashley S. *Estimation of mortality and morbidity risk in vascular surgery using POSSUM and the Portsmouth predictor equation.* Br J Surg 1999; **86**:471-474.

61 Wilson J, Woods I, Fawcett J, Whall R, Dibb W, Morris C, McManus E. *Reducing the risk of major elective surgery: randomised control trial of perioperative optimisation of oxygen delivery.* BMJ 1999; **318**:1099-1103.

62 *Guidelines for the management of colorectal cancer.* Royal College of Surgeons and the Association of Coloproctology of Great Britain and Ireland. London, 1996.

63 Pell J, Stonebridge P (on behalf of the Scottish Vascular Audit Group). *Association between age and survival following major amputation.* Eur J Vasc Eurovasc Surg 1999; **17**:166-169.

Appendix A - Glossary

Definition of the 1997/98 sample groups

Children: those aged less than 16 years, i.e. until the day preceding the 16th birthday, at the time of death.

The Elderly: those aged 90 years and over, i.e. from the day of the 90th birthday, at the time of death.

Admission category *(NCEPOD definitions)*

Elective: at a time agreed between the patient and the surgical service.

Urgent: within 48 hours of referral/consultation.

Emergency: immediately following referral/consultation, when admission is unpredictable and at short notice because of clinical need.

American Society of Anesthesiologists (ASA) classification of physical status

ASA 1: a normal healthy patient.

ASA 2: a patient with mild systemic disease.

ASA 3: a patient with severe systemic disease that limits activity but is not incapacitating.

ASA 4: a patient with incapacitating systemic disease that is a constant threat to life.

ASA 5: a moribund patient who is not expected to survive for 24 hours with or without an operation.

Classification of operation *(NCEPOD definitions)*

Emergency: Immediate life-saving operation, resuscitation simultaneous with surgical treatment (e.g. trauma, ruptured aortic aneurysm). Operation usually within one hour.

Urgent: Operation as soon as possible after resuscitation (e.g. irreducible hernia, intussusception, oesophageal atresia, intestinal obstruction, major fractures). Operation within 24 hours.

Scheduled: An early operation but not immediately life-saving (e.g. malignancy). Operation usually within three weeks.

Elective: Operation at a time to suit both patient and surgeon (e.g. cholecystectomy, joint replacement).

Recovery and special care areas *(Association of Anaesthetists of Great Britain and Ireland definitions)*

High dependency unit: A high dependency unit (HDU) is an area for patients who require more intensive observation, treatment and nursing care than can be provided on a general ward. It would not normally accept patients requiring mechanical ventilation, but could manage those receiving invasive monitoring.

Intensive care unit: An intensive care unit (ICU) is an area to which patients are admitted for treatment of actual or impending organ failure, especially when mechanical ventilation is necessary.

Recovery area: A recovery area is an area to which patients are admitted from an operating theatre, and where they remain until consciousness has been regained, respiration and circulation are stable and postoperative analgesia is established.

Appendix B - Abbreviations

A&E ... Accident & Emergency
AAA ... Abdominal aortic aneurysm
ACE ... Angiotensin-converting enzyme
AF ... Atrial fibrillation
AP ... Anteroposterior
APLS ... Advanced Paediatric Life Support
AQ ... Anaesthetic questionnaire
ARDS ... Adult respiratory distress syndrome
ASA ... American Society of Anesthesiologists
ATLS ... Advanced Trauma Life Support
BAPS ... British Association of Paediatric Surgeons
BK ... Below knee
BP ... Blood pressure
CCF ... Congestive cardiac failure
CCST ... Certificate of Completion of Specialist Training
CESDI ... Confidential Enquiry into Stillbirths and Deaths in Infancy
CHI ... Commission for Health Improvement
CPAP ... Continuous positive airway pressure
CT ... Computerised tomography
CVA ... Cerebrovascular accident
CVP ... Central venous pressure
DGH ... District general hospital
DIC ... Disseminated intravascular coagulopathy
DU ... Duodenal ulcer
DVT ... Deep vein thrombosis
ECG ... Electrocardiogram
ELBW ... Extremely low birthweight
ENT ... Ear nose and throat
ERCP ... Endoscopic retrograde cholangiopancreatography
EUA ... Examination under anaesthesia
GA ... General anaesthesia
GCS ... Glasgow coma score
GI ... Gastrointestinal
GIT ... Gastrointestinal tract
GP ... General practitioner
HDU ... High dependency unit
ICP ... Intracranial pressure
ICU ... Intensive care unit
IHD ... Ischaemic heart disease
IM ... Intramuscular
IMV ... Intermittent mandatory ventilation
IPPV ... Intermittent positive pressure ventilation
IV ... Intravenous
LA ... Local anaesthesia
LAS ... Locum appointment, service
LAT ... Locum appointment, training
LIF ... Left iliac fossa
LMA ... Laryngeal mask airway
LVF ... Left ventricular failure
MI ... Myocardial infarction
MRI ... Magnetic resonance imaging
NCCG ... Non-consultant career grade
NEC ... Necrotising enterocolitis
NG ... Nasogastric
NHS ... National Health Service
NICE ... National Institute for Clinical Excellence
NICU ... Neonatal intensive care unit
NSAID ... Non-steroidal anti-inflammatory drug
ODP ... Operating department practitioner
OGD ... Oesophagogastroduodenoscopy
OPCS ... Office of Population Censuses and Surveys
PCA ... Patient controlled analgesia
PD ... Peritoneal dialysis
PEG ... Percutaneous endoscopic gastrostomy
PEP ... Pulmonary embolism prevention
PICU ... Paediatric intensive care unit
PM ... Postmortem
POSSUM ... Physiological and operative severity score for enumeration of mortality and morbidity
P-POSSUM ... Portsmouth predictor equation
RCA ... Royal College of Anaesthetists
RTA ... Road traffic accident
SASM ... Scottish Audit of Surgical Mortality
SC ... Subcutaneous
SCBU ... Special care baby unit
SHO 1,2 ... Senior house officer, year 1 or 2
SpR 1,2,3,4 ... Specialist registrar, year 1, 2, 3 or 4
SQ ... Surgical questionnaire
TPN ... Total parenteral nutrition
TPR ... Temperature pulse and respiration
TURBT ... Transurethral resection of bladder tumour
TURP ... Transurethral resection of prostate
VLBW ... Very low birthweight
WCC ... White cell count

Appendix C - NCEPOD Corporate structure

The National Confidential Enquiry into Perioperative Deaths (NCEPOD) is an independent body to which a corporate commitment has been made by the Associations, Colleges and Faculties related to its areas of activity. Each of these bodies nominates members of the Steering Group.

Steering Group

(as at 1 October 1999)

Chairman
Mr John Ll Williams

Members

Mrs M Beck	*(Royal College of Ophthalmologists)*
Dr J F Dyet	*(Royal College of Radiologists)*
Dr H H Gray	*(Royal College of Physicians of London)*
Dr P Kishore	*(Faculty of Public Health Medicine)*
Mr G T Layer	*(Association of Surgeons of Great Britain and Ireland)*
Professor V J Lund	*(Royal College of Surgeons of England)*
Dr J M Millar	*(Royal College of Anaesthetists)*
Dr A J Mortimer	*(Royal College of Anaesthetists)*
Mr J H Shepherd	*(Royal College of Obstetricians and Gynaecologists)*
Dr P J Simpson	*(Royal College of Anaesthetists)*
Mr M F Sullivan	*(Royal College of Surgeons of England)*
Professor P G Toner	*(Royal College of Pathologists)*
Professor T Treasure	*(Royal College of Surgeons of England)*
Dr D J Wilkinson	*(Association of Anaesthetists of Great Britain and Ireland)*
Mr J Ll Williams	*(Faculty of Dental Surgery, Royal College of Surgeons of England)*

Observers

Dr V Chishty	*(Department of Health - England)*
Mr R Jones	*(Institute of Health Services Management)*
Dr P A Knapman	*(Coroners' Society of England and Wales)*

NCEPOD is a company limited by guarantee, and a registered charity, managed by Trustees.

Trustees

Chairman	Mr J Ll Williams
Treasurer	Dr J N Lunn Dr J Lumley Mr M F Sullivan

Clinical Coordinators

The Steering Group appoint the Principal Clinical Coordinators for a defined tenure. The Principal Clinical Coordinators lead the review of the data relating to the annual sample, advise the Steering Group and write the reports. They may also from time to time appoint Clinical Coordinators, who must be engaged in active academic/clinical practice (in the NHS) during the full term of office.

Principal Clinical Coordinators

Anaesthesia	Dr G S Ingram
Surgery	Mr R W Hoile

Clinical Coordinators

Anaesthesia	Dr A J G Gray Dr K M Sherry
Surgery	Mr K G Callum Mr I C Martin

Funding

The total annual cost of NCEPOD is approximately £500,000 (1998/99). We are pleased to acknowledge the support of the following, who contributed to funding the Enquiry in 1998/99.

Department of Health (England)
Welsh Office
Health and Social Services Executive (Northern Ireland)
States of Guernsey Board of Health
States of Jersey
Department of Health and Social Security, Isle of Man Government
BMI Healthcare
BUPA
Community Hospitals Group
Nuffield Hospitals
PPP/Columbia
Benenden Hospital
King Edward VII Hospital, Midhurst
St Martin's Hospitals
The Heart Hospital
The London Clinic

This funding covers the total cost of the Enquiry, including administrative salaries and reimbursements for Clinical Coordinators, office accommodation charges, computer and other equipment as well as travelling and other expenses for the Coordinators, Steering Group and advisory groups.

Appendix D - Data collection and review methods

The National Confidential Enquiry into Perioperative Deaths (NCEPOD) reviews clinical practice and aims to identify remediable factors in the practice of anaesthesia, all types of surgery and other invasive procedures. The Enquiry considers the quality of the delivery of care and not specifically causation of death. The commentary in the reports is based on peer review of the data, questionnaires and notes submitted; it is not a research study based on differences against a control population, and does not attempt to produce any kind of comparison between clinicians or hospitals.

Scope

All National Health Service and Defence Secondary Care Agency hospitals in England, Wales and Northern Ireland, and public hospitals in Guernsey, Jersey and the Isle of Man are included in the Enquiry, as well as many hospitals in the independent healthcare sector.

Reporting of deaths

NCEPOD collects basic details on all deaths in hospital within 30 days of a surgical procedure, through a system of local reporting. The Local Reporters (Appendix E) in each hospital are often consultant clinicians, but this role is increasingly being taken on by information and clinical audit departments who are able to provide the data from hospital information systems. When incomplete information is received, the NCEPOD administrative staff contact the appropriate medical records or information officer, secretarial or clinical audit staff.

Deaths of patients in hospital within 30 days of a surgical procedure (excluding maternal deaths) are included. If Local Reporters are aware of postoperative deaths at home they also report them. A surgical procedure is defined by NCEPOD as:

"any procedure carried out by a surgeon or gynaecologist, with or without an anaesthetist, involving local, regional or general anaesthesia or sedation".

Local Reporters provide the following information:

- Name of Trust/hospital
- Sex/hospital number/NHS number of patient
- Name of hospital in which the death occurred (and hospital where surgery took place, if different)
- Dates of birth, final operation and death
- Surgical procedure performed
- Name of consultant surgeon
- Name of anaesthetist

Sample for more detailed review

The data collection year runs from 1 April to 31 March. Each year, a sample of the reported deaths is reviewed in more detail. The sample selection varies for each data collection year, and is determined by the NCEPOD Steering Group (see Appendix C).

NCEPOD may, on occasion, collect data about patients who have survived more than 30 days after a procedure. These data are used for comparison with the data about deaths, or to review a specific aspect of clinical practice. Data from other sources may also be used.

The perioperative deaths which fell within the sample groups for 1997/98 were those where the patient was aged under 16 years, or 90 years and over, at the time of death.

For each sample case, questionnaires were sent to the consultant surgeon or gynaecologist and consultant anaesthetist. These questionnaires were identified only by a number, allocated in the NCEPOD office. Copies of operation notes, anaesthetic records, fluid balance charts and postmortem reports were also requested. Surgical questionnaires were sent directly to the consultant surgeon or gynaecologist under whose care the patient was at the time of the final operation before death. When the Local Reporter had been able to identify the relevant consultant anaesthetist, the anaesthetic questionnaire was sent directly to him or her. However, in many cases this was not possible, and the local tutor of the Royal College of Anaesthetists was asked to name a consultant to whom the questionnaire should be sent. Copies of the questionnaires used in 1997/98 are available from the NCEPOD office on request.

Consultants

NCEPOD holds a database, regularly updated, of all consultant anaesthetists, gynaecologists and surgeons in England, Wales and Northern Ireland.

Analysis and review of data

The NCEPOD administrative staff manage the collection, recording and analysis of data. The data are aggregated to produce the tables and information in the reports; further unpublished aggregated data is available from the NCEPOD office on request. All data are aggregated to regional or national level only, so that individual Trusts and hospitals cannot be identified.

Advisory groups

The NCEPOD Clinical Coordinators (see Appendix C), together with the advisory groups for anaesthesia and surgery, review the completed questionnaires and the aggregated data. The members of the advisory groups are drawn from hospitals in England, Wales and Northern Ireland. The advisory group in pathology reviews postmortem data from the surgical questionnaires as well as copies of postmortem reports.

Production of the report

The advisory groups comment on the overall quality of care within their specialty and on any particular issues or individual cases which merit attention. These comments form the basis for the published report, which is prepared by the Coordinators, with contributions from the advisors. The report is reviewed and agreed by the NCEPOD Steering Group prior to publication.

Confidentiality

NCEPOD is registered with the Data Protection Registrar and abides by the Data Protection Principles. All reporting forms, questionnaires and other paper records relating to the sample are shredded once an individual report is ready for publication. Similarly, all patient-identifiable data are removed from the computer database.

Before review of questionnaires by the Clinical Coordinators or any of the advisors, all identification is removed from the questionnaires and accompanying papers. The source of the information is not revealed to any of the Coordinators or advisors.

Appendix E - Local Reporters

The following list shows Local Reporters as at 1 October 1999, with NHS Trusts listed according to regional divisions in place at that date. It should be noted that regional boundaries have changed since the 1997/98 data collection period described in this Report.

We appreciate that there are many clinical audit and information departments involved in providing data, although we have in many cases named only the consultant clinician nominated as the Local Reporter.

Eastern

Addenbrooke's .... Dr D. Wight

Basildon & Thurrock General Hospitals .... Dr S.G. Subbuswamy

Bedford Hospital .... Mrs S. Blackley

East Hertfordshire .... Dr A. Fattah

Essex Rivers Healthcare .... Mrs A. Bryan

Hinchingbrooke Health Care .... Dr M.D. Harris

Ipswich Hospital .... Mr I. Lennox

James Paget Hospital .... Dr M.J. Wilkinson

King's Lynn & Wisbech Hospitals .... Miss J.M. Rippon

Luton & Dunstable Hospital .... Dr D.A.S. Lawrence

Mid-Essex Hospital Services .... Mr A.H.M. Ross *(Broomfield Hospital)*; Dr S.G. Subbuswamy *(St Andrew's Centre)*

Mount Vernon & Watford Hospitals .... Dr R. Smith

Norfolk & Norwich Health Care .... Dr A.J.G. Gray

North Hertfordshire .... Dr D.J. Madders

Papworth Hospital .... Dr M. Goddard

Peterborough Hospitals .... Dr P.M. Dennis

Southend Hospital .... Ms W. Davis

St Albans & Hemel Hempstead .... Dr A.P. O'Reilly

The Princess Alexandra Hospital .... Dr R.G.M. Letcher

West Suffolk Hospitals .... Mrs V. Hamilton

London

Barnet and Chase Farm Hospitals .... Dr J. El-Jabbour *(Edgware General Hospital & Barnet General Hospital)*; Dr W.H.S. Mohamid *(Chase Farm Hospital)*

Bart's and The London .... Dr D.J. Wilkinson *(St Bartholomew's Hospital)*; Dr K. Wark *(London Chest Hospital)*; Dr P.J. Flynn *(The Royal London Hospital)*

Bromley Hospitals .... Dr A. Martin

Chelsea & Westminster Healthcare .... Ms J. Tranter

Ealing Hospital .... Dr C. Schmulian

Epsom and St Helier .... Dr D.M. Thomas *(Epsom General Hospital)*; Dr E.H. Rang *(St Helier Hospital)*

Forest Healthcare .... Dr K.M. Thomas

Greenwich Healthcare .... Mr S. Asher

Guy's & St Thomas' Hospital .... Dr. B. Hartley *(Guy's Hospital)*; Mr W. Owen *(St Thomas' Hospital)*

Hammersmith Hospitals .... Professor G.W.H. Stamp

Havering Hospitals .... Ms C. Nicholls

Hillingdon Hospital .... Dr F.G. Barker

Kings Healthcare .... Ms L. Cregan

Kingston Hospital .... Mr P.D. Willson

Mayday Health Care .... Mr C. Fernandez

Moorfields Eye Hospital .... Professor P. Luthert

Newham Healthcare .... Dr C. Grunwald

North Middlesex Hospital .... Dr K.J. Jarvis

North West London Hospitals .... Dr G. Williams
(Northwick Park Hospital & St Mark's Hospital)
Dr C.A. Amerasinghe
(Central Middlesex Hospital)

Queen Mary's Sidcup .... Dr E.J.A. Aps

Redbridge Health Care .... Dr P. Tanner

Royal Brompton & Harefield .... Professor D. Denison
(Royal Brompton Hospital)
Mr J. Thomas
(Harefield Hospital)

Royal Free Hampstead .... Dr J.E. McLaughlin

Royal Marsden .... Dr J. Williams

Royal National Orthopaedic Hospital .... Ms J. Lapidge

St George's Healthcare .... Dr C.M. Corbishley

St Mary's .... Ms R.A. Hittinger

The Great Ormond Street Hospital for Children .... Dr A. Mackersie

The Homerton Hospital .... Ms B. Davies

The Lewisham Hospital .... Dr G. Phillip

University College London Hospitals .... Ms A.E. Glover
(Middlesex Hospital & University College Hospital)
Mrs J.A. Sullivan
(The National Hospital for Neurology & Neurosurgery)

West Middlesex University Hospital .... Dr R.G. Hughes

Whittington Hospital .... Dr S. Ramachandra

North West

Aintree Hospitals .... Dr W. Taylor

Blackburn, Hyndburn & Ribble Valley Healthcare .... Mr R.W. Nicholson

Blackpool Victoria Hospital .... Dr K.S. Vasudev

Bolton Hospitals .... Dr S. Wells

Burnley Health Care .... Mr D.G.D. Sandilands

Bury Health Care .... Dr E. Herd

Central Manchester Healthcare .... Dr E.W. Benbow

Chorley & South Ribble .... Dr M. Calleja

Christie Hospital .... Miss S.T. O'Dwyer

Countess of Chester Hospital .... Dr P.R.M. Steele

East Cheshire .... Dr A.R. Williams

Halton General Hospital .... Dr K. Strahan

Liverpool Women's Hospital .... Ms C. Fox

Manchester Children's Hospitals .... Dr M. Newbould

Mid Cheshire Hospitals .... Miss H. Moulton

Morecambe Bay Hospitals .... Dr R.W. Blewitt
(Royal Lancaster Infirmary)
Dr V.M. Joglekar
(Furness General Hospital)

North Manchester Health Care .... No named reporter

Oldham .... Dr M.W. Atkinson

Preston Acute Hospitals .... Dr C.M. Nicholson

Rochdale Healthcare .... Dr M. Bradgate

Royal Liverpool & Broadgreen University Hospitals .... Mr I.B. McColl

Salford Royal Hospitals .... Mrs E. Craddock

South Manchester University Hospitals .... Dr J. Coyne
(Withington Hospital)
Dr P.S. Hasleton
(Wythenshawe Hospital)

Southport and Ormskirk Hospitals .... Mr A.D. Johnson
(Ormskirk & District General Hospital)
Dr S.A.C. Dundas
(Southport & Formby District General Hospital)

St Helens & Knowsley Hospitals .... Ms G. Moses

Stockport Acute Services .... Dr P. Meadows

Tameside Acute Care .... Dr A.J. Yates

The Cardiothoracic Centre Liverpool .... Mr M. Jackson

The Royal Liverpool Children's .... Mrs P.A. McCormack

Trafford Healthcare .... Dr B.N.A. Hamid

Walton Centre for Neurology & Neurosurgery .... Dr J. Broome

Warrington Hospital .... Dr M.S. Al-Jafari

Wigan & Leigh Health Services .... Ms S. Tarbuck

Wirral Hospital .... Dr M.B. Gillett

Wrightington Hospital .... Mr A.D. Johnson

Northern & Yorkshire

Airedale .... Dr J.J. O'Dowd

Bradford Hospitals .... Dr C.A. Sides

Calderdale Healthcare .... Mr R.J.R. Goodall

Carlisle Hospitals .... Dr E.D. Long

City Hospitals Sunderland .... Miss K. Ramsey

Dewsbury Health Care .... Dr P. Gudgeon

East Yorkshire Community Healthcare .... Mr G. Britchford

East Yorkshire Hospitals .... Mr G. Britchford

Gateshead Health .... Dr A. McHutchon

Harrogate Healthcare .... Miss A.H. Lawson

Huddersfield .... Dr H.H. Ali

North Durham Healthcare .... Dr D. Wood

North Tees and Hartlepool .... Mr I.L. Rosenberg
(North Tees General Hospital)
Mrs A. Lister
(Hartlepool General Hospital)

Northallerton Health Services .... Dr D.C. Henderson

Northumbria Healthcare .... Dr F. Johri
(North Tyneside General Hospital)
Dr J.A. Henry
(Wansbeck General Hospital & Hexham General Hospital)

Pinderfields & Pontefract Hospitals .... Dr I.W.C. Macdonald

Royal Hull Hospitals .... Mr M. Whittle

Scarborough & North East Yorkshire Health Care .... Dr A.M. Jackson

South Durham Healthcare .... Ms C. Evans

South Tees Acute Hospitals .... Mrs L. Black

South Tyneside Healthcare .... Dr K.P. Pollard

The Leeds Teaching Hospitals .... Dr C. Abbott
(Leeds General Infirmary)
Mr S. Knight
(St James's University Hospital & Seacroft Hospital)

The Newcastle upon Tyne Hospitals .... Dr M.K. Bennett
(Freeman Hospital)
Miss D. Robson
(Royal Victoria Infirmary & Newcastle General Hospital)

West Cumbria Health Care .... Dr R.G. Ghazala

York Health Services .... Dr C. Bates

South East

Ashford & St Peter's Hospital .... Mr R.H. Moore
(St Peter's Hospital)
Dr J.C. Dawson
(Ashford Hospital)

Brighton Health Care .... Mr M. Renshaw

Dartford & Gravesham .... Dr A.T.M. Rashid

East Kent Hospitals .... Mrs B.M. Smith
(Queen Elizabeth the Queen Mother Hospital)
Dr C.W. Lawson
(Buckland Hospital & William Harvey Hospital)
Mr M. Guarino
(Kent & Canterbury Hospital)

Eastbourne Hospitals .... Mrs P. Jones

Frimley Park Hospitals .... Dr G.F. Goddard

Hastings & Rother .... Mr S. Ball

LIVERPOOL JOHN MOORES UNIVERSITY AVRIL ROBARTS LRC TEL. 0151 231 4022

Heatherwood &
Wexham Park Hospitals .... Dr M.H. Ali

Isle of Wight Healthcare .... Ms S. Wilson

Kent & Sussex Weald .... Dr G.A. Russell

Kettering General Hospital .... Dr B.E. Gostelow

Medway Maritime .... Mrs J.L. Smith

Mid Kent Healthcare .... Mr J. Vickers

Mid-Sussex .... Mr P.H. Walter
(Hurstwood Park Neurological Centre)
Dr P.A. Berresford
(Princess Royal Hospital)

Milton Keynes General .... Dr S.S. Jalloh

North Hampshire Hospitals .... Ms A. Timson

Northampton General Hospital .... Dr A.J. Molyneux

Nuffield Orthopaedic Centre .... Dr P. Millard

Oxford Radcliffe .... Dr P. Millard
(The Churchill Hospital,
The Radcliffe Infirmary &
The John Radcliffe Hospital)
Dr N.J. Mahy
(Horton Hospital)

Portsmouth Hospitals .... Dr N.J.E. Marley

Royal Berkshire &
Battle Hospitals .... Dr R. Menai-Williams

Royal Surrey County Hospital .... Mrs G. Willner

South Buckinghamshire .... Dr M.J. Turner

Southampton University Hospitals .... Dr A. Bateman

Stoke Mandeville Hospital .... Dr A.F. Padel

Surrey & Sussex Healthcare .... Ms C. Parkinson
(East Surrey Hospital)
Dr C. Moon
(Crawley Hospital)

The Queen Victoria Hospital .... Mrs D.M. Helme

The Royal West Sussex .... Mr J.N.L. Simson

Winchester & Eastleigh Healthcare .... Dr R.K. Al-Talib

Worthing & Southlands Hospitals .... Mrs J. Tofield

South West

Dorset Community .... Dr A. Anscombe

East Gloucestershire .... Dr W.J. Brampton

East Somerset .... Dr J.P. Sheffield

Gloucestershire Royal .... Dr B.W. Codling

North Bristol .... Ms A. Griffiths
(Southmead Hospital)
Dr N.B.N. Ibrahim
(Frenchay Hospital)

Northern Devon Healthcare .... Dr J. Davies

Plymouth Hospitals .... Dr C.B.A. Lyons

Poole Hospital .... Dr D.S. Nicholas

Royal Bournemouth &
Christchurch Hospitals .... Mr E. Robbin

Royal Cornwall Hospitals .... Mr R. Johnson

Royal Devon &
Exeter Healthcare .... Dr R.H.W. Simpson

Royal United Hospital Bath .... Ms L. Hobbs

Salisbury Health Care .... Dr C.E. Fuller

South Devon Healthcare .... Dr D.W. Day

Swindon & Marlborough .... Mr M.H. Galea

Taunton & Somerset .... Dr B. Browne

United Bristol Healthcare .... Mr J. Murdoch
(St Michael's Hospital)
Dr E.A. Sheffield
(Bristol Royal Infirmary)
Dr M. Ashworth
(Bristol Royal Hospital for Sick Children)
Mr S. Cook
(Bristol Eye Hospital)

West Dorset General Hospitals .... Dr A. Anscombe

Weston Area Health .... Dr M.F. Lott

Trent

Barnsley District
General Hospital .... Dr M.A. Longan

Bassetlaw Hospital &
Community Services .... Dr P.A. Parsons

Central Nottinghamshire Health Care .... Dr I. Ross

Central Sheffield University Hospitals .... Dr S. K. Suvarna

Chesterfield & North Derbyshire Royal Hospital .... Dr P.B. Gray

Doncaster Royal Infirmary & Montagu Hospital .... Dr G. Kesseler

Glenfield Hospital .... Mrs S. Clarke

Grantham & District Hospital .... Dr D. Clark

Leicester General Hospital .... Mr M.J.S. Dennis

Leicester Royal Infirmary .... Mr R. Mowbray

Lincoln & Louth . . . . .Mr E.O. Amaku
(Louth County Hospital)
Dr J.A. Harvey
(Lincoln County Hospital)

North East Lincolnshire .... Dr W.M. Peters

Northern General Hospital .... Dr S.K. Suvarna

Nottingham City Hospital .... Ms B. Egginton

Pilgrim Health .... Ms S. Cosgriff

Queen's Medical Centre Nottingham UniversityHospital .... Dr J.A. Jones

Rotherham General Hospitals .... Mr R.B. Jones

Scunthorpe & Goole Hospitals .... Dr C.M. Hunt

Sheffield Children's Hospital .... Dr I. Barker

Southern Derbyshire Acute Hospitals .... Mr J.R. Nash

The King's Mill Centre for Health Care Services .... Ms J. Jenkins

West Midlands

Alexandra Healthcare .... Dr L. Brown

Birmingham Children's Hospital .... Dr P. Ramani

Birmingham Heartlands & Solihull .... Dr M. Taylor

Birmingham Women's Healthcare .... Dr T. Rollason

Burton Hospitals .... Dr N. Kasthuri

George Eliot Hospital .... Dr J. Mercer

Good Hope Hospital .... Dr J. Hull

Hereford Hospitals .... Dr F. McGinty

Kidderminster Health Care .... Dr G. Kondratowicz

Mid Staffordshire General Hospitals .... Dr V. Suarez

North Staffordshire Hospital .... Dr T.A. French

Robert Jones & Agnes Hunt Orthopaedic Hospital .... Mrs C. McPherson

Royal Shrewsbury Hospitals .... Dr R.A. Fraser

Sandwell Healthcare .... Mrs I. Darnley

South Warwickshire General Hospitals .... Mr M. Gilbert

The City Hospital .... Dr S.Y. Chan

The Dudley Group of Hospitals .... Dr S. Ghosh

The Princess Royal Hospital .... Dr R.A. Fraser

The Royal Orthopaedic Hospital .... Mr A. Thomas

The Royal Wolverhampton Hospitals .... Dr J. Tomlinson

University Hospital Birmingham .... Professor E.L. Jones

Walsall Hospitals .... Dr Y.L. Hock

Walsgrave Hospitals .... Dr J. Macartney

Worcester Royal Infirmary .... Mr A. Singfield

Northern Ireland

Altnagelvin Hospitals .... Dr J.N. Hamilton

Armagh & Dungannon .... Mr B. Cranley

Belfast City Hospital .... Mrs A. McAfee

Causeway .... Dr C. Watters

Craigavon Area Hospital Group .... Mr B. Cranley

Down Lisburn . . . . .Mrs M. Gilgunn
(Downe Hospital)
Dr B. Huss
(Lagan Valley Hospital)

Green Park Healthcare .... Dr J.D. Connolly

Mater Hospital Belfast .... Dr P. Gormley

Newry & Mourne .... Mr B. Cranley

Royal Group of Hospitals & Dental Hospitals .... Ms M. Toner

Sperrin Lakeland .... Dr F. Robinson
(Tyrone County Hospital)
Dr W. Holmes
(Erne Hospital)

Ulster Community & Hospitals .... Dr T. Boyd

United Hospitals .... Mr I. Garstin
(Antrim Hospital)
Mr P.C. Pyper
(Mid-Ulster Hospital)
Mr D. Gilroy
(Whiteabbey Hospital)

Wales

Bro Morgannwg .... Dr A. Dawson
(Neath General Hospital)
Dr A.M. Rees
(Princess of Wales Hospital)

Carmarthenshire .... Dr L.A. Murray
(Prince Philip Hospital)
Dr R.B. Denholm
(West Wales General Hospital)

Ceredigion & Mid-Wales .... Mrs C. Smith

Conwy & Denbighshire .... Dr B. Rogers

Gwent Healthcare .... Ms R. Howell
(Royal Gwent Hospital & St Woolos Hospital)
Dr R.J. Kellett
(Nevill Hall Hospital)

North East Wales .... Dr R.B. Williams

North Glamorgan .... Mrs A. Shenkorov

North West Wales .... Dr M. Hughes

Pembrokeshire & Derwen .... Dr G.R. Melville Jones

Pontypridd & Rhondda .... Dr D. Stock

Swansea .... Dr S. Williams
(Singleton Hospital)
Dr A. Dawson
(Morriston Hospital)

University Hospital of Wales & Llandough .... Mrs M. Keenor
(Cardiff Royal Infirmary)
Dr R. Attanoos
(Llandough Hospital)
Dr A.G. Douglas-Jones
(University Hospital of Wales)

Defence Secondary Care Agency

The Royal Naval Hospital, Haslar .... Dr N. Carr

Guernsey / Isle of Man / Jersey

Guernsey .... Dr B.P. Gunton-Bunn

Isle of Man .... Ms E. Clark

Jersey .... Dr H. Goulding

BMI Healthcare
(from 1 April 1998)

Alexandra Hospital .... Mrs P. Enstone

Bath Clinic .... Mrs E.M. Jones

Beardwood Hospital .... Ms A. Walmsley

Beaumont Hospital .... Mrs C. Power

Bishops Wood Hospital .... Ms D. Dorken

Chatsworth Suite, Chesterfield & N Derbyshire .... Ms S. Darbyshire

Chelsfield Park Hospital .... Ms C. Poll

Clementine Churchill Hospital .... Ms S. Latham

Droitwich Spa Hospital .... Mrs P. Fryer

Esperance Private Hospital .... Ms S. Mulvey

Fawkham Manor Hospital .... Miss C. Stocker

Goring Hall Hospital .... Ms A. Bailey

Harbour Hospital .... Ms S. Prince

London Independent Hospital .... Ms J. Jones

Meriden Wing, Walsgrave Hospital .... Ms C. Ayton

Nuneaton Private Hospital .... Mrs A. Garner

Park Hospital .... Ms S. Quickmire

Princess Margaret Hospital .... Mrs J. Bevington
Ridgeway Hospital .... Mrs R. Butler
Sandringham Hospital .... Mr S. Harris
Sarum Road Hospital .... Ms Y.A. Stoneham
Saxon Clinic .... Ms V. Shiner
Shirley Oaks Hospital .... Ms S. White
The Blackheath Hospital .... Mrs C. Pagram
The Chaucer Hospital .... Mrs G. Mann
The Chiltern Hospital .... Ms J. Liggitt
The Garden Hospital .... Ms L. Sharp
The Hampshire Clinic .... Ms R. Phillips
The Highfield Hospital .... Ms P. Shields
The Manor Hospital .... Mrs S. Otter
The Paddocks Hospital .... Ms S. Hill
The Priory Hospital .... Dr A.G. Jacobs
The Runnymede Hospital .... Mrs P. Hill
The Sloane Hospital .... Mrs U. Palmer
The Somerfield Hospital .... Ms N. Poulson
The South Cheshire Private Hospital .... Mrs S. Hughes
The Thornbury Hospital .... Mrs J. Cooper
Werndale Private Hospital .... Ms A. Morgan
Winterbourne Hospital .... Ms S. Clark

BUPA

BUPA Alexandra Hospital .... Ms R. Stephens
BUPA Belvedere Hospital .... Mr S.J. Greatorex
BUPA Cambridge Lea Hospital .... Ms M. Vognsen
BUPA Chalybeate Hospital .... Ms M. Falconer
BUPA Dunedin Hospital .... Mrs C. Bude
BUPA Fylde Coast Hospital .... Mrs D. Hodgkins
BUPA Gatwick Park Hospital .... Mrs D. Wright
BUPA Hartswood Hospital .... Ms S. Fraser-Betts
BUPA Hospital Bushey .... Ms L. Adair
BUPA Hospital Cardiff .... Dr A. Gibbs
BUPA Hospital Clare Park .... Ms M. Wood
BUPA Hospital Elland .... Ms M.E. Schofield
BUPA Hospital Harpenden .... Ms B. Hayter
BUPA Hospital Hull & East Riding .... Ms A. Meyer
BUPA Hospital Leeds .... Mr D. Farrell
BUPA Hospital Leicester .... Mrs C.A. Jones
BUPA Hospital Little Aston .... Mr K. Smith
BUPA Hospital Manchester .... Ms A. McArdle
BUPA Hospital Norwich .... Ms J. Middows
BUPA Hospital Portsmouth .... Ms J. Ward
BUPA Murrayfield Hospital .... Miss J.C. Bott
BUPA North Cheshire Hospital .... Miss A.L. Alexander
BUPA Parkway Hospital .... Mrs M.T. Hall
BUPA Roding Hospital .... Ms D. Brett
BUPA St. Saviour's Hospital .... Mrs E. Biddle
BUPA South Bank Hospital .... Miss A. Tchaikovsky
BUPA Wellesley Hospital .... Mrs L. Horner
The Glen Hospital .... Miss M. O'Toole

Community Hospitals Group
(from 1 April 1998)

Ashtead Hospital .... Ms R. Hackett
Duchy Hospital .... Ms D. Martin
Euxton Hall Hospital .... Ms B. Dickinson
Fitzwilliam Hospital .... Ms S. Needham
Fotheringhay Suite .... Ms G. Jones
Fulwood Hall Hospital .... Ms C. Aucott

Mount Stuart Hospital .... Ms J. Abdelrahman

New Hall Hospital .... Ms H.L. Cole

North Downs Hospital .... Mrs M. Middleton

Oaklands Hospital .... Ms S. Croston

Oaks Hospital .... Ms M. Gallifent

Park Hill Hospital .... Ms D. Abbott

Pinehill Hospital .... Mrs J. Benson

Renacres Hall Hospital .... Ms L. Proffitt

Rowley Hall Hospital .... Ms L. Serginson

Springfield Hospital .... Ms J. Inggs

The Berkshire Independent Hospital .... Ms J. McCrum

The Rivers Hospital .... Ms K. Handel

The Yorkshire Clinic .... Ms J. Sands

West Midlands Hospital .... Ms F. Allinson

Winfield Hospital .... Ms M. Greaves

Woodland Hospital .... Mr I. Fraser

Nuffield Hospitals

HRH Princess Christian's Hospital .... Ms S. Fisher

Mid Yorkshire Nuffield Hospital .... Mrs J. Halliwell

Suffolk Nuffield Hospital .... Ms S. Verow

The Acland Hospital .... Miss C. Gilbert

The Birmingham Nuffield Hospital .... Miss E. Loftus

The Bournemouth Nuffield Hospital .... Mrs S. Jackson

The Chesterfield Nuffield Hospital .... Miss P.J. Bunker

The Cleveland Nuffield Hospital .... Ms D. Thornton

The Cotswold Nuffield Hospital .... Mrs J.T. Penn

The Duchy Nuffield Hospital .... Ms L. Wilcock

The East Midlands Nuffield Hospital .... Mrs C. Williams

The Essex Nuffield Hospital .... Mrs B.M. Parker

The Exeter Nuffield Hospital .... Mrs A. Turnbull

The Grosvenor Nuffield Hospital .... Mrs J.L. Whitmore

The Huddersfield Nuffield Hospital .... Miss S. Panther

The Hull Nuffield Hospital .... Ms B. Mendham

The Lancaster & Lakeland Nuffield Hospital .... Mrs K. McKay

The Newcastle Nuffield Hospital .... Ms D. Thornton

The North London Nuffield Hospital .... Miss J. Ward

The North Staffordshire Nuffield Hospital .... Mr D. Allison

The Nuffield Hospital Leicester .... Mrs S. Harriman

The Nuffield Hospital Plymouth .... Mrs T. Starling

The Purey Cust Nuffield Hospital .... Mr J. Gdaniec

The Shropshire Nuffield Hospital .... Mrs S. Crossland

The Somerset Nuffield Hospital .... Mrs J.A. Dyer

The Sussex Nuffield Hospital .... Mrs F. Booty

The Thames Valley Nuffield Hospital .... Mrs J. Shimell

The Tunbridge Wells Nuffield Hospital .... Mr R. Muddiman

The Warwickshire Nuffield Hospital .... Mrs J. Worth

The Wessex Nuffield Hospital .... Mrs V. Heckford

The Woking Nuffield Hospital .... Ms K. Barham

The Wolverhampton Nuffield Hospital .... Mr B. Lee

The Wye Valley Nuffield Hospital .... Mrs W.P. Mawdesley

PPP/Columbia
(from 1 April 1998)

The Harley Street Clinic .... Ms S. Thomas

The Portland Hospital for Women and Children .... Miss A.D. Sayburn

The Princess Grace Hospital .... Mrs D. Hutton

The Wellington Hospital .... Mr R. Hoff

St Martin's Hospitals

Devonshire Hospital .... Miss C. Cowley

London Bridge Hospital .... Ms Y. Terry

The Lister Hospital .... Mrs J. Norman

Other Independent Hospitals

Benenden Hospital .... Mr D. Hibler

King Edward VII Hospital, Midhurst
(from 1 April 1998) .... Dr J. Halfacre

The Heart Hospital
(from 1 October 1998) .... Ms C. Westland

The London Clinic .... Mrs K. Perkins

Appendix F - Participants

Consultant anaesthetists

These consultant anaesthetists returned at least one questionnaire relating to the period 1 April 1997 to 31 March 1998. We are not able to name all of the consultants who have done so as their names are not known to us.

Abbott M.A.
Abercrombie C.A.
Adley R.
Aitkenhead A.R.
Akhtar T.M.
Akinbole S.
Al-Hasani A.
Albin M.Z.
Alexander M.A.
Allen J.G.
Allison N.
Allt-Graham J.
Allum T.G.
Almond S.J.
Alsop E.
Anandanesan J.
Anderson J.
Anderson S.K.
Andrews J.I.
Appleby J.N.
Archer P.L.
Arrowsmith A.E.
Ashurst N.H.
Avery A.F.
Bagshaw O.
Bailie R.
Bainton A.B.
Baker G.M.
Balachandra K.
Baldwin L.N.
Ballard P.K.
Bamber M.
Bankov A.
Banks I.C.
Barker G.L.
Barrett P.
Barrett R.F.
Barron E.K.
Barry P.
Bashir P.M.
Bavister P.H.
Beck G.N.
Bembridge J.L.
Bennett A.
Bennett M.W.R.
Berry C.
Bew S.
Bhadresha R.
Bhar D.
Bhaskar H.K.
Bickford-Smith P.J.
Billingham I.S.
Bird T.M.
Bishton I.
Blumgart C.
Blundell M.D.
Boaden R.W.
Borman E.
Bourne J.A.
Bousfield J.D.
Bowhay A.
Bowley C.J.
Boyd T.
Boyd V.
Boys J.E.
Bracey B.J.
Bradburn B.G.
Bradfield H.G.C.
Brampton W.
Bramwell R.G.B.
Branch K.G.
Bray R.J.
Brice D.D.
Brim V.B.
Broadway J.W.
Bromley P.
Brooks A.M.
Brown J.
Brown R.
Brown R.M.
Bryan G.
Bryant M.T.T.
Buckland R.W.
Buist R.J.
Bullock R.E.
Bunsell R.P.
Burcher L.
Burgess A.J.
Byrne W.F.
Calleja M.A.
Calvert S.
Campbell F.A.
Campbell W.I.
Canton J.L.
Carnie J.C.
Carter J.A.
Casey W.F.
Catling J.S.
Chadwick I.S.
Chamberlain M.E.
Chambers J.J.
Chapman J.M.
Charlton A.J.
Charway C.L.
Cheema S.
Childs D.
Chishti J.M.
Christian A.S.
Chung S.K.N.
Clarke F.
Clarke T.N.S.
Clyburn P.
Coates D.
Coe A.J.
Coghill J.C.
Coniam S.W.
Conn A.G.
Conn D.
Conyers A.B.
Cook J.H.
Cook M.H.
Cooper P.D.
Copp M.
Cory C.E.
Cossham P.S.
Cotter J.
Coultas R.J.
Counsell D.
Coutinho W.B.
Craddock S.C.
Cranston A.J.
Creagh-Barry P.
Criswell J.C.
Crooke J.W.
Cross R.
Cutler P.G.
Dalal A.
Dalgleish J.G.
Daly P.E.
Dash A.
Daugherty M.O.
Daum R.E.O.
Davey A.J.
David A.
Davidson A.
Davies E.
Davies J.R.
Davies M.
Davies M.H.
Davies P.R.F.
Dawson A.D.G.
Day C.
Day C.D.
Daya H.
De Lima J.
De Mello W.F.
De Zoysa S.L.
Deacock S.
Dearlove O.
Dennis A.
Derbyshire D.R.
Deulkar U.V.
Devlin E.G.
Dexter T.
Dhariwal N.K.
Dickson D.
Dickson D.E.
Dinsmore J.
Dixon J.
Dixon J.L.
Dobson P.M.S.
Dodds C.
Donald F.
Dowdall J.W.
Drewery H.
Driemal S.
Dua R.
Duggal K.
Durcan T.
Duthie A.M.
Dwyer N.
Edmends S.
Edmondson L.
Edmondson W.C.
Elliott D.J.
Elton J.
Eustace R.W.
Evans C.S.
Evans G.
Evans K.
Evans M.L.
Ewah B.N.
Ewart M.C.
Fairfield J.E.
Fairfield M.
Fairley C.J.
Farquharson D.
Fenner S.
Ferguson A.
Field L.
Fischer H.B.J.
Fisher M.F.
Florence A.M.
Flynn M.J.

Forrest E.
Forster D.M.
Francis R.I.
Frater R.A.S.
Frerk C.
Friend J.
Furniss P.
Gabbott D.A.
Gademsetty M.K.
Galea P.J.
Galway J.E.
Gammanpila S.W.
Ganado A.
Ganepola S.R.
Gannon J.
Gargesh K.
George A.
Ghosh S.
Gibson J.S.
Gill K.J.
Gill S.S.
Girgis M.
Glover D.J.
Goddard G.F.
Goddard J.
Goodwin A.P.E.
Goold J.E.
Goulden P.
Gouldson R.
Grant I.C.
Gray A.J.G.
Gray D.
Gray H.S.J.
Grayling G.G.
Gregory M.
Gregory M.A.
Griffiths R.B.
Grummitt R.
Haden R.M.
Hammond J.
Harding S.A.
Hargrave S.A.
Hargreaves R.
Harper J.
Harper N.
Harris J.W.
Harris R.W.
Harrison C.A.
Harrison K.M.
Harrod S.
Harvey P.B.
Harwood R.J.
Hasan M.A.
Hawkins D.J.
Hawkins S.
Hawkins T.J.
Haycock J.C.
Head-Rapson A.
Heath M.L.
Hebblethwaite R.
Hegde R.T.
Helwa S.A.I.
Henderson R.
Heriot J.
Herrema I.H.
Hester J.B.
Hill A.
Hill H.
Hill S.
Hitchings G.M.
Hoad D.J.
Hobbs A.
Hodkinson J.N.
Hollis J.N.
Hollister G.R.
Hood G.
Houghton K.
Howard R.F.
Howell E.
Howell P.J.
Howell R.S.C.
Hudecek I.P.
Hughes J.
Hughes K.R.
Hull J.
Humphries C.
Hunter S.J.
Huss B.K.D.
Hutchinson H.T.
Iskander L.N.
Iyer D.
Jackson A.S.
Jackson D.G.
Jackson E.
James I.
James R.H.
Jameson P.
Jamieson J.R.
Jappie A.G.
Jardine A.D.
Jarvis A.P.
Jayaratne B.
Jayson D.W.
Jena N.M.
Jenkins J.R.
Jephcott G.
Jingree M.
John R.E.
Johnson C.J.H.
Johnson G.
Johnson T.W.
Johnston H.M.L.
Johnstone R.D.
Jones C.
Jones D.F.
Jones M.J.
Jothilingam S.
Kalia P.
Kapila A.
Kapoor S.C.
Kay P.M.
Keeler J.
Keep P.J.
Kelly E.P.
Kelsall P.
Kendall A.P.
Kent A.P.
Kettern M.A.
Khanna V.K.
Khiroya R.C.
Kiching A.
Kidd J.
Kilpatrick S.M.
King T.A.
Kipling R.M.
Kirby I.J.
Kirton C.
Koehli N.
Kong A.
Kotur C.F.
Koussa F.
Kraayenbrink M.A.
Krishnan A.
Kulasinghe N.
Kumar C.M.
Lack J.A.
Laishley R.
Lamb J.
Lamberty J.
Landon K.
Langham B.T.
Lanigan C.
Lawes E.G.
Leach A.B.
Leibler L.
Leith S.
Lesser P.J.A.
Lethbridge J.R.
Lewis P.
Lewis R.P.
Lintin D.J.
Lloyd-Thomas A.
Loader B.W.
Loan P.B.
Lockwood G.
Logan A.D.
Logan S.W.
Longan M.A.
Loughnan B.
Lowe D.
Lowe S.S.
Lowrie A.
Loyden C.F.
Ludgrove T.
Lung C.P.C.
Luxton M.C.
Lynch C.G.M.
McAteer E.J.
McAteer E.M.
McAteer M.P.
McCann N.
McConachie I.W.
McCrirrick A.
McCulloch W.J.D.
McDonald P.
McGregor R.R.
McHutchon A.
MacIntosh K.C.
Mackay C.J.
Mackenzie S.I.P.
Mackersie A.
MacKinnon J.C.
McLeod T.J.
McSwiney M.
Madden A.P.
Madej T.H.
Maher O.A.
Mann S.
Manus N.J.
Marczak A.
Marshall A.G.
Marshall F.P.F.
Martin A.J.
Martin D.
Martin V.
Mason R.A.
Masri Z.
Matheson H.A.
Matheson K.H.
Mathias I.M.J.
Mathur N.K.
Mawson P.J.
May A.J.
Meakin G.
Mehta R.M.
Mendonca L.M.
Messer C.
Metias V.F.
Mettam I.
Michael S.
Michel M.
Michelska B.M.
Milaszkiewicz R.M.
Millar S.W.
Miller R.I.
Mills P.J.
Milne I.S.
Mimpriss T.J.
Moony R.N.E.
Morcos W.E.
Morgan G.A.R.
Morle D.V.A.
Morris K.
Morris S.
Moss P.
Mostert M.J.
Moulla F.
Mowbray M.J.
Mudie L.L.
Mulvein J.T.
Murdoch L.
Murray F.P.
Murray-Wilson A.
Murthy B.
Mwanje D.K.
Nagi H.
Nalliah R.S.C.
Nancekievill M.L.
Nandi K.
Naqushbandi K.
Nash P.J.
Nathanson M.H.

Navaratnarajah M.N.
Nevantaus J.
Newbegin H.
Newman P.
Newman V.J.
Nicholls B.J.
Noble H.
Norley I.
Norton P.M.
Nosseir M.
Notcutt W.G.
Nott M.R.
Nunn G.
O'Connor B.
O'Dwyer J.
O'Sullivan K.A.
Okell R.W.
Olivelle A.
Olver J.J.
Onugha C.O.
Pac Soo C.
Page V.
Palin P.H.
Park G.R.
Park W.G.
Parke T.
Parkin G.
Parmar N.
Parry H.M.
Patel P.
Pateman J.A.
Paterson G.M.C.
Pavlou S.P.
Payne J.F.
Penfold N.
Peters C.G.
Phillips B.
Phillips K.A.
Phillips P.D.
Platt N.
Plummer R.B.
Pocklington A.G.
Porter G.E.
Porterfield A.J.
Power K.J.
Power S.J.
Powney J.G.
Price V.
Prince G.D.
Pryle B.
Purcell-Jones G.
Pyne A.
Radford P.
Raithatha H.H.
Raitt D.G.
Ramachandra V.
Randall N.P.C.
Randall P.J.
Rao D.S.
Rao J.J.
Rao M.V.S.N.
Raphael G.
Raveendran K.
Ravenscroft P.J.
Rawle P.R.
Razis P.A.
Redman D.R.O.
Rees D.G.
Reid M.F.
Renshaw A.J.N.
Richmond D.J.H.
Riddell G.S.
Rimell P.J.
Rittoo D.B.
Roberts F.L.
Robertson S.M.
Robinson F.P.
Saba G.
Saddler J.M.
Sagar D.A.
Sahal B.B.
Sainsbury M.
Samuels T.A.
Sanchez A.
Sanders D.
Sandhar B.
Sansome A.
Sarginson R.E.
Schofield N.M.
Schwarz P.A.
Scott P.V.
Scott R.B.
Searle J.F.
Sellwood W.G.
Selwyn D.A.
Shah R.N.N.
Shambrook A.S.
Shanks A.B.
Shanmuganathan K.
Shanthaklimar R.E.
Sharpe R.
Sharples A.
Shaw T.C.
Shaw T.J.I.
Shawket S.
Shribman A.J.
Siddiqui S.A.
Sides C.A.
Simpson P.J.
Skelly A.M.
Skinner J.B.
Smith C.
Smith M.
Smith M.B.
Smith N.
Smith P.
Smith Q.
Smyth D.
Smyth P.R.F.
Soskin M.
Spargo P.
Sprigge J.S.
Srivatsa S.M.
Stafford M.A.
Stanford B.J.
Stannard C.
Stanton J.M.
Starkey C.
Steer B.
Steven C.M.
Stevens J.
Stockwell M.A.
Stray C.M.
Stuart-Taylor M.
Stubbing J.F.
Studd C.
Styles J.T.
Summerfield R.J.
Sumner E.
Sury M.
Swayne P.
Sweeney J.E.
Swinhoe C.F.
Tarpey J.J.
Tarr T.J.
Tayler D.H.
Taylor A.J.
Taylor E.
Taylor M.
Taylor R.H.
Thomas D.G.
Thomas V.J.E.
Thompson M.C.
Thorn J.L.
Thornberry A.
Thorniley A.
Thornley B.
Thornton R.J.
Thorpe C.
Tierney N.M.
Tighe S.
Till C.
Timmins A.C.
Titoria M.
Tofte B.C.
Tordoff S.
Trotter T.
Turner G.A.
Turner M.A.
Turtle M.J.
Tweedie D.G.
Twigley A.J.
Twohig M.M.
Uncles D.R.
Vallance H.
van Miert M.
Van Ryssen M.E.P.
Vanner R.G.
Venkataraman P.
Vickers A.P.
Vine P.R.
Waddell T.
Walker H.A.C.
Walker I.
Walker M.A.
Walmsley A.J.
Walsh E.M.
Walton D.P.
Wandless J.G.
Ward M.E.
Ward R.M.
Ward S.
Warnell I.H.
Watson D.M.
Watt J.
Watt T.
Weatherill D.
Webster R.E.
Wee M.
Weiner P.C.
Weldon B.
Weston G.A.
White M.J.
White W.D.
Whitehead E.M.
Whitehead J.P.
Whiteley S.
Wilkins C.J.
Wilkinson M.B.
Willatts D.G.
Williams D.J.M.
Williams P.
Williams V.
Williams W.D.
Wilson A.J.
Wilson I.G.
Wilson J.
Windsor J.P.W.
Wolfe M.J.
Wolff A.
Wood D.W.
Wood K.
Woodall N.M.
Wort M.
Wraight W.J.W.
Wray G.
Wright E.
Wright M.M.
Yaqoob M.
Yarwood G.
Yate B.
Yates D.W.
Yoganathan S.
Yogasakaran B.S.
Young P.N.
Youssef H.
Zideman D.A.
Zych Z.

LIVERPOOL
JOHN MOORES UNIVERSITY
AVRIL ROBARTS LRC
TEL. 0151 231 4022

Appendix G - Participants

Consultant surgeons and gynaecologists

These consultant surgeons and gynaecologists returned at least one questionnaire relating to the period 1 April 1997 to 31 March 1998.

Abberton M.
Abraham J.
Achary D.M.
Adair H.M.
Ahmed N.
Ainscow D.A.P.
Al-Khatib M.
Al-Sabti A.
Albert D.
Albert J.S.
Aldam C.H.
Alderson D.
Alexander D.J.
Ali A.L.
Ali Q.K.
Allan A.
Allardice J.
Allerton K.
Allum R.L.
Amery A.H.
Anderson J.T.
Anderson R.J.L.
Anderton J.M.
Andrew D.R.
Angel J.C.
Antrobus J.N.
Appleton G.V.N.
Appleyard I.
Arafa M.
Archer I.A.
Armitage T.G.
Ashour H.
Atrah S.G.
Attarra G.A.
August A.
Aukland P.
Avill R.
Backhouse C.M.
Bailey C.M.
Baker A.S.
Bakran A.
Bale R.S.
Bamford D.
Banan H.
Banerjee A.K.
Banks A.J.
Barker J.R.
Barrett D.
Barrie W.W.
Barrington R.L.
Barros D'Sa A.A.B.
Battersby R.D.E.
Bedford A.F.
Beeden A.G.
Belham G.
Bell J.R.
Bentley P.G.
Berry A.R.
Berstock D.A.
Bett N.J.
Bhamra M.S.
Bickerstaff D.R.
Binfield P.M.
Binns M.S.
Bintcliffe I.W.L.
Birch N.
Bircher M.D.
Bishop C.C.R.
Blake G.
Blake J.R.S.
Blakeway C.
Blayney J.D.M.
Blewitt N.
Blower A.
Boardman K.P.
Bodey W.N.
Boeree N.R.
Bollen S.
Bolton J.P.
Bonnici A.V.
Bowen J.C.
Boyd N.A.
Bracegirdle J.
Bracey D.J.
Bradley J.G.
Bradley P.J.
Bransom C.J.
Brigg J.K.
Brightwell A.P.
Brignall C.
Britton B.J.
Brooks S.
Brooks S.G.
Brough W.A.
Brown C.
Brown G.J.A.
Browning N.
Bruce J.
Bryan S.
Bryant M.J.
Bryson J.R.
Buckles J.A.C.
Buick R.G.
Bunker T.D.
Burd A.
Burge D.M.
Burkitt D.
Burton V.W.
Butler-Manuel A.
Cain D.
Cairns D.W.
Calvert C.H.
Calvert P.T.
Campbell J.K.
Campbell P.
Campbell W.B.
Carden D.G.
Carr R.T.W.
Carty N.J.
Carvell J.E.
Castillo A.A.
Cavanagh S.P.
Chadwick C.J.
Chan R.N.W.
Channon G.M.
Chant A.D.B.
Chapman D.F.
Chapman J.A.
Chapman P.G.
Charnley G.J.
Charnley R.M.
Chaudhry S.M.
Cheatle T.R.
Checketts R.G.
Cherry R.J.
Chester J.
Chissell H.
Churchill M.A.
Citron N.D.
Clark D.W.
Clarke D.
Clarke J.M.F.
Clay N.R.
Clegg J.F.
Clifford R.P.
Clothier P.R.
Cobb A.G.
Cobb R.A.
Coen L.D.
Colin J.F.
Collin J.
Collins R.E.C.
Conybeare M.E.
Cooke T.J.C.
Cooper J.C.
Cooper Wilson M.
Corbett W.A.
Cord-Udy C.
Corfield A.P.
Cox P.J.
Coxon J.E.
Crabbe D.C.G.
Crane P.W.
Crawford P.J.
Crawford R.
Creedon R.
Crerand J.
Crighton I.L.
Cross A.T.
Crumplin M.K.H.
Curley P.J.
Curry R.C.
Curwen C.
D'Arcy J.C.
Da Costa O.
David H.G.
Davies G.
Davies M.
Davies R.M.
Dawson K.
De Boer P.G.
de Kiewiet G.P.
De La Hunt M.N.
Deacon P.B.
Deakin M.
Deliss L.J.
Desai K.
Dewar E.P.
Dhingra D.
Dickson G.H.
Dilworth G.R.
Dixon J.H.
Docherty D.O.
Dodds R.
Donell S.T.
Donovan A.G.
Douglas D.L.
Dowd G.S.E.
Drabble E.
Drake D.P.
Dunn M.
Dunning J.
Dyson P.H.P.
Earlam R.J.
Earnshaw J.J.
Earnshaw P.
Eastwood D.M.
Eaton A.C.
Ebizie A.O.
Eckersley J.R.T.
Edge P.
Edwards M.H.

Edwards P.
Elem B.
Elguindi M.
Elliott B.
Elliott M.J.
Ellis S.
Ellul J.P.
Elsworth C.F.
Emery R.J.
English P.J.
Evans C.M.
Evans G.
Evans G.H.
Evans J.
Evans M.J.
Evans P.
Everson N.W.
Eyres K.
Fahmy N.R.M.
Fairbank A.C.
Farhan M.J.
Farndon J.R.
Fearn C.B.
Feggetter J.G.W.
Feneley R.C.L.
Ferguson G.H.
Fergusson C.M.
Fernandes A.
Fernandez G.N.
Fewster S.
Fiddian N.J.
Field E.S.
Field J.
Field R.E.
Finnis D.
Fitzgerald J.A.W.
Flowerdew A.F.
Fordyce M.J.F.
Forrest L.
Fortes Mayer K.D.
Foster G.E.
Fourie L.R.
Fowler J.
Freedlander E.
Freedman L.S.
Gale D.
Gallagher P.
Gammall M.M.
Garlick N.I.
Gartell P.C.
Gerber C.
Geroulakos G.
Ghali N.N.
Gibb P.
Gibbin K.P.
Gibbons C.L.M.
Gibbons C.P.
Gibbs A.N.
Gibson M.J.
Gibson R.J.
Gie G.A.
Gilbert H.W.
Gill P.J.
Gillham N.R.
Gillies R.M.
Goldman M.D.
Goodman A.J.
Gornall P.
Gough A.L.
Goulbourne I.A.
Grace D.L.
Graham G.P.
Grant H.
Gray M.
Greaney M.G.
Greatrex G.H.
Green G.A.
Green T.
Gregory P.
Griffith M.J.
Griffiths D.A.
Griffiths M.
Griffiths R.W.
Gupta A.K.
Gwynn B.R.
Hahn D.M.
Haines J.F.
Hall C.
Hall G.
Hall R.
Hall R.I.
Hall S.W.
Hallett J.P.
Halliday A.G.
Halliday J.A.
Hambidge J.E.
Hamer D.B.
Hamilton G.
Hamlyn P.J.
Hanafy M.
Hardy J.R.
Harkness W.F.J.
Harrison D.J.
Harrison N.W.
Harrison R.A.
Harrison T.A.
Hart C.T.
Hart R.O.
Hartley M.
Harvey M.H.
Hasan S.T.
Hawthorn I.E.
Hayes A.G.
Haynes I.G.
Hayward R.
Heald R.J.
Heath D.V.
Heather B.P.
Henderson A.
Henderson J.J.
Hendrickse C.
Hershman M.
Higginson D.W.
Hindley C.J.
Hinves B.L.
Hobbs N.
Hockley A.D.
Holbrook M.C.
Homer-Vanniasinkam S.
Hook W.E.
Hopcroft P.W.
Hornby R.
Horner J.
Horrocks M.
Houghton P.W.J.
Housden P.
Howard A.C.
Howell C.J.
Howell F.R.
Huddy S.P.J.
Hughes S.
Hui A.
Humphrey C.S.
Hunt D.M.
Hunter J.B.
Hunter S.
Hurst P.A.
Hussain T.
Hutchinson I.F.
Hyder N.
Iftikhar S.Y
Imray C.H.E.
Ingoldby C.J.H.
Innes A.
Ions G.K.
Irwin A.
Isbister E.
Iyer S.V.
Jacobs L.G.H.
Jaffe V.
Jaffray B.
Jain S.
James S.E.
Jamieson A.M.
Jamison M.H.
Jane M.
Jefferiss C.D.
Jeffery P.J.
Jeffery R.S.
Jessop J.
John T.
Johns A.M.
Johnson S.R.
Johnson-Nurse C.
Jones D.R.
Jones G.M.
Jones J.R.
Jones M.W.
Jones P.
Jones P.A.
Jones R.N.
Jones W.A.
Kaisary A.V.
Kaltsas D.S.
Kanvinde R.
Kapadia C.R.
Kapadia K.B.
Kashi H.
Kashif F.
Kathuria V.
Keith A.O.
Kelly J.F.
Kelly M.J.
Kennedy R.H.
Kenny N.W.
Kerin M.J.
Kerr P.
Kerrigan D.
Kershaw C.J.
Ketzer B.
Keys G.W.
Khan M.
Khan M.A.A.
Khan M.Z.G.
Khan O.
Kiely E.
Kinder R.B.
Kirk S.
Kirkpatrick J.N.P.
Klosok J.K.
Knox A.J.S.
Knudsen C.J.M.
Kong K.C.
Kourah M.A.
Krikler S.
Krishnamurthy G.
Lafferty K.
Lahoti O.
Laidlaw I.
Lambert D.
Lambert M.E.
Lambert W.G.
Lamont G.
Lander A.
Lane R.H.S.
Langkamer G.
Lavelle J.R.
Lawrance R.J.
Lawrence D.
Lawson A.
Lazim T.R.
Lee J.O.
Lees P.D.
Leese T.
Leighton S.E.J.
Leinhardt D.
Leitch J.
Lennard T.W.J.
Lennox M.S.
Leopold P.W.
Lewis J.L.
Lewis P.
Leyshon R.L.
Limb D.L.
Linsell J.C.
Livingstone B.N.
Livingstone J.
Lloyd D.A.
Loeffler M.
Logan A.M.
Losty P.
Lovegrove J.

Lynch M.C.
Lyttle J.A.
McAuliffe T.B.
McCarthy D.
Macdonald D.A.
MacDonald R.C.
MacFie J.
McGee H.
MacKay N.N.S.
Mackenney R.P.
McLatchie G.
McLoughlin S.J.
McMahon M.J.
McPartlin J.F.
McPherson G.A.D.
Madden N.P.
Maheson M.V.S.
Majkowski R.S.
Makar A.
Makin C.A.
Mal R.K.
Mani G.V.
Marks S.M.
Marsh G.
Marshall G.
Marshall J.
Marshall P.D.
Marston R.A.
Marx C.L.
Mason M.C.
Matanhelia S.S.
Mathur A.
Maxwell H.A.
Maxwell W.A.
May A.R.L.
May P.
Maybury N.K.
Mayer A.D.
Meadows T.H.
Meehan S.E.
Menzies D.
Mercurius-Taylor L.A.
Meyrick Thomas J.
Miles J.B.
Miller A.J.
Miller G.A.B.
Miller J.G.
Milling M.A.P.
Mills C.L.
Milton C.M.
Misra D.
Modgill V.K.
Moftah F.S.
Mohammed A.
Mok D.W.H.
Monsell F.P.
Monson J.R.T.
Montgomery P.Q.
Montgomery R.J.
Montgomery S.C.
Moore A.J.
Moran B.
Moran C.G.
Morrell M.T.
Morris M.A.
Mosquera D.A.
Moss A.L.H.
Moss M.C.
Mowbray M.A.S.
Muddu B.N.
Mughal M.M.
Muir L.
Munro E.N.
Murphy J.
Murray J.M.
Nadarajan P.
Nahabedian A.
Nairn D.S.
Nanu A.
Nash A.G.
Nasra S.
Natali C.
Naylor H.G.
Needoff M.
Nejim A.H.
Nelson I.W.
Newman R.J.
Nicholas R.J.
Niezywinski W.A.
Noble J.G.
Nolan J.F.
North A.D.
Nour S.
Novell J.R.
O'Doherty D.
O'Dowd J.K.
O'Riordan B.
O'Sullivan D.G.
Orr M.M.
Ostick D.G.
Owen E.R.T.
Packer G.
Pailthorpe C.A.
Palmer J.G.
Palmer J.H.
Parikh D.H.
Parkinson R.
Parmar H.V.
Patel A.D.
Peet T.N.D.
Pegg D.J.
Pena M.A.
Pennie B.
Petri J.
Pettit S.H.
Pickard P.
Pierro A.
Pigott H.W.S.
Pike J.
Pittam M.R.
Pobereskin L.H.
Pooley J.
Poskitt K.R.
Postlethwaite J.C.
Poston G.J.
Potts S.R.
Powell B.W.
Powell J.M.
Power R.
Pozo J.L.
Pradhan N.S.
Prince H.G.
Pring D.
Pritchett C.J.
Pryor G.A.
Punt J.A.G.
Puntis M.C.A.
Quaile A.
Radford P.J.
Rahman H.
Rainey H.A.
Rajasekaran J.
Raman R.
Ranaboldo C.
Rance C.H.
Rangecroft L.
Rao S.
Ratliff D.A.
Ratnatunga C.P.
Ravi S.
Read C.
Reasbeck P.G.
Rees M.
Reissis N.
Richards P.
Richardson D.
Riley D.
Roberts J.P.
Roberts-Harry J.
Robson M.J.
Rooker G.D.
Ross K.R.
Rothwell N.
Roushdi H.
Rowles J.
Rowntree M.
Rowson N.J.
Royle S.
Rutter P.C.
Sacks N.P.M.
Sagar S.
Saidiah Y.C.
Sainsbury J.R.C.
Salam A.
Saleh M.
Sandeman D.R.
Sansom J.R.
Saran D.
Sarin R.
Sarker A.K.
Sarson D.
Sayegh E.F.
Scammell B.
Schizas C.
Schranz P.J.
Scott A.D.N.
Scott B.W.
Scott I.
Scott I.H.K.
Scott R.A.P.
Scott W.A.
Sefton G.K.
Sell P.J.
Sellu D.
Sethia B.
Sethia K.K.
Shafighian B.
Shah V.
Shaikh N.A.
Shami K.
Shanahan M.D.G.
Shankar N.
Shankarappa Y.K.S.
Shanker J.
Shanker J.Y.
Shannon M.N.
Sharif D.
Sharp D.J.
Shaw D.L.
Shawis R.N.
Shea J.G.
Shearman C.P.
Shedden R.G.
Shepperd J.A.N.
Sheridan W.G.
Sherlock D.J.
Sherman I.W.
Sherry P.G.
Shinkfield M.
Shrivastava M.
Shrotria S.
Sida H.Y.
Simison A.J.M.
Simson J.N.
Singhal K.
Sivapragasam S.
Skene A.
Skinner P.W.
Skipper D.
Slater R.N.S.
Smallwood J.
Smith D.N.
Smith E.
South L.M.
Spaine L.
Spence R.A.
Spencer R.F.
Spivey C.J.
Squire B.R.
Stallard M.C.
Staniforth P.
Stanley D.
Stapleton S.
Stassen L.F.A.
Steele S.C.
Stephen I.B.M.
Stewart H.D.
Stewart M.
Stirrat A.N.
Stoddard C.J.
Stoker T.A.M.
Stokes M.

UNIVERSITY
ARTS LRC
0151 231 4022

Stollard G.E.
Stott M.A.
Stuart A.E.
Studley J.
Sudlow R.A.
Sutaria P.D.
Swift R.I.
Szypryt E.P.
Taams K.
Tait W.F.
Taktak S.G.
Tang D.
Tasker T.P.B.
Taylor G.J.
Taylor J.L.
Taylor L.J.
Taylor M.
Thacker C.R.
Themen A.E.G.
Thomas D.M.
Thomas P.A.
Thomas P.B.M.
Thomas T.L.
Thompson D.
Thompson H.H.
Thompson R.L.E.
Thompson S.K.
Thomsitt J.
Thomson A.A.G.
Thomson H.J.
Thomson W.H.F.
Thorneloe M.H.
Thorpe A.C.
Tibrewal S.
Tindall S.F.
Todd R.C.
Tolley N.
Trevett M.
Trimmings N.P.
Tsang T.T.
Tsang V.
Tucker J.K.
Tudor R.G.
Turnbull T.J.
Turner A.
Turner A.G.
Turner P.G.
Tuson K.W.R.
Twiston-Davies C.W.
Twyman R.
Upadhyay S.
Van Der Walt P.
Vaughan R.
Vaughan-Lane T.
Vickers R.H.
Villar R.N.
Vloeberghs M.H.
Vowden P.
Vyas J.
Waddington R.T.
Wakeman R.
Walker A.J.
Walker C.
Walker D.I.
Walker S.J.
Wallace R.G.H.
Walsh A.K.M.
Walsh M.E.
Wand J.S.
Ward D.C.
Warren P.
Waterfield A.H.
Watkins R.M.
Watts M.T.
Way B.G.
Webster D.J.T.
Weeber A.
Wenger R.J.J.
West C.G.H.
Weston P.M.T.
Wetherell R.G.
Wheeler R.
Whiteley G.S.W.
Whittaker M.
Widdison A.L.
Wilde G.P.
Wilkins D.C.
Willett K.
Williams C.
Williams D.J.
Williams G.T.
Williams H.M.
Wilson N.M.
Wilson N.V.
Winson I.G.
Wise D.I.
Wise K.S.H.
Withanage A.S.
Wojcik A.
Womack N.
Woods W.
Woolf V.
Wray C.C.
Wyatt M.G.
Wyman A.
Wynne K.S.
Yeates H.A.
Yeung C.K.
Zahir A.G.
Zaman M.M.
Zeiderman M.R.